T0305350

High-Probability Trade Setups

Founded in 1807, John Wiley & Sons is the oldest independent publishing company in the United States. With offices in North America, Europe, Australia, and Asia, Wiley is globally committed to developing and marketing print and electronic products and services for our customers' professional and personal knowledge and understanding.

The Wiley Trading series features books by traders who have survived the market's ever-changing temperament and have prospered—some by reinventing systems, others by getting back to basics. Whether a novice trader, professional, or somewhere in-between, these books will provide the advice and strategies needed to prosper today and well into the future.

For a list of available titles, please visit our web site at www.WileyFinance.com.

High-Probability Trade Setups

A Chartist's Guide to Real-Time Trading

TIM KNIGHT

WILEY

John Wiley & Sons, Inc.

Published by John Wiley & Sons, Inc., Hoboken, New Jersey.
Published simultaneously in Canada.

ProphetCharts used with permission from TD Ameritrade.

For general information on our other products and services or for technical support, please contact our Customer Care Department within the United States at (800) 762-2974, outside the United States at (317) 572-3993 or fax (317) 572-4002.

Wiley also publishes its books in a variety of electronic formats. Some content that appears in print may not be available in electronic books. For more information about Wiley products, visit our web site at www.wiley.com.

Library of Congress Cataloging-in-Publication Data:

Knight, Tim, 1966–
   High-probability trade setups : a chartist's guide to real-time trading / Tim Knight.
      p. cm. – (Wiley trading series)
   Includes index.
      ISBN 978-1-118-02225-2 (hardback); ISBN 978-1-118-11296-0 (ebk); ISBN 978-1-118-11295-3 (ebk); ISBN 978-1-118-11297-7 (ebk)
   1. Stocks–Prices–Charts, diagrams, etc.   2. Stocks–Charts, diagrams, etc.   3. Investment analysis.
4. Speculation.   I. Title.
   HG4638.K553 2011
   332.63'2042–dc22

                                                                                    2011014260

Printed in the United States of America

10 9 8 7 6 5 4 3 2 1

For E&S
May you always be the best of friends

Contents

About the Author   **xiii**

PART I   **An Overview**   **1**

CHAPTER 1   **A Primer on Chart Setups**   **3**

     The Bulls versus the Bears   4
     Why Is a Prediction Valuable?   4
     A Word on Shorting   6
     Support and Resistance   7
     What Happens When Prices Punch Through?   8
     History Repeats Itself   11
     When Patterns Work Together   13
     How to Use This Book   14

CHAPTER 2   **My Personal Trading Journey**   **15**

     Earliest Interest in the Markets   15
     Beginning with the Crash   16
     Technical Tools   17
     Prophet's Beginning   18
     The Internet Makes Its Appearance   18
     Enter Alex and JavaCharts   19
     Project Kandinsky   21
     The Slope of Hope   22
     Lessons Learned   22
     ProphetCharts Lives   23
     The Three Steps   24

PART II   **The Patterns**   **31**

CHAPTER 3   **Ascending Triangles**   **33**

     Definition of the Pattern   33
     Psychology behind the Pattern   35

	Examples	35
	Summary	43
CHAPTER 4	**Ascending Wedges**	**45**
	Definition of the Pattern	45
	Psychology behind the Pattern	47
	Examples	47
	Summary	53
CHAPTER 5	**Channels**	**55**
	Definition of the Pattern	55
	Psychology behind the Pattern	57
	Examples	57
	Summary	68
CHAPTER 6	**Cup with Handle**	**69**
	Definition of the Pattern	69
	Psychology behind the Pattern	70
	Examples	72
	Longer-Term Examples	75
	Summary	79
CHAPTER 7	**Descending Triangles**	**81**
	Definition of the Pattern	81
	Psychology behind the Pattern	83
	Examples	83
	Summary	89
CHAPTER 8	**Descending Wedges**	**91**
	Definition of the Pattern	91
	Psychology behind the Pattern	92
	Examples	93
	Summary	102
CHAPTER 9	**Diamonds**	**103**
	Definition of the Pattern	103
	Psychology behind the Pattern	105

	Examples	105
	Summary	110
CHAPTER 10	**Fibonacci Fans**	**111**
	Definition of the Pattern	111
	Psychology behind the Pattern	113
	Examples	114
	Summary	126
CHAPTER 11	**Fibonacci Retracements**	**129**
	Definition of the Pattern	130
	Examples	132
	Summary	139
CHAPTER 12	**Flags**	**141**
	Definition of the Pattern	141
	Psychology behind the Pattern	142
	Examples	143
	Summary	153
CHAPTER 13	**Gaps**	**155**
	Definition of the Pattern	155
	Psychology behind the Pattern	157
	Examples	158
	Summary	174
CHAPTER 14	**Head and Shoulders**	**175**
	Definition of the Pattern	175
	Psychology behind the Pattern	176
	The Importance of the Neckline	177
	Examples	178
	Summary	197
CHAPTER 15	**Inverted Head and Shoulders**	**199**
	Definition of the Pattern	199
	Psychology behind the Pattern	201
	The Importance of the Neckline	202
	Examples	202
	Summary	215

CHAPTER 16   Multiple Bottoms   **217**

    Definition of the Pattern   217
    Psychology behind the Pattern   219
    Examples   220
    Summary   230

CHAPTER 17   Multiple Tops   **231**

    Definition of the Pattern   231
    Psychology behind the Pattern   233
    Examples   233
    Summary   241

CHAPTER 18   Pennants   **243**

    Definition of the Pattern   243
    Psychology behind the Pattern   244
    Examples   245
    Summary   253

CHAPTER 19   Rounded Bottoms   **255**

    Definition of the Pattern   255
    Psychology behind the Pattern   256
    Examples   257
    Summary   265

CHAPTER 20   Rounded Tops   **267**

    Definition of the Pattern   267
    Psychology behind the Pattern   269
    Examples   270
    Summary   278

CHAPTER 21   Support Failure   **279**

    Definition of the Pattern   279
    Psychology behind the Pattern   280
    Examples   281
    Summary   299

CHAPTER 22   Automatic Patterns   **301**

    Patterns in ProphetCharts   302
    Working with the Results   307

	Pattern Failures	314
	Putting the Patterns to Work	315

PART III   **Trading and You**   **317**

CHAPTER 23   **Setting Stops**   **319**

General Guidelines	319
Below Support	320
Above Resistance	320
Above Trendline	321
Below Trendline	321
Most Recent Low	322
Most Recent High	322
Special Cases	323

CHAPTER 24   **On Being a Bear**   **325**

The Philosophy of Shorting	325
Practical Guide to Short Selling	326
Exchange-Traded Funds	328
Puts for Leveraged Profits	330
The Philosophy of Shorting	332

CHAPTER 25   **A Guide to Real-Life Trading**   **337**

Trading Rules	337
How to Open a Position	338
How to Hold a Position	341
How to Close a Position	343
Time and Money	343
There Is No Holy Grail	344
Closing Thoughts	345

Index	**347**

About the Author

Tim Knight is a hedge fund manager and the founder of Prophet Financial Systems (now owned by TD Ameritrade), rated by *Forbes* magazine and *Barron's* as the number-one online site for technical analysis. He also writes the popular blog Slope of Hope (www.slopeofhope.com). Prior to starting Prophet.net, he was Vice President of Products for Montgomery Securities investment bank, where he helped develop Macintosh-based traders' workstations before the development of Web trading. Knight has traded for over 20 years, primarily using technical analysis and price charts, and has written 20 other books. He lives with his family in Palo Alto, California.

PART I

An Overview

CHAPTER 1

A Primer on Chart Setups

T his is a book about chart setups and how they can make you a more profitable trader. I have been involved in trading for a quarter-century, and during almost that entire time, I have used charts and technical analysis as the basis of my investing decisions. This book endeavors to show you meaningful, clear examples of the most powerful chart patterns so that you can commit them, and their importance, to memory.

Technical analysis is the study of past price movement for the purpose of predicting future price movement, which, if done correctly, can lead to substantial trading profits. The prices studied are typically those of financial instruments such as stocks, commodities, and foreign currencies. But no matter what market is being studied, the underlying principles are the same. Specifically:

- A price chart is the most perfect representation of the balance of buyers and sellers for any given entity.
- Prices tend to move in trends and patterns which, based on historical analysis, can lead to statistically meaningful probabilities of future price movement.
- The skilled examination of a price chart can guide a trader as to how long he should remain in a trade and when he should exit.

No matter what you trade, technical analysis can make you a better and more profitable trader. Price charts will consistently provide the most truthful picture that can be had of a tradable object, because everything that can be publicly known or speculated is already built into the graph. You will never get the same pure representation of a stock (or anything else) from a broker, a newsletter writer, or an analyst. A chart is as good as it gets. How much good that chart can do for *you* depends on your own skill and objective analysis.

THE BULLS VERSUS THE BEARS

Before we get into price charts—and there will be hundreds of them in this book—let's examine the basics about what forms a price chart in the first place: sellers (the supply) and buyers (the demand). It should also be noted at the outset that almost all the examples in this book will be of stocks, but the same rules and methods are appropriate for any form of financial instrument.

When buyers are more powerful than sellers, prices move up. When sellers are more powerful than buyers, prices move down. This tug-of-war, in these simple terms, is behind the trillions of dollars that get traded every week of the year. Buying power represents an excess of demand which will, because of simple market dynamics, inflate price levels.

What many people tend to forget is that every time a trade is placed, each side believes that they are right and the other side of the transaction is wrong. When person A buys stock from person B, person A believes the stock is going to go up in price (meaning B is selling too cheap) and person B believes he would rather have the cash than the stock (meaning A is buying an overvalued, or at least fully valued, stock).

As a group, the individuals who believe a given instrument is going to move higher in price are the bulls, whereas the opposing camp, believing prices for the same instrument will drop, are the bears. And the war between the bulls and the bears, fought over many thousands of different stocks, options, and commodities every day, is what creates price movement. Analyzing that movement with skill is what will give you a substantial edge in the markets you trade.

This book seeks not so much to interpret what those wiggles of movement mean. Instead, it seeks to illustrate for you, with example after real-life example, how these patterns as a whole have played out in actual trading. History tends to repeat itself, and recognizing the meaning of a well-formed pattern will be a great ally in your trading career.

WHY IS A PREDICTION VALUABLE?

The astonishing thing about technical analysis is not only how far out its predictive power goes, but also how, even with a future full of unknowns, it still seems able to see its way clear to make a meaningful prediction. A staggering number of great forces can wreak havoc with financial markets—scandals, war, governmental chaos, interest rates, terrorist attacks, earnings surprises, the social climate, financial meltdowns, and so forth.

Through it all, the knowledgeable chartist can see what others cannot see and know what seems unknowable.

Let's take a real-life example with a very long timespan: the Dow Jones Industrial Average over a period of more than a century. Figure 1.1 has two Fibonacci fans drawn on it (don't worry if you are not familiar with that term; it is explained later in this book). These fans are drawn from an extreme low to an extreme high. The first is drawn from the low in 1903 (called the Rich Man's Panic) to the peak of the Roaring Twenties bull market in 1929. The second is drawn from the depths of the depression in 1932 to the peak of the Internet bubble in January 2000.

FIGURE 1.1 The Dow Jones Industrial Average from 1900 to 2005, enhanced with two Fibonacci fans.

There is a variety of astounding things to note in this chart:

- The point where the two major lines intersect in 1974 predicted the precise bottom of the massive 1973–1974 bear market.
- The steady climb from 1990 to 1995 was perfectly bounded by two of the fan lines.
- Most impressive of all, the ultimate market top in 2000 was established by the first fan (which, remember, began 97 years before).

Figure 1.2 is a close-up view of late 1999 and early 2000; as you can see, the almost century-old fan line creates impressive resistance to these prices moving higher on four different occasions. If we owned stocks at that time, this would be a vital warning signal that the top was established.

FIGURE 1.2 Highlighted here are four instances when the Dow bounced off the fan line established over a century earlier.

This is an extreme example, but the point is that being able to gain insight into the most likely future of a particular price is a vehicle for real trading profits. It is an edge that those not using charts lack.

A WORD ON SHORTING

There are many places in this book where we refer to *shorting* a particular stock or *being short* a stock. It is valuable to understand this terminology, in case you do not already. I also have a personal fondness for shorting stocks, so there will be more examples of short setups in this book than you might expect.

Most people participating in a market are *long* the market; that is, they own the security with the hope that the price will go up. So if a person owns 1,000 shares of Apple Computer (AAPL) which he bought at $250 per share, and later sells it for $290 per share, he has made $40,000 based on the long position (a $40 per share gain times 1,000 shares).

A person who is short a security has done things backwards: He first sells a security he does not own for a certain price with the hope that the price will go *down*. The reason people are able to sell stock they do not own (essentially giving them a negative number of shares) is that their broker has so much of the stock already that it is available to sell with the promise that, at some point, it will be repurchased to replace the shares that were sold.

Taking the example of Apple again, an individual might sell short 1,000 shares of Apple at $290 per share. If the stock fell to $250 and the trader *covered* the position (that is, bought 1,000 shares of the stock, thus making the broker whole), he would have made $40,000 just as the other trader did, only he would have done it in the other direction.

The advantages and disadvantages of shorting markets will be discussed in a special section later in this book, but the principal benefit of shorting is that you can take advantage of a *falling* market as well as a *rising* one. If you are at the beginning of a bear market, and you can only buy stocks, it will be very difficult to make money (inverse ETFs and put options notwithstanding). If you are able to short stocks at high prices and then buy them back later at low prices, you can make money in either an up or down market.

The key disadvantage to shorting stocks is that all the big money is made by going *long*. The most you can ever make with a short position is 100 percent (that is, if the stock goes to $0.00, which almost never happens), whereas the most you can make with a long position is unlimited. You can definitely make profits shorting markets, but unless you are a brilliant options trader, you will never get rich being a bear (that is, a person betting on a market going down).

SUPPORT AND RESISTANCE

The world of technical analysis can seem overwhelming to many. There are hundreds of complex mathematical indicators, studies, patterns, and rules. But there is absolutely no reason good charting has to be complicated. A trader can set aside all of the complexity and focus on some solid basics, starting with the ideas of support and resistance.

You will find the themes of support and resistance to be the backbones (almost literally) of every single setup in this volume.

To illustrate this, think back to the classic playground-based children's game Red Rover. In case you don't remember it, kids split up into two groups, and each group forms a line by holding hands, so that there are two parallel lines of children facing each other across a field. Then one team calls out, "Red Rover, Red Rover, send Skylar (or some other kid's name) right over!" and the named child rushes headlong into the other line, trying to break through. If she busts through the line, she gets to choose a person to join her team.

This image of *breaking through* is exactly what support and resistance are all about, because in the grown-up world of trading, buyers of securities tend to mass at certain price levels. And those owners will hold the line at those prices if the security tries to go above (in the case of resistance) or below (in the case of support).

Let's take a simple, hypothetical example. Suppose a given stock traded at between $4.95 and $5.05 for many months. Day after day, week after week, it stayed in this range, accumulating owners of the stock at around the $5 level. Let's go on to assume the company has some good news, and the stock goes up to $6, but subsequent profit-taking pushes the stock back down again.

Given this circumstance, you can rest assured that it's unlikely the stock is going to drop beneath the $5 level. The reason is that there's a huge number of owners at that level, and they are simply *not* going to sell. Fear and greed are the primary drivers of any market, and in this case, greed is going to come first (meaning the owners are telling the market "I refuse to sell my stock at this price for a breakeven trade; I want a profit"). If something remarkable happens and it shoves the stock down to, say, $4.50, the fear starts to take hold ("I am worried my losses will get even worse, so I'm going to sell now while I still have the chance"), which means the selling will feed on itself.

Expressed in economic terms, the stock price found equilibrium at the $5 level, thus amassing a large number of owners. If the stock price challenges that level again, equilibrium will once more take hold, stabilizing the price. The people owning stock at this level constitute resistance—the Red Rover line will hold fast, unless a very powerful force punches through it.

Support, therefore, is a price level at which prices are prone to stay above. Resistance is a price level at which prices are prone to stay below. So these are reliable levels at which we can count on a pause in price movement, unless the levels are violated, which is where the real action is.

WHAT HAPPENS WHEN PRICES PUNCH THROUGH?

One time when outsized profits can be made is when prices push through either support or resistance and break out. The longer a price has been trying to push through a certain price level, the more momentum it will have if it finally does make it through (imagine our Red Rover game again, and picture a particularly eager youngster who has tried ten times to get through the line and is more determined than ever to do so on this turn).

Figure 1.3 is an example of how potent this is. The first half of the stock chart for ALVR shows prices bouncing between about $2.00 and $2.50. For month after month the stock was completely stagnant, and buyers were accumulating at these levels.

There were several attempts to push through resistance (represented by the horizontal line), but they failed . . . until the midpoint of the graph, in April.

FIGURE 1.3 After breaking out of a saucer pattern, ALVR blasted ahead on much bigger volume to a 500 percent gain in about a year.

At that point, three important things happened: (1) buyers overcame sellers, pushing prices above resistance; (2) volume increased as excitement began to build around the stock; and (3) when some profit-taking took place, prices eased back, *but they did not go beneath the former line of resistance*. From that point, the stock moved up about 500 percent in the course of a year.

The concept of how resistance can change into support (and vice versa) is critical to your understanding when reading a chart. Any sort of line—be it a trendline, a channel, or a horizontal line—has two faces to it: support and resistance. Once prices cross a line, the nature of that line changes.

Let's take another look at resistance to see how valuable it is to have an awareness of price behavior at certain levels. Figure 1.4 shows the chart for Chesapeake Energy (symbol CHK) over a period of about half a year. Early on, the price was blasting skyward to a new high, then it slumped down through August. It then regained its footing and mounted a new assault on higher prices, but it was repelled again at about the same level. A couple of months later, in November, a third attempt was made to push past the $34 barrier, but it failed a third time. You can imagine the exasperation of the owners of this stock as they watched their stock being shoved away from higher prices again and again.

FIGURE 1.4 This is known as a triple top, where a new high happens three times, but the price can't get above it. Once the attempts at overcoming this resistance failed, the stock collapsed.

What the market was telling the owners of this stock was: "The price is probably not going to go any higher." The supply of stock (those selling it) represented what is known as overhead resistance. Perhaps some people who bought earlier at $34 promised themselves that the moment the stock recovered to a breakeven level, they would get out. Perhaps most people felt the stock was fully valued at $34. The reasons really don't matter; the fact is that over a six-month period, there was an invisible line drawn on the stock chart through which prices simply could not pass.

What happened afterward is very interesting: Far from pushing above the $34 price, the stock instead started collapsing. As Figure 1.5 shows, CHK withered away from $34 per share to about 50 cents, almost a 99 percent decline. Clearly the stock had worse problems than a triple top, but the important point here is that the market was *telling* the owners of the stock something, and the triple top was a warning that this was a stock to sell, not keep.

FIGURE 1.5   After its triple top, CHK went on to a nearly 99 percent decline in price.

HISTORY REPEATS ITSELF

Another tenet of technical analysis is that human behavior doesn't change, and therefore price behavior doesn't change. If a certain pattern is predictable now, it will be just as predictable 10 years from now.

An excellent illustration of this on a single chart is Figure 1.6. The stock shown here is Red Hat (symbol RHAT) over a four-year period. For all of 2002 and most of 2003, RHAT was forming a rather large *cup with handle* pattern, indicated by the horizontal line. When it broke above this pattern, the stock just about tripled in price.

After it peaked, RHAT sank for about a year before establishing another pattern. This time, the pattern was quite similar, only smaller. And once again, after it broke above the pattern, the stock soared (this time to "only" double its breakout price, which is typical of a smaller pattern).

As you can see, once you train your eyes to find patterns and understand what the important price points are, you can take advantage of what are relatively predictable price movements.

There are a variety of factors that dictate the power of a breakout from a particular pattern. One is the pattern itself, because some patterns are simply more potent and reliable than others. Another is the volume accompanying the price movement; a stock

FIGURE 1.6 Patterns can—and often do—repeat themselves in the same chart.

moving higher on stronger and stronger volume is far more attractive than a stock moving the same direction on anemic volume. Yet another factor is the length of the pattern. A breakout from a three-year-old saucer is going to have a lot more fireworks than a breakout from a tiny two-week saucer.

Figure 1.7 provides an illustration of both (a) repetition and (b) pattern size equaling potency. The chart is the Russell 2000. The symbol is $RUT. This chart actually shows several patterns within a larger pattern. The broad pattern, shown by the two almost parallel lines, is an ascending channel. This index makes a series of higher highs (bumping up against the upper line) and higher lows (bouncing off the lower line). So the index is in a general uptrend.

Within this pattern, though, are three smaller patterns, all of which are progressively smaller versions of the first. If you look at the shape of the prices beneath the horizontal line, you can see that this price movement is virtually identical in all three instances, although the second pattern is smaller than the first, and the third pattern is smaller still.

What's interesting, of course, is what happens after the prices break above each horizontal line—the stock moves higher. But not only can we see the stock moving higher, we can also observe that the amount it goes up is a little less each time. This is an example of how the *oomph* of the push upward is closely related to how sizeable the pattern is in the first place.

FIGURE 1.7 An ascending channel and, within that pattern, three nearly identical patterns indicated by the horizontal lines.

WHEN PATTERNS WORK TOGETHER

A pattern on its own can be a good indicator of future price direction, but when two patterns work in concert, pointing to the same direction, it can add even more credence to the prediction.

The patterns need not be similar, although they can be. For example, the right shoulder of a head and shoulders pattern might itself be a smaller head and shoulder pattern. Or you might find two bullish patterns (or bearish patterns) appearing on the same chart in approximately the same time frame.

Figure 1.8 is an example of this. The stock is the Utility HOLDRS Trust (symbol UTH). There are two bearish situations shown here: The first is that UTH broke beneath an extremely long ascending trendline, which indicates a possible change in direction from bullish to bearish. As the price meandered along during the last few months of 2005 and the first few months of 2006, it formed a very well-defined head and shoulders pattern whose neckline it pierced. Since these two patterns were both bearish and happened roughly in the same period, it made a doubly bearish argument for UTH's direction.

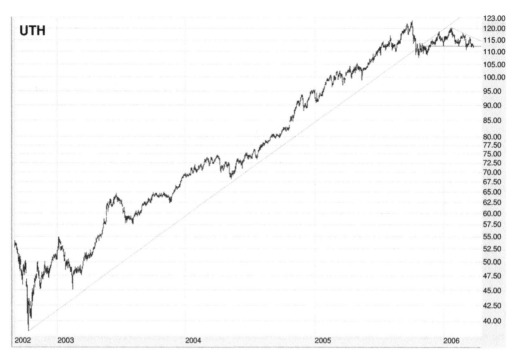

FIGURE 1.8 This chart shows two patterns in action—an ascending trendline, which was violated, and a head and shoulders pattern.

HOW TO USE THIS BOOK

This book has three principal purposes.

First, it is intended as a solid introduction to the principals and philosophy of technical analysis. This chapter was a big step in that direction, and throughout the book you will find a lot of background about the *why* behind the patterns shown.

Second, it is organized to be a teaching tool, presenting all the important patterns of technical analysis so that you can identify, interpret, and discuss with some familiarity any of the important graph types contained herein. The order in which you read these sections isn't important, because each one stands on its own as an overview of the given pattern.

And third, it is meant to be an ongoing reference for you, long after you've completed reading it. If you think you spot a certain pattern on a chart, grab this book and refer to the appropriate section. Look at past examples and discern the similarities and differences to the pattern you are considering. Having reviewed this history, you can then decide if it still makes sense to take action.

I've enjoyed charting and trading for many, many years. I hope that this book helps enrich your own trading life and provides you with added profits for years to come.

CHAPTER 2

My Personal Trading Journey

You might be wondering what my own history with trading has to do with a book about trading setups. I have three purposes in describing my own experience with the world of trading:

1. Every trader has a story, and I think it's helpful to understand a particular trader's narrative to better grasp what they have to say about the markets.
2. My experiences with trading occurred during some of the most extraordinary times in financial history—the Internet boom, the dot-com crash, the housing bubble, and the Great Recession.
3. Through the years, a lot of people have asked me to tell the Prophet story (that is, the founding and growth of my finance-oriented Internet company). Since so many people around the world use ProphetCharts, I believe it may be interesting to some readers to read about the history of the business.

EARLIEST INTEREST IN THE MARKETS

As a boy, growing up in the suburbs of Louisiana in the late 1970s, I had no exposure to anything resembling a stock chart. My family didn't have the kind of money that would have made such a thing relevant in the household, and the malaise of the 1970s made stocks seem absolutely passé in the world. Oil and gold were where the money was at, and equities were dead as far as most people were concerned. Even the esteemed magazine *BusinessWeek* declared "The Death of Equities."

I do have a couple of memories from those days however, which in retrospect do resonate with my later interest in trading. One of them was the PBS program *Wall Street Week*, hosted by Louis Rukeyser. As a child, what appealed to me about that show was its opening theme. The music, the images of traders jostling with their order tickets strewn on the floor, the lights of the ticker tape whizzing by—all of them seemed exciting and a million miles away from the humid torpor of Louisiana.

The second relevant memory I have is of raindrops. Specifically, watching the raindrops on the outside of the car's window wiggle up and down as I was being driven somewhere during my childhood. My affection for real-time streaming charts reminds me of this, because I was always mesmerized by trying to guess where a certain drop would wiggle next. You could call it chaos theory meeting the precipitation of the Deep South.

I moved away from all that rain when my family left for California in the summer of 1979. Although I didn't realize it at the time, I was moving to a place where the earliest rumblings of the personal computer revolution were taking place. In my math class, the teacher proudly announced that we'd be getting some computers. A few months later, we finally got them—a handful of Commodore PET machines, which looked as though they came from the set of *Star Trek*'s original television series.

Early in 1980, I convinced my parents to get me a computer of my own—a TRS-80 Model 1 with Level 2 BASIC and a whopping 16 kilobytes of memory. During the next few years, I engaged in all manner of computer-oriented activities: I learned to program, I wrote articles and software reviews (which was a great way for the teenaged me to get free games from manufacturers who were eager to get publicity), and I wrote my first book—*The World Connection*—when I was 16 years old. The book was about how everyone in the future would be connected electronically via computers and would engage in communications, commerce, and information exchange—not a bad prediction for a 16-year-old Louisiana boy back in 1983.

BEGINNING WITH THE CRASH

By the time I was entering college, I had written over a dozen books, and they had provided me with sufficient cash to pay my way through school, buy a nice sports car, rent a condo, and make a couple of lousy investments. In those days, limited partnerships were all the rage, and I put $5,000 into a firm that raised houseplants in Hawaii (I wish I was making this up, but I am not) and $10,000 into a firm called Sky Tech that was going to put flat panel screens in airplanes (an idea that eventually flowered, but was about 15 years too early). Both investments wound up worthless.

In 1987, the stock market was riding high, and America had fallen in love with equities in the preceding five years. I gathered up enough money to invest, and I finally was ready to take the plunge. I opened up an account with Fidelity, deposited my money, and made my first trade on October 19, 1987. If that doesn't ring a bell for you, it is the date of the Black Monday crash, when the Dow lost over 500 points in one day (which would be like the Dow crashing *thousands* of points today). My first trade was in Apple Computer, the company where I worked, and my success as an investor was off to a less-than-propitious start. Even though one of the most basic rules of trading is "Don't average down" (that is, don't buy a stock on which you've lost money merely to reduce your overall cost basis), I did precisely that in December 1987, when Apple was even cheaper, and in the end, I wound up making a profit.

I was drawn to the idea of looking at charts to make trading decisions, and I bought a trio of books that got me hooked: *Secrets for Profiting in Bull and Bear Markets* (Stan Weinstein), *How to Make Money in Stocks* (William O'Neill), and *Technical Analysis of Stock Trends* (Edwards & McGee). The last book, which is considered the bible of technical analysis, accompanied me on my honeymoon. A somewhat famous photograph of me, asleep in bed with the book on my chest, made the rounds years later.

Although computers were gaining in popularity, not many people were using programs for charting. As computer-savvy as I was, I subscribed to the *Daily Graphs* service, which was a printed book of U.S. equity charts that came out once a week from *Investor's Business Daily* (William O'Neill's organization). I can still remember eagerly flipping through the pages of graphs on weekends, marking those I found of interest.

TECHNICAL TOOLS

After a few years at Apple, I joined the investment bank Montgomery Securities in San Francisco. My joining the firm had nothing to do with trading or stocks—I went there to manage a product called MarketMax, which was a Macintosh-based trader's workstation. I confess I found the trading floor terrifically exciting, but my job had to do with providing technology to those traders, not being a trader myself.

Back in 1990, MarketMax was a very powerful system. It had streaming portfolio pages, live news, streaming charts, and many other leading-edge features. The only problem was that pretty much no one on Wall Street used Macintosh computers. Back then the Macintosh was considered the tool of illustrators and desktop publishers, and if you were on Wall Street, you used a Sun workstation (or Bloomberg terminal, or Quotron, or any other computer that didn't have an Apple logo on it).

So the MarketMax system really didn't sell very well at all, and after about a year, I joined a nine-person outfit in Los Altos called Technical Tools, run by a fellow named Chris Cooper. Whereas MarketMax was an expensive workstation intended for institutional traders, Technical Tools products were geared strictly for the retail crowd. What they sold was data, and as dry as that may sound, it was a gateway to a really exciting universe of traders.

I learned there were a couple of major products out there for at-home traders who wanted to do technical analysis—MetaStock (from Equis International, now owned by Reuters) and TradeStation (from Omega Research, which today is a publicly traded company under the symbol TRAD). It was the business of Technical Tools to provider users of these systems with historical daily data, historical tick (that is, intraday) data, and daily updates via modem. Keep in mind this was 1991, before the public Internet existed and when having a 1,200-baud modem was considered cutting edge.

One day, a fellow came in to our little office to buy every data product we sold. For this little business, most sales averaged $50 or so. This person bought our entire daily database, our entire tick database, and all our utilities products. It was a multithousand-dollar sale, and it got our attention.

I later found out the visitor, Andy Bechtolsheim, was the cofounder of Sun Microsystems, and he was working on a system to try to beat the stock market, since he now had plenty of personal wealth to manage (although he would have vastly more later, when he became Google's first investor).

PROPHET'S BEGINNING

Early in 1992, due to management changes at Technical Tools, I left the company and was trying to decide what to do next. I was an entrepreneur at heart, and I wanted to create a company similar to Technical Tools. However, I didn't have the cash to start such an operation.

Somehow—I'm not quite sure how—Andy learned about my dreams, and he called me at home wondering if I'd be interested in having him fund my startup idea. I was thrilled, of course, and I set to work on a business plan. As I did so, I pondered what to call the company. I finally landed on the name "Prophet" for three reasons—first, it suggested money; second, it suggested seeing into the future; and third, it was seven letters long, which I considered lucky. Prophet was born as a business on July 1, 1992, and its purpose was to provide historical data and daily updates to individual traders.

As with most small businesses, the excitement of starting up soon gave way to the slow process of building up an enterprise, one customer at a time. After a year, things were going along decently, and we accumulated enough cash to move into a nicer office. Shortly after doing so, we were burglarized. They took it all—the computers, the modems, the backup tapes—everything that we had spent the past year building. It was worse than being back at proverbial square one.

We spent many months recovering from that disaster, and during that time, I did a lot of my own programming to keep things going. Incredibly, even in those circumstances, we landed our first commercial deal. America Online licensed our data and daily updates for a fee that, over the long haul, added up to a very sizable amount, and they used that raw data to provide their own charts to customers.

THE INTERNET MAKES ITS APPEARANCE

Prophet was hard up for cash in those days, and my former boss from Technical Tools contacted me and said he was starting a new business called Quote.com, and he needed some office space. I rented out one of the rooms of our office to him, and once he was set up, he showed me on his computer how he could see pictures from Hawaii on a thing called a browser via something called the World Wide Web.

Given my decade in computers, and the fact I had been using modems since 1981, you would assume I would have been riveted by this whole Internet thing he was showing me, but I didn't really get it, and I wasn't really interested. After all, what was the big deal about looking at pictures from someone else's computer? It would take a couple of years for the Internet to finally make sense to me. (I should also note that Chris sold Quote.com a few years later for over $80 million, demonstrating the rewards of timing plus talent.)

In the meantime, I moved Prophet out of its nice office into a spare room of my house, since we were just about broke. Our employees had been reduced to me (working from my home) and one woman (working from hers), and we split technical and customer service duties, respectively. The amazing thing is that this is when the business started really doing well. The customers didn't know (or care) what our office looked like, and with expenses close to zero, it wasn't long before the company was throwing off almost nothing but profits.

The Internet was getting more and more attention from the press, and things completely boiled over in 1995 when Netscape went public. It was high time for Prophet to be on the Web, so I put together my own web site called ProphetData.com in order to describe and promote our goods and services to the trading community. In 1996, I took things a step further by writing my own charting program (which, given my limited programming skills, could even be considered a distant ancestor of ProphetCharts).

A company in the next town, Menlo Park, had started a business providing investment newsletters via the Internet. The company was called Investools, and they licensed our charts. Prophet continued to grow, and in 1998 the CEO of Investools proposed buying us out. I was interested in doing so, but Andy Bechtolsheim said that he'd rather put more money into the business and see me really do something with it (proving again the adage that it's easiest to get money when you don't need it).

ENTER ALEX AND JAVACHARTS

As 1999 began, Prophet once again was in a position to look for a real office (liberating my house for more common domestic activities) as well as some real engineers (as opposed to someone like me, who can program, but certainly has never pretended to be an engineer).

One of the first engineers we hired was a contractor from Ukraine named Alexander Dobrovolski. Alex's English was very limited, but his programming talent and mental acuity were astonishing. Alex and I found it cumbersome to try to speak to one another, so usually when I wanted to talk, I would instead fire up a DOS window and just start typing sentences to him. He would reply in kind.

As Alex became more acquainted with what we did, he and several other engineers transformed the hodgepodge of little programs I had written into an integrated system. He was working toward developing our first charting applet, dubbed JavaCharts, which would finally put Prophet on the proverbial map. Although the term SAAS didn't really exist at the time (that is, Software As a Service), what was happening was that Prophet was transforming itself from a data outfit to an SAAS company.

The first time we recognized that we were making serious headway was when *Forbes* gave us the top spot on their list of Web Sites for Traders. A year later, in 2002, *Barron's* gave us a similar award by deeming us the best Technical Analysis Site on the Web. We continued to win these awards for years to come.

Prophet had grown to 15 people (a few of whom are shown in Figure 2.1, which is from a portion of our trade show booth), and it was time to find a larger office space. At that time, we had set up shop in a converted hair salon, since office space was extremely hard to find. As we were all working to change the world of financial data and charting, not a week would go by that someone didn't walk in the door wanting to get their hair styled.

Since the landlord wanted to redevelop the property, we had to move yet again. There was absolutely no office space to be had in Palo Alto, so we rented a house that was also zoned for commercial use. The Internet bubble had burst, but the real estate bubble had yet to get word of this, so we found ourselves spending $17,000 per month on an unimpressive century-old house in downtown Palo Alto.

FIGURE 2.1 Prophet's trade show booth featured some of our early employees.

The free publicity from the mentions in *Forbes* and *Barron's* garnered attention from some companies interested in purchasing the business. One of the most interested parties was a large energy concern from Houston called Enron, which considered buying us as part of its own EnronOnline business. Happily, the all-stock transaction never came to fruition.

With all the good things that were happening with our growing little company, tragedy struck us in early November 2002. Alex, who had already started working on JavaCharts' successor (code-named Kandinsky) was working late, as he always did, on Friday night. At about 8 P.M., he finally decided to head home to his wife and son. No one was with him but, knowing Alex, I imagine he was either reading or lost in thought as he crossed Alma Street to get to his vehicle. A car struck him, threw him in the air, and killed him. The hit-and-run driver was never found, and Alex—who, more than anyone, was the technical heart of the business—was gone.

PROJECT KANDINSKY

The weeks following Alex's death were occupied partly with finding someone who could try to fill his very large shoes. We finally found a fellow from San Francisco who was quite brilliant and was ready to pick up the Kandinsky project. Prophet also moved out of its very-overpriced house into a much larger, proper office, as we had about twenty people working at Prophet (now renamed Prophet.net) and were happy to pay a lower price for a much nicer facility.

ProphetCharts came out in 2004, and even in its first version, it was terrific. It had a much better user interface, was far more expandable, and did away with many of the limitations that JavaCharts users found confining. ProphetCharts was the crown jewel of both the Prophet.net web site and the company.

In February of 2004, I approached our largest licensee, optionsXpress, about buying the business. They were very interested, and we got about 90 percent of the way through the acquisition process before it was abandoned. I then approached another one of our licensees, Investools, which also had strong interest. (This wasn't the same Investools mentioned earlier, but was instead an investor education company based in Utah that had, some years before, acquired the Menlo Park–based outfit, as well as its moniker.)

On January 26, 2005, Investools acquired Prophet Financial Systems, and for the first time in over 13 years, I found myself working for a company that I didn't own.

I was the Vice President of Technology at Investools, and our mission was to create, from scratch, the new Investor Toolbox that their tens of thousands of students would be using. ProphetCharts would be at the center of the Toolbox, and many of the adjunct technologies we had created over the years would also be included.

Although managing such a large project took plenty of my attention, I still found the need to express myself independently, so I started writing a blog in March 2005 called Technically Speaking. In it, I took snapshots of charts I found of interest and wrote about them. Initially, my blog had just a few readers, and I considered it little more than a personal trading diary.

Over the months, as word got out that the guy who had started Prophet was writing a trading blog, more readers were attracted to the site, and I was surprised and excited to soon pass the 1,000-readers mark. It wouldn't be very long before I was getting tens of thousands of page views every trading day.

THE SLOPE OF HOPE

The growth of the blog was very organic, and I shaped the online culture to be one where fellow traders could share ideas in an atmosphere of respect and learning (in contrast with many other trading blogs, which at the time resembled something out of *Animal House* or *Lord of the Flies*).

Blogging on a regular basis reminded me how much I enjoyed writing, so I decided to put together a book for traders about how to use ProphetCharts. There was no other book that documented ProphetCharts, and with so many users around the world, I felt there was a need for such a volume. *Chart Your Way to Profits* came out in 2007 (from John Wiley & Sons), and the stock market, coincidentally, was nearing its highest point in history.

In my own trading, I have always leaned heavily bearish. That is, I really enjoy and do better in markets that are falling as opposed to rising. I'm not sure why this is, but after many years of trading, I definitely know this to be the case. Trading in the markets of 2003 through 2007 was very frustrating as a bear, but as the Dow crossed 14,000 late in 2007, cracks were starting to appear.

The first crack happened before the Dow finally peaked. On February 27, 2007, the Chinese market fell hard, and the Dow responded by falling over 500 points. The readers of my blog—which I had renamed The Slope of Hope, to reflect my bearish sentiment—were very excited that the market was finally starting to turn down. This downturn was temporary, however, and the Dow jumped over 2,000 more points following the bottom on March 14.

The summer of 2007 revealed a few more cracks in the market, but even as the Dow started slipping during the summer, it surged once again to mark its ultimate high on October 11. Even though no one knew it at the time, the Dow was to begin a drop that would wipe out over half its value. What was about to take place in the financial world would have struck most market observers in 2007 as utterly unthinkable.

Over the next 16 months, the market moved down in violent lurches. It was not all straight down, of course, since many countertrend rallies took place, but—as a bear—the autumn of 2008 was the best trading period of my life. My own accounts were up several hundred percent, and most of those gains took place within a very short amount of time.

LESSONS LEARNED

Because I was trading so actively, I started to explore other disciplines and techniques that I had only heard about before. One of these was the Elliott Wave. During the bear market, it seemed to have an almost magical ability to spot turning points. Regrettably, my own experience with this method after the market started to turn higher was a negative one. Elliott Wave is notoriously subjective and prone to revisionist interpretation, and in my own experience, I gradually found it to have absolutely no predictive value for my own trading.

I was also drawn to the ideas of cycles, which are usually shown as sine waves of various lengths that collectively cluster on major turning points. Here again, there was no holy grail. Methods such as this can predict, as the joke goes, 170 of the past three bear markets. Divining general market direction measured over a period of months or years continues to be very difficult for most traders, and I am no exception.

During this time, however, I did learn a couple of valuable lessons. One of them had to do with not fighting the Fed, and another had to do with the importance of percentages.

"Don't fight the Fed" is one of the most common rules you will find in any trader's list. As the market fought its way back in 2009 and 2010, I assumed that the only real tool the Fed had at its disposal was interest rates. That is, once they had reduced interest rates to zero, they would be "out of bullets," and the market could finally move in its own direction.

With the introduction of quantitative easing, QE2, POMO, and many other multi-trillion-dollar programs, it was quite evident that interest rates are but *one* tool in the Fed's vast arsenal. As trite as the rule "Don't fight the Fed" appears to be, it is nonetheless good advice. Heed it well.

As for percentages, this comes down to an important reason why, in the long run, bulls outrun bears. A stock can only go down 100 percent, and even the savviest bear is fortunate to short a stock that goes down 25 percent. A long position, on the other hand, can go up by hundreds or even thousands of percent. If you short Pier One at $10, it might go to 10 cents, but the percentage move going from ten cents to $10 is orders of magnitude more powerful. (Pier One, symbol PIR, did indeed enjoy a move similar to this in the 2009 recovery.)

As the market was getting crushed in late 2008 and early 2009, a person purchasing $1,000 each of 50 randomly chosen, battered stocks would have found himself much richer in the coming months. Even if a few of these stocks went bankrupt, which is rare for a common stock, many of the others provided multihundred-percent gains that more than made up for the handful of failures. Gobbling up stocks after a brutal bear movement sounds elementary, but it can work wonders.

PROPHETCHARTS LIVES

Early in 2010, the Prophet.net web site was shut down for good, and a few months after that, the Palo Alto office was closed. It was a little sad for me to see Prophet disappear, but I knew that ProphetCharts was still in very good hands, since its owners provided it on both the thinkorswim trading platform as well as the Investor Toolbox web site. Tens of thousands of people around the world used the product every day, and it is entirely likely that, in years to come, hundreds of thousands of people will be doing so.

My own trading journey continues with ProphetCharts every day. Three years after *Chart Your Way to Profits* came out, my publisher introduced the second edition of the book, which covered its many new features. As many books as I had written over the years, I had never had a second edition of anything, so this was an exciting accomplishment for me.

Now that you've read some things about my own history building Prophet as a business and ProphetCharts as a product, let's explore how I go about the day-to-day business of trading.

THE THREE STEPS

When we created the Prophet.net web site, it was oriented around three successive themes—Explore, Analyze, and Manage. That is, a trader first seeks out opportunities via exploration, scrutinizes those ideas via technical analysis, and then acts upon and manages those positions in a real trading account. The follow sections will describe how I go about these tasks in my own trading.

Explore

This is the first stage of the investment process: seeking out stocks that fit a specific criteria in order to establish well-organized watch lists that serve as the fodder for a refined set of executable trades. This is hardest when you are first starting out, since you are dealing with a blank slate, but as your trading matures, you will assemble a reliable family of ticker symbols to use as the source of your financial instruments.

The assumption is that you have a place for the stocks that you decide to track to reside. In other words, you need access to what is commonly known as a watch list. Watch lists are typically short, named lists that behave like file folders where you can keep ticker symbols organized. Watch lists might have names such as "Momentum Stocks" or "Biotechnology" or "Short Sale Candidates." It is these lists that, over time, you will populate with ticker symbols that you find of interest.

One good place to get started is with a ticker list of major index components. For example, you might go to Google and type "S&P 100 Components," and you will have instant access to the list of 100 stocks that comprise that index. The NASDAQ 100 is another good candidate, since it will, by definition, contain a list of actively traded ticker symbols that isn't so long as to be unwieldy.

Another good source for ideas is the daily list of big market movers. You can find this kind of top 10 list on most finance sites and in many charting programs. In ProphetCharts, there is a module called Chart Toppers that is constantly updated with the stocks that fit in these categories:

- **Percent Gainers:** stocks up the most in percentage terms.
- **Dollar Gainers:** stocks up the most in absolute dollar terms.
- **New 52wk Highs:** stocks that have hit a new yearly high during the day.
- **Dollar Losers:** most down in absolute dollar terms.

- **Percent Losers:** most down in percentage terms.
- **Most Active:** stocks with the highest volume quantity.

Looking at this list at the end of each trading day usually garners you one or two interesting stocks that you aren't yet following. Of course, going through dozens and dozens of stocks each day, particularly when they are going to be the same from day to day, can be a waste of time, so making use of a filter can be helpful. In the case of Chart Toppers, there is a handy filter (Figure 2.2) that lets you establish minimum and maximum values for the price and volume and, importantly, lets you exclude the symbols that you are already following in your watch lists. This means you will only be presented with the most likely candidates for new ideas.

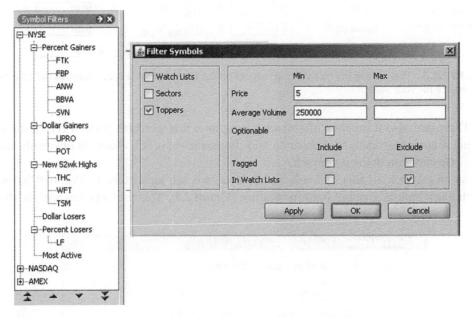

FIGURE 2.2 Chart Toppers is updated constantly to show which securities are moving at the most dramatic rates.

As you build your watch lists, the need to add more and more symbols will diminish, since you will already have a good collection from which to choose. Indeed, it will be just as important to trim away symbols that are no longer of interest, since looking at them regularly will be a waste of your time. As you go about your trading life, however, you will also get trading ideas from finance-oriented articles and blogs that you frequent. Some blogs even feature the ability to e-mail you the best ideas that their readers offer up for that day. You may want to subscribe to some of these free services to keep a regular flow of new ideas coming your direction.

Another category of free service for exploration is scanning tools and filters (Figure 2.3). One trip to a search engine with the term *free stock screener* will yield more complementary screeners than you would ever need, and some of the more popular ones, such as Microsoft's, have a surprisingly good feature set. Using these screeners is quite intuitive, since you merely enter the criteria (or, in some cases, drag the graphical elements to establish your parameters) and let the screener do the work for you.

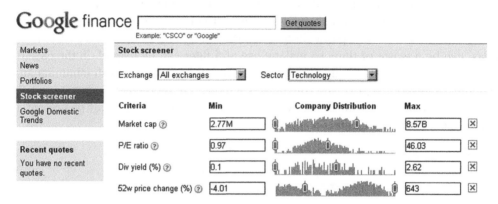

FIGURE 2.3 There are many free stock screeners on the Internet that let you establish the criteria you require for your search.

There are also a number of software programs that perform pattern recognition. Having a computer analyze thousands and thousands of stock charts is obviously far more efficient than doing it yourself.

As an example of this technology, however, we can again turn to ProphetCharts, which has a built-in Prophet Patterns feature (Figure 2.4). This tool lets you analyze the

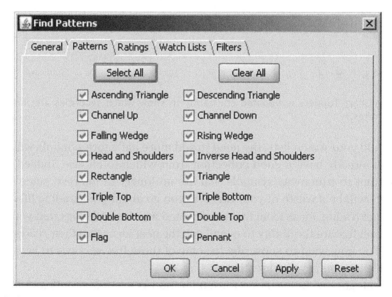

FIGURE 2.4 Prophet Patterns is built into ProphetCharts and can seek out the existence of technical patterns anywhere in the price database.

entire stock database for any of sixteen classic technical patterns. Importantly, it lets you filter out symbols that you are already following in other watch lists so that you can focus only on new ideas. You can also filter based on price, volume, whether or not the stock is optionable, and what rating it has (based on the quality of the pattern).

As you can see, building up a library of watch lists isn't difficult, considering all the resources available to you for little or no charge. Having a well-organized and well-populated database of symbols is crucial to availing yourself of profitable trading opportunities.

Analyze

Now that you have a base of stocks to work with, it's time to put your analytical skills to work. Of course, the two camps of analysis are fundamental (dealing with earnings, management, balance sheets, cash flow, and the like) and technical. Since this book is oriented toward chart patterns, its focus obviously is going to be on the technical side.

ProphetCharts is the basis of my own analysis, and even though it has hundreds of technical studies built in, I tend to focus on chart patterns instead of technical indicators for my own trading decisions. The topic of chart patterns is the basis of this book, so we will be exploring my favorite patterns soon.

For me, ProphetCharts has two principal roles for my trading: (1) it provides a clean, easy-to-embellish chart from which I can divine trading decisions (and, importantly, stop-loss levels); and (2) it gives me a mechanism to keep my trading ideas organized. This is a vital step, particularly if you intend to trade a large quantity of positions.

The watch list module is the nexus for managing all this information. My own watch lists have the following names and functions shown next. How you organize your lists is, of course, totally up to you, but this may give you some ideas for how to structure your symbols.

- **Assess:** This is where the major indexes go, such as $INDU, $SPX, $OEX, and so on. There are also a few important indicators such as $VIX.
- **Assess Two:** Here are the symbols for important market indicators that aren't quite as crucial as those in Assess, such as interest rates ($TNX), foreign exchange rates (EUR/USD, USD/JPY), and a few major ETFs (such as EEM, IWM, and SPY).
- **Core List:** This is by far the largest list, containing about 1,000 equities. Anything in this list is something I follow but which I am not watching closely. I usually go through this list once a day to extract candidates.
- **Bear Pen:** Here is the holding area for items I am considering selling short. The desired price at which I'd like to short may be some distance away, but by being in this list, the symbol gets much closer attention than it would if it were sitting in the Core list.
- **Bull Pen:** Similarly, here is the holding area for items I am considering buying.
- **Candidates Short:** When something in Bear Pen is at a desirable price, I move it into this watch list, which is the batting cage, so to speak, for positions that I intend to sell short.

- **Candidates Long:** Likewise, items from Bull Pen are moved into this watch list once I am ready to actually purchase them.
- **Long Positions:** When I have a true long position in my portfolio, the symbol winds up here. Any given symbol is only in one list at one time.
- **Short Positions:** When I have a short position, the symbol is moved from Bear Pen into this list.
- **ETFs:** Finally, I sequester the 160 exchange-traded funds I follow into a special watch list, and I have tagged (that is, bold-faced) the 40 or so ETFs that I want to look at on a daily basis.

This organization makes my trading life much easier, particularly since I may have over 100 positions "live" in my portfolio at any given moment. You probably will not track this many positions, but the preceding method of moving symbols from place to place will save you a lot of time and allow you to focus on actually looking at the handful of charts that demand your attention.

Manage

The management of your positions focuses on managing two possible outcomes for each position in your portfolio: (1) the prospect of profits, which you must decide when to take; and (2) the prospect of a loss, or a reduced profit, by your stop-loss level being hit. As for managing your profits, determining how much cash to take out of a position is clearly a case-by-case decision. As for minimizing losses (or preserving profits) via stop-loss orders, it is vital, in my opinion, that you keep your stops fresh, by making relatively frequent updates, taking into account the latest information on the price chart.

I typically update my own stops once every two or three days, since I want to try to minimize risk and lock in profits as much as I reasonably can. Toward this end, I have put together a spreadsheet of all my positions so that I can closely monitor my risk. Of course, managing risk through stop-loss prices is imperfect, since there is no guarantee that a position will not gap in price far away from your stop. For instance, if you are long AAPL, and you have a stop-loss at $300, and one day the company announces bad news and the stock opens at $250, the fact that your stop-loss was at $300 doesn't earn you back that $50 per share. You will simply be taken out at the current market price.

In spite of this imperfection, big gaps are relatively unusual and normally occur only when companies are taken over at rich premiums or have surprising earnings news (either good or bad). You can create a spreadsheet similar to mine to manage your own positions, and doing so is actually quite constructive, since it will help you get a better grasp on good portfolio management. By no means does your spreadsheet have to be a copy of the one I put together, but for some ideas, here are the principal rows in my Positions spreadsheet and their meanings.

(a) **Symbol:** The ticker symbol.

(b) **Stop:** The stop-loss price; that is, the specific price at which a market order will be triggered to get out of a position. For long positions, the stop is below the current market prices, and for short positions, the stop is above the current market price.

(c) **Last:** This is the most recent price for the security. Now this is where using the macro function in Excel can be handy, since it can fetch the price for you. Populating your spreadsheet with stock price information is something I'll leave to you, since it varies depending on the broker you use or the subscriptions to data services you may have. At a minimum, you could hand-enter this data once a day.

(d) **% Chg:** This is the day's percentage change for the security.

(e) **Stop Risk:** This, for me, is one of the most important columns on the spreadsheet, since it shows the percentage difference between the current price and the current stop-loss level. I like to see a fairly small figure here, rarely exceeding 5 percent. I'm most comfortable with about a 2 percent to 3 percent figure here.

(f) **Entry:** The price paid for the position.

(g) **Polarity:** This is +1 if the position is long and –1 if the position is short.

(h) **Target $:** This is a hand-entered value of how big I would like the position to be.

(i) **Calc Quant:** This is a computed value derived by dividing the figure in (h) by the current price in (c), showing the quantity in shares needed.

(j) **Tgt Pos:** This is a hand-entered figure of the quantity of shares I want for the position; normally it is very close to the figure in (i), but I usually round the figure up or down a little to make it cleaner (as opposed to having positions of 193 shares, 279 shares, and so forth).

(k) **Live Pos:** This is also a hand-entered figure of the quantity of shares that are actually live and in position.

(l) **% of Pos:** This figure is (k) divided by (j), and the value is usually equal to 100 percent. However, if you *scale in* to a position, you might have only a portion of the target position established as a live position, and this column helps you track which items are not at 100 percent yet.

(m) **Position:** The dollar value of the position, which is the figure in (k) times (c).

(n) **Net P/L:** This is the net profit or loss, calculated by multiplying the quantity in (k) by the difference in price between (f) and (c).

(o) **P/L %:** This is the net profit or loss in percentage terms, which is (n) divided by (m).

(p) **Entry Risk:** This is the risk based on the entry price, which is the percentage difference between the stop at (b) and the entry price at (e).

(q) **True Risk:** This is the more important risk, and it is the percentage difference between the stop at (b) and the last price at (c).

As you can see, the spreadsheet can be as complicated as you like. The objective isn't to make it complex, of course. The goal is to get a clear picture of your positions and risk profile. There are many other possibilities for cells in such a spreadsheet, including the total number of short and long positions, what your total risk is, the ratio of longs to shorts, and so on. As you develop your spreadsheet, it will take on a life of its own, and you may find the need to tweak it from time to time to incorporate features that you hadn't considered before.

Trading is a very personal experience, and the techniques, tools, charts, watch lists, and spreadsheets you create are all of your design. Don't be intimidated by the possibilities, since persevering in these tasks will not only be educational for you as a trader but will also help reduce the overall risk of taking on something which is admittedly risky—speculating in the financial markets.

We will now turn our attention to the principal focus of this book, which is historical price patterns, their results, and their nuances. Use the following chapters as a reference, and feel free to peruse them in any order that interests you. This book is intended to be used as a reference again and again, and very little expertise is required to understand the concepts presented in any one section.

PART II

The Patterns

CHAPTER 3

Ascending Triangles

When a security is ascending in price, forming a series of higher lows (the ascending trendline) and identical highs (the horizontal line above it), and it is already in a general uptrend, it is forming an ascending triangle pattern. This pattern is a continuation pattern—that is, this pattern is a bullish pattern when formed in the context of a trend that is already bullish.

DEFINITION OF THE PATTERN

The pattern has several criteria, and symbol TDG shown in Figure 3.1 provides a good example. First, you should have an ascending trendline acting as support; second, you should have a horizontal line representing the overhead supply of the stock that is slowly being eaten away by new buyers; and third, you should have a breakout above the horizontal line.

Volume can play a role too, although it isn't shown in this example. Volume typically dries up as these patterns progress, because traders are losing interest in the security since it evidently isn't breaking out but is merely in the slow process of accumulation. If and when a breakout occurs, then volume should spike higher, evidence of the fact that the overhead supply (formerly at the horizontal line) has been dispensed with, and a hoard of new buyers (or reenergized former buyers) are sweeping in to purchase the security.

The chart in Figure 3.1 climbs a hearty 62 percent after its breakout before it has any meaningful retracement. If you want to establish an estimated target for a stock that has broken out of an ascending triangle, measure the different between the lowest and highest parts of the triangle and add that to the horizontal line. For instance, if the low price was about $25 (as is the case in this example), and the high price was $35, then the target price would be $35 (that is, $35 plus the difference between $25 and $35, $10, which yields $45).

FIGURE 3.1 This is the chart for Transdigm Group (symbol TDG), which surged after its breakout from the ascending triangle formation.

You should also remember this pattern is synonymous with the term *right-angle triangle*, since you could form a complete triangle by connecting the leftmost points of the two existing lines. The volume doesn't need to descend for this pattern to be valid, but the uptrend should be established, because this is a continuation, not a reversal, formation.

PSYCHOLOGY BEHIND THE PATTERN

First keep in mind that, as a continuation pattern, a stock forming an ascending triangle is already in an uptrend and, by and large, has a relatively happy population of owners of the stock.

The stock ascends, reaches a certain price level, and backs away. It backs away because the sellers overwhelm the buyers, and the price cannot ascend any farther. These sellers represent either overhead supply (former purchasers of the stock at this level that want to get out) or simply want to get out at a price they feel is the highest the stock is likely to achieve in the near term.

The stock ascends again, reaching the same level, and it fades away. Owners and new buyers are getting somewhat weary of the stock's inability to make them money, but the selling dries up at a price higher than before, establishing a *higher low* for the chart.

Yet again, the stock price moves up to the same level and sells off. Volume is getting lower and lower, because fewer and fewer people are interested in participating in a security that can only seem to reach a certain price level and no higher. However, yet another "higher low" is made, which is constructive.

During the stock's fourth push higher, it pushes past the horizontal line, and people get excited. Current owners buy more stock, now that it is finally doing something interesting. Bystanders who were waiting for a breakout leap in. The volume is much higher, and the stock lurches forward before selling off again. The selling sinks the price, but it reaches approximately the same level as the horizontal line (if not a little bit below) before stabilizing.

Now that the line representing resistance has not transformed into a support line, more buyers accumulate at this price level, and the stock pushes to a new high. Now the pattern is finally complete, those who wanted to get out of the stock have been satisfied, and the current block of owners of this security are happy to finally see their holdings lurching forward in value.

EXAMPLES

What follows are several real-life examples of the ascending triangle taking place. These will serve as helpful templates as you encounter new instances of this pattern during your own trading.

Exide Technologies

Figure 3.2 shows Exide (symbol XIDE) jump toward $8.40 and then sink away. It pushes higher to the same level and then sinks once again to a higher low. On its third attempt,

FIGURE 3.2 Symbol XIDE broke out, very briefly dipped beneath its top line, and then gapped higher. A modest amount of "wiggle room" when setting stops can sometimes keep you in a valuable position like this, since it only took a couple of days to move firmly higher.

Pattern Start: 10/29/2007   Breakout Price: $8.40   Percentage Increase: 134%
Breakout: 2/1/2008   Peak Price: $19.66

it pierces the $8.40 level but, importantly, it sinks a little beneath this line in the ensuing two days before gapping higher and starting its trip to a 134 percent increase in price.

This illustrates the importance of not having overly tight stops, particularly when a pattern first breaks out. If you are waiting for a break above $8.40, and you buy the stock at $8.45, you don't need to set your stop at exactly $8.39 just because that's under the breakout point. You instead might want to put in an initial amount of "wiggle room"—for example, 5 percent would permit the stock to dip to 7.98 without getting stopped-out.

Echelon Corporation

The chart in Figure 3.3 shows that the number of touch-points for the horizontal line and ascending line don't have to be equal. For this example, the stock makes four failed

FIGURE 3.3 Here ELON provides some confusion for traders, since it broke above $9 and soon thereafter dipped beneath the breakout. Two weeks later, it finally provided a breakout that stuck.

Pattern Start: 1/5/2009   Breakout Price: $9.00   Percentage Increase: 67%
Breakout: 7/20/2009   Peak Price: $15.00

attempts to cut through the line at $9, but there are only two touch-points on the ascending line. As long as the pattern itself can still be confined to a triangle, the number of points doesn't really matter (provided, of course, there are at least two of them!)

We also see, as is common, that the initial breakout is followed by a penetration back into the triangle. As long as the price doesn't actually cut beneath the ascending trendline, the pattern can still be considered intact. If your stops are too stringent, you will get stopped out of opportunities that ultimately move substantially higher in value.

SBA Communications

Utility companies aren't known for dramatic price moves, but a 37 percent increase in price in a short amount of time, as shown in Figure 3.4, is still impressive. The target move of $5 was actually achieved twice over, as SBAC moved from $27 to $37.

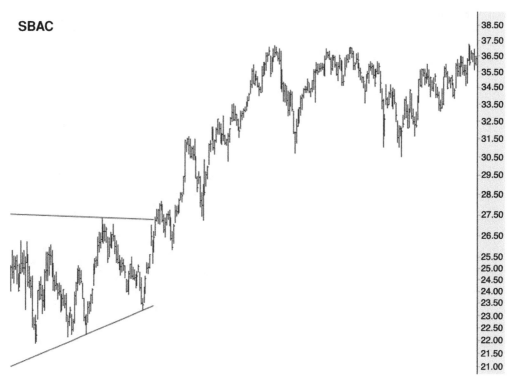

FIGURE 3.4   Once again we have an example of a "quick dip" by way of SBAC.

Pattern Start: 4/9/2009   Breakout Price: $27   Percentage Increase: 37%
Breakout: 9/16/2009   Peak Price: $37

Brookfield Asset Management

For the sake of easy identification and consistency, it is best to look for ascending triangles that have a horizontal line as their top, but as you become more experienced with pattern identification, you can allow for some leeway with this rule. In Figure 3.5, the top line of the triangle is tilted slightly higher. This is actually positive for the stock, since it underscores the positive bias of the price. The drawback to this violation of the pattern's basic definition is that it undercuts the notion of a strong price breakout once a very clear level of resistance becomes an equally clear level of support.

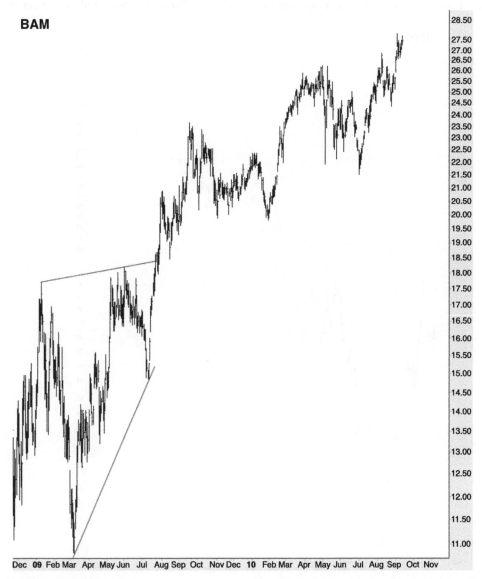

FIGURE 3.5 Symbol BAM illustrates that you can allow some latitude for the breakout line to not be perfectly flat.

Pattern Start: 1/9/2009   Breakout Price: $18.50   Percentage Increase: 27%
Breakout: 7/23/2009   Peak Price: $23.50

Rockwell Automation, Inc.

Rockwell Automation, Inc.

A very clean example is shown in Figure 3.6, which also sports a slightly ascending line for the top. There are a couple of interesting properties to note about this chart: (1) it is a very clean breakout without any retracement below the breakout line; and (2) although it is a good ascending triangle, it also strongly resembles a cup with handle pattern (covered in a different section of this book). These are both bullish patterns,

FIGURE 3.6 Symbol ROK could be viewed as both an ascending triangle as well as a very tall cup with handle pattern, both of which are bullish.

Pattern Start: 1/6/2009   Breakout Price: $34   Percentage Increase: 82%
Breakout: 7/20/2009   Peak Price: $62

so they agree that the direction of the stock is going to be higher. The 82 percent lift in the stock's price following the breakout affirms the power of both these patterns in this instance.

Louisiana-Pacific Corporation

Both lines in Figure 3.7 conform to the definition of the ascending triangle pattern, as it features a flat line at $8.12 and ascending line with two touchpoints. As is apparent

FIGURE 3.7 LPX has a target price of $11, which is slightly exceeded here.

Pattern Start: 9/11/2009   Breakout Price: $8.12   Percentage Increase: 66%
Breakout: 2/20/2010   Peak Price: $13.44

from the examples in this section, the price after an ascending triangle breakout is prone to a modest retracement and penetration back within the pattern. The target price is a little above $11, and the stock pushes above $13 before relaxing. You may find it most profitable in your own trading to close out half the position once the target price is met and retrain the other half (with increasingly tight stops) to enjoy any supplementary profits that might be garnered from better prices.

China Yuchai

It's been mentioned several times that this is a continuation pattern. Let's take a look at a very well-formed ascending triangle that takes place in the wrong context—that is, outside the bounds of an upwardly trending market. (See Figure 3.8.)

FIGURE 3.8 Because this pattern is not in an uptrend, it fails badly, even though CYD's ascending triangle was very clean when examined outside of its context.

In this case, both the ascending trendline and the horizontal line have four touch-points, very neatly defining the triangle. In the fifth attempt to move higher, the stock shoots above the triangle, pushing quickly higher in just two days. Things start going wrong, however. The price sinks beneath the breakout price, and continues to sink, penetrating where the ascending trendline would be if it were extended to the right. After a sharp downturn, it tries again to move higher, but it fails to even meet its recent high, and it begins sinking again, this time dropping below its recent low. The stock continues dropping, and by the time the damage is done, the stock has plunged from about $11.50 to $2.50.

This emphasizes the importance of viewing a pattern in the proper and supportive context. An inverted head and shoulders pattern isn't very meaningful at the top of a stock chart that has already risen dramatically; a head and shoulders pattern doesn't mean much if a stock has already plunged from $20 to 50 cents; and an ascending triangle doesn't really matter if a market has been falling or trading flat for a long time.

SUMMARY

You have learned a number of lessons about ascending triangles that can be applied to most technical patterns, including these four: (1) you can allow for some leeway from the rigid definition; (2) you can also allow a few percentage points in price movement for the retracement to take place; (3) volume during the pattern formation isn't imperative, but during the breakout, it is quite important; and (4) for continuation patterns, it is important that the pattern appear within the proper supportive context in order for it to have meaning.

The ascending triangle is relatively easy to identify and has a cleanly defined target price. The more you look at the examples in this book, the more you will train your eyes to spot similar patterns in your own charts.

CHAPTER 4

Ascending Wedges

When price bars are confined by an ascending trendline beneath and another trendline above, and these lines converge on the right side, this is called an ascending wedge. The pattern highlights price action that, although moving higher, is becoming increasingly confined. Because the lower trendline is the most vulnerable to being violated, this pattern is a reliable bearish indicator when and if the price bars slip beneath support. This pattern has a close relative in the form of the descending wedge, which is covered in another chapter.

DEFINITION OF THE PATTERN

The pattern requires just two lines: Both of them are ascending, but they are not parallel. Instead, they converge on the right side, although the price bars may break beneath the lower trendline well before this intersection.

Figure 4.1 shows Banco Santander (symbol STD), which went down 44 percent in price after its ascending wedge was broken. Take note that the price didn't just plunge straight down after the pattern broke. On the contrary, the stock went on to a new high a few weeks thereafter. However, the pattern's long formation and break to the downside was an important harbinger of the forthcoming movement of the stock, which was decidedly to the downside.

STD

FIGURE 4.1 STD's ascent was long-lived and substantial before it finally gave in to selling pressure.

PSYCHOLOGY BEHIND THE PATTERN

Because the prices are generally ascending during the formation of an ascending wedge, holders of the stock are increasingly optimistic and bullish about its prospects. The nature of this pattern, however, is one in which the strength of the movement higher loses energy until such time as the supporting trendline can no longer bear the *weight* of those who want to sell the stock.

The tell-tale sign of this pattern is the upper trendline, because the distance between the *higher lows* of the lower trendline and the *higher highs* of the upper trendline becomes more and more narrow. Buyers simply are unable to give the stock as much lift with each successive push higher, and once the price breaks beneath the lower trendline, the mass of buyers (who until this time were happily watching their profits increase) may make a rush for the exits by way of sell orders.

Even if such a stampede doesn't take place, the fact is that the cleanly defined uptrend has been broken, and the stock is vulnerable to a sell-off, since those following the trend no longer have a rational technical reason to hold on. This temptation to sell can become widespread, and if people start acting on that temptation, then the selling can feed on itself.

EXAMPLES

Here are five actual instances of ascending wedges taking place in U.S. stock markets.

Arkansas Best Corporation

Here in Figure 4.2 we have a simple example of an ascending wedge. The lower trendline spans from April to September of 2009, and the resistance trendline above it is at a less sharp angle. It would be many months before these lines would converge, but as long as the price breaks out of the pattern before this intersection, the pattern can be considered complete.

Although this stock fell from about $29 to $24 after the initial break, it would take several months of meandering before it finally dipped below $19 in the summer of 2010. The important thing to note about this chart is that the broad direction of the stock changed, and that change was signaled by the termination of the ascending wedge.

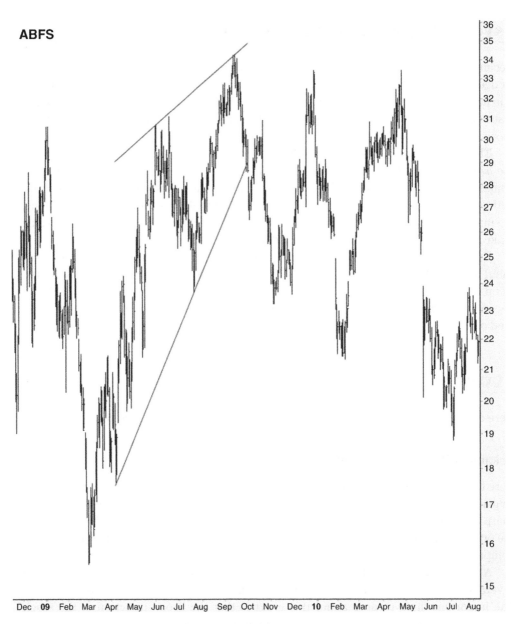

FIGURE 4.2 The violation of the lower trendline commenced the beginning of a new, broad pattern in price that was downward in spite of a series of significant buying spurts.

Pattern Start: 4/7/2009   Break Price: $29   Price Drop: 38%
Pattern Break: 9/30/2009   Postbreak Low: $18

On Assignment, Inc.

On Assignment, Inc. (symbol ASGN), charted in Figure 4.3, illustrates a more dramatic plunge following an ascending wedge, and there is no retracement following the price break, meaning that only those who were already in the trade (or got aboard quickly) reaped the full benefit of this drop; others didn't have a second chance.

The ascending wedge can act as a reversal pattern (changing a bullish uptrend to a downtrend) or a continuation pattern (representing an upward pause in a general

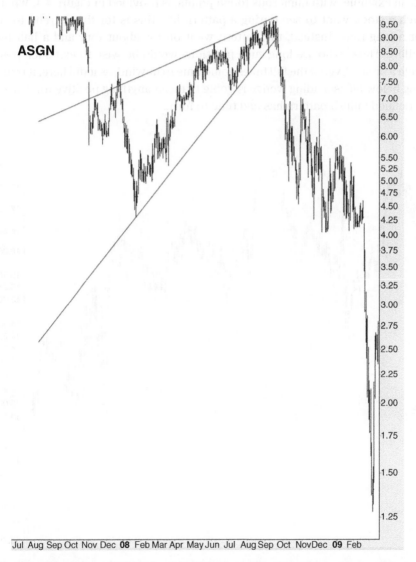

FIGURE 4.3 There was no looking back for this chart once the pattern was complete.

Pattern Start: 1/24/2008   Break Price: $9   Price Drop: 86%
Pattern Break: 9/23/2008   Postbreak Low: $1.30

downward-moving trend). For ASGN, this wedge was a continuation pattern, since the stock had been falling already during 2007. The stock made an impressive countertrend rally from about $4.75 to about $9.50, then it broke the uptrend at about $9. From there, it dropped almost to penny-stock status, losing 86 percent by late February of 2009.

Duke Energy Corporation

A very clean example, with numerous touch-points, is provided in Figure 4.4. What owners of such a stock want to see during a pattern like this is for the uptrend to remain intact for a long time. Instead, the pattern went on for about four and a half months before failing. Those who are long such positions would be wise to exit such positions during such a break. Even if the fall takes some time to unwind, as it did here, it is unlikely that falling below an ascending wedge is going to mean anything positive for prices until a clearly defined bullish pattern has had time to form.

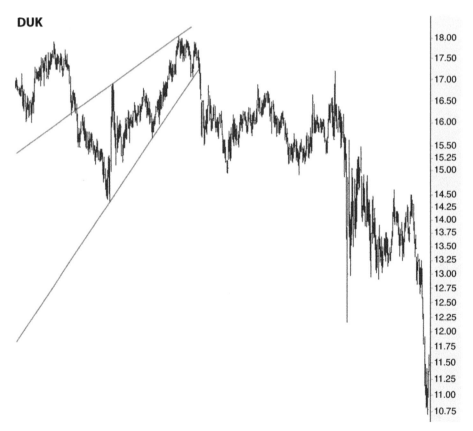

FIGURE 4.4 Serious selling didn't start taking place for several months after this ascending wedge was broken.

Pattern Start: 8/30/2007   Break Price: $16.50   Price Drop: 36%
Pattern Break: 1/17/2008   Postbreak Low: $10.50

Emulex Corporation

Using measured targets can be a risk-reducing way of taking profits off the proverbial table when you are trading, but as mentioned elsewhere in this book, it may be best, depending on your tolerance for risk, to take only partial profits when a simple measured target has been achieved and leave the balance of the position in place (using frequently refreshed stop-loss levels).

Take Figure 4.5, for instance. The standard for measuring price moves is to take the extremes in price of the pattern—in this instance, $13 and $17—and compute their difference. Next, you subtract this difference from the breaking point, which is $15.50.

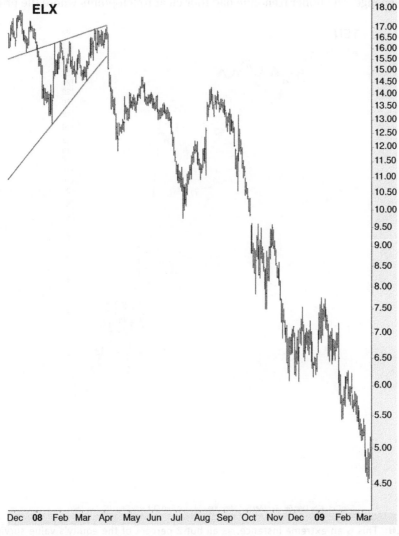

FIGURE 4.5 This stock experienced a waterfall decline for nearly a year before it stabilized.

Pattern Start: 1/2/2008   Break Price: $15.50   Price Drop: 71%
Pattern Break: 4/4/2008   Postbreak Low: $4.50

That yields a price target of $11.50, which is relatively modest but which makes sense, considering the pattern's small size. However, the stock kept falling to $4.50 in a relatively orderly series of lower lows and lower highs. Even if profits were taken on a portion of the position once $11.50 was reached, the trade overall would have been much more profitable by simply keeping the stop-loss fresh and letting the stock's downward movement reach its potential.

Tenneco, Inc.

The final example in this chapter, Figure 4.6, is the most dramatic of all with respect to percentage change. The upper trendline had four clear touch-points where the price was

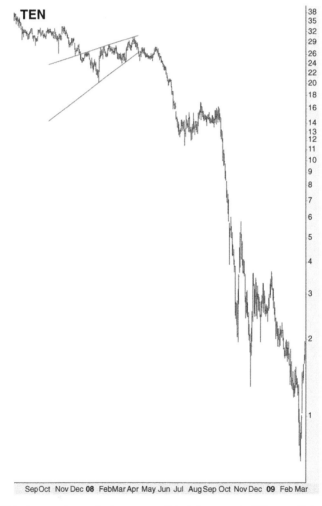

FIGURE 4.6 This is an extreme instance, as all but 2 percent of the equity's value survived the plunge.

Pattern Start: 12/28/2007   Break Price: $26.50   Price Drop: 98%
Pattern Break: 4/11/2008   Postbreak Low: $0.50

trying to push higher, but it could not get past the ascending line of resistance. The lower trendline had three touch-points, the final of which failed and permitted the stock to drift sideways for a couple of weeks.

Once outside the confines of the pattern, the price began falling heartily from about $26 to about half that price. At that point it stabilized for over a month, giving panicked bulls an opportunity to either make an exit or, for those so inclined, to buy more of a stock that now seemed to be on sale. Regrettably for those with long positions, the selling was not over, and the downtrend resumed in an even more powerful fashion until a full 98 percent of the stock's price at the pattern breakdown was eliminated.

It is very rare to see a stock move this dramatically, but the very well-defined ascending wedge gave a strong sell signal once the price pattern was broken.

SUMMARY

Wedges can be one of the easier patterns to spot, but they can also be one of the more challenging to trade. Unlike patterns with more clearly defined zones of support and resistance, the ascending wedge can allow prices for drift for weeks or even months after the pattern has been complete. In most instances, however, even a stubborn stock that is trying to push higher will not exceed its peak price point from the pattern itself, and you can remain in the short position even while the stock bides its time. As long as the pattern is well defined and is evidently broken, you can consider a price failure beneath an ascending wedge to be a reliably bearish trading signal.

CHAPTER 5

Channels

The channel pattern is one of the easiest to identify, although it is not very common. It consists of a pair of parallel trendlines that confine a stock's price for a meaningful length of time. One of the interesting things about this pattern is that it can serve three different purposes: It can provide a series of buying and shorting opportunities as it oscillates within the pattern; it can serve as a buy signal when broken to the upside; and it can serve as a sell signal (or short signal) when broken to the downside.

The reason channels are fairly rare is because a stock's uptrend or downtrend is usually too random or biased in a particular direction to create a clean trend. Ideally, the price movement between these two trendlines will represent a sine wave, with the price rallying up to resistance, stalling, and then selling off to support. The more times it does this, the more useful it is as a tool for swing trade opportunities, and the more potent it is when it finally does break in one direction or another, as it is bound to do eventually.

DEFINITION OF THE PATTERN

A channel is made up of two trendlines that are more or less parallel. They may be ascending or descending, and if you use a high-end charting program such as ProphetCharts, you can make use of the Channel tool to establish those boundaries with just three data points. Most channel objects can also show the median line (that is, a third parallel line between the other two) and also lines for the 25 percent and 75 percent levels (which are, in turn, between the upper and median trendlines and the lower and median trendlines).

The price should have at least two touch-points on each of the two trendlines in order to qualify as a channel, and the trendlines should be parallel (giving a few degrees of latitude; if it's much more than this, you are looking at a wedge pattern or a broadening pattern instead). At some point, the price will break out of the channel, because no channel trend lasts forever. When the price finally does this, you may also consider that a buy or sell signal, depending on which side of the channel prices emerge.

An example of a channel is in Figure 5.1, which shows the price of CurrencyShares Euro Trust (symbol FXE), the exchange-traded fund for the Euro/U.S. dollar cross-rate. This shows three touch-points on the top line and two touch-points on the bottom. Once it is clear that a channel has been established, you can take advantage of this by going long the security with each instance of prices hitting support and taking your profits when the resistance line is hit. If you want to be particularly aggressive, you can even sell the security short (in other words, reverse your position) at resistance, cover the short at support, and yet again go long the security.

FIGURE 5.1 The ETF for the EUR/USD foreign exchange cross-rate bounced for months within this channel, providing both long and short opportunities.

Keeping this kind of trading going can be profitable for a while, but, as has been said, the channel will be guaranteed to break either up or down at some point, and you must be prepared to get out of your *cycle trades* when this happens. Indeed, when the channel is finally broken, you might elect to make a trade of a large size in the direction of the breakout.

PSYCHOLOGY BEHIND THE PATTERN

When a security is trading within a channel, there is a tug-of-war taking place between buyers and sellers, and for whatever reason, the party with the most strength keeps changing on a fairly regular basis. For instance, the buyers may be more aggressive for three weeks, and then a certain high price is achieved (which might be a higher high or a lower high, depending on the channel's direction), at which time the sellers get the upper hand and create more selling pressure than the buyers can handle, thus pushing prices back down to support.

If the channel is ascending, then the stock is generally being accumulated over the long haul, and buyers generally have more strength than the sellers. A break above an ascending channel shows an exceptional amount of buying strength, whereas a break below such a channel illustrates that the buying power is no longer able to sustain the angle of the price's growth.

A descending channel exhibits a stock that is generally weak but that keeps attracting buyers who believe they are getting a bargain of sorts. As the stock falls toward resistance, more nervous owners will decide the risk is not worth it and will abandon the stock, but eventually enough buyers come in to reverse the trend and continue the oscillation of the price to the upside. Prices snapping below a descending channel are giving in to the selling pressure and may be entering a hard fall, whereas prices pushing above and away from the descending channel are signaling a trend change, now that all the weak hands have been cleaned out of the security.

EXAMPLES

Channels are relatively easy to spot, but the following examples should help train your eyes what to seek.

Amazon.com, Inc.

One of the strongest stocks in the first decade of the twenty-first century was Amazon. Of course, Amazon also was very strong during the Internet bubble of the late 1990s and, near its peak, its founder Jeff Bezos was on the cover of *Time* magazine as Man of the Year. As the stock plunged during 2000 and 2001, the cover story was pointed out as a contrarian indicator, and some people felt that Amazon might go the way of Pets.com and simply plummet into oblivion.

Clearly, this was not the case, as Amazon had real staying power, and the stock found stability by 2002. Beginning in that year, the stock established its first touch-point on the line that would later be recognized as its supporting trendline. It moved steadily from $15 to about $60, establishing the first point of its resistance line, sold off for two and half years to about $25, stabilized, and then started a new uptrend.

This up-and-down pattern lasted for an entire decade, and even during those individual up-and-down cycles there were smaller up-and-down cycles that traders may have exploited as well. But the extraordinarily wide, broad uptrend was the safest way for more conservative traders to use AMZN as a vehicle for profits.

Suppose, for instance, a person in 2008 wanted to own Amazon, but he didn't know what would represent a good buying price. After all, the stock was falling, like most other stocks, in late 2008, and those not equipped with charts or the requisite knowledge would have no idea where Amazon would find support, except for a guarantee that it would not go below $0.

This channel pattern, however, indicated that a price close to $35 would be a touchpoint on the ascending trendline. If it broke this line, the long position should be abandoned, and a trader might want to instead wait for $25, which was the prior major low. This was not necessary, however, because the stock formed a V-shaped bottom and moved up, almost uninterrupted, to a quadrupling of price.

There's another interesting aspect about this chart, and that is the horizontal line shown in Figure 5.2. This line, at about $100, seemed to represent resistance for the stock, particularly since it was the former high price. A surprisingly good earnings report blasted the stock above this zone, and within a few weeks, the price perfectly touched the resistance trendline. It continued to make small pushes down and up, but always above the horizontal line (its former resistance) and below the upper trendline (resistance that remained for many, many years).

FIGURE 5.2 Even with a stupendous burst above the horizontal line, the AMZN price still remained contained in the ascending channel.

It's worth pointing out that a person going long or short a stock, even exactly at one of the trendlines, isn't guaranteed a profit. Imagine a person selling AMZN short late in 2009 at about $145, which was the point reached soon after the tremendous push above that horizontal line. The stock did indeed fall, but then it reversed and went on to a higher high. It fell again even further, but once more pushed to an even higher high. A person holding this short position, hoping the stock would obediently fall back to the lower support line would have been frustrated and disappointed. Indeed, although this chart does not show it, the price wound up pushing above this decade-long channel, illustrating that Amazon was even stronger than this broad uptrend suggested.

Harris Corporation

Besides taking advantage of the ups and downs of price action within a channel, you can also make use of a breakout. One of the more potent forms of breakout is from within the confines of a descending price channel, as shown in Figure 5.3. This stock, symbol HRS, was in a very long-term downtrend, lasting from 1978 to 1992—a decade and a half.

There were a couple of great buying opportunities of HRS during the downtrend in 1982 and 1990, but these were within the bounds of the channel. When the price made its fifth and final assault on the resisting trendline in 1992, it emerged from its 15-year price prison and commenced a climb of over 300 percent. Analyzing this signal would be simple for someone following this channel, simply because an emergence from the

FIGURE 5.3 The breakout above the resistance trendline was a strong buy signal in 1982.

Pattern Start: 5/9/1978   Break Price: $5.37   Percentage Change: 309%
Pattern Break: 10/20/1992   Postbreak Price: $22

channel above resistance (especially for such a long-term chart) was a clear buy signal. It stair-stepped its way to a series of higher highs and higher lows for years to come.

When looking at the big picture, you can see the trend of this stock actually changed late in 1990, two years before the breakout. But that would have been impossible to know at the time. A more conservative trader looking for confirmation of a trend change would have taken his cue from the penetration of the long-standing resistance line, even though the stock had already doubled by the time the breakout took place.

Citi Trends

The chart of symbol CTRN, shown in Figure 5.4, is another instance of a breakout providing a buy signal, but this one would require a bit more intestinal fortitude since the breakout was followed by a rather large retracement before it finally moved higher.

FIGURE 5.4 Citi Trends hit its supporting trendline many more times than its resisting trendline, but in the end, the buyers overcame the sellers and the stock recaptured its former price level.

Pattern Start: 8/9/2007   Break Price: $14.50   Percentage Change: 93%
Pattern Break: 2/1/2008   Postbreak Price: $28.93

The breakout took place at $14.50 on February 1, 2008, and the stock moved to $17. It dipped back to the breakout price, moved to $17 again, and then fell to just beneath $13. Whether or not a trader stayed with this position would depend on where the stop-loss was placed (assuming they had one). A good position for a stop-loss in this instance would have been the most recent *higher low* that had taken place before the breakout, which was at about $12.50. The fact that the price stayed well above this level meant that another higher low was being established, which is constructive to a bullish breakout.

By April, the stock had not only recovered but had also provided a handsome gap-up in price, which was another confirmation of the new bullish direction. CTRN enjoyed a 93 percent gain before its next significant weakness.

iShares MSCI Brazil Index

A price break beneath a channel is just as actionable as a price break above, and CH-5 illustrates this point with a long-term graph of EWZ, which is the exchange-traded fund for Brazilian stocks. The ascending channel was in place for six years, with an unbroken string of higher highs and higher lows. The final higher high took place in the first half of 2008, and the stock descended to the supporting line.

A trader looking at the chart at this time would naturally and correctly assume a buying opportunity was at hand. After all, the stock was in a very long-term uptrend, and past instances of prices that approached support had provided excellent returns on long positions for six years running. That same trader, assuming his stop-loss order was in place, would have been taken out of the position at a loss, since EWZ broke its long-term support at the point that is circled.

The same trader could make two decisions at this point. He could either step aside, remaining unaffiliated with the stock, since there was no actionable bullish trade. He could also decide it was a good opportunity to sell the stock short, since the failure of such a sizable pattern implied the potential for a big move downward.

The price fell from $63 at its break to $23 at its bottom, a 63 percent decline. An even more aggressive trader might have purchased some long-term puts on EWZ, yielding a much more substantial percentage gain (naturally with an equal amount of added risk).

FIGURE 5.5 This channel was in its sixth year when it finally broke down.

Pattern Start: 6/20/2002   Break Price: $63   Percentage Change: −63%
Pattern Break: 8/12/2008   Postbreak Price: $23

Incyte Corporation

Downward breakouts can be meaningful with both ascending channels, as shown in Figure 5.5, and descending channels, as illustrated by Figure 5.6. The stock, Incyte (symbol INCY), had been in an uptrend in 2007 and early 2008, but it began reversing and established a descending channel with three touch-points on each of its channel's trendlines. The big break came on December 6, 2007.

When a stock breaks above a pattern, it can retrace back to the breakout point and below. For similar reasons, a stock that drops beneath a pattern can recover its immediate losses and provide a second chance for either those in long positions to escape, or for those wishing to go short the stock a chance to get into the position. We see this take place with INCY, as its plunge beneath $4 was quickly followed by a list in price to the point precisely beneath where the lower trendline would be touching. This was the last chance for longs to get out and for bears to get on board, as the drop was much faster afterward.

FIGURE 5.6 The supporting trendline offered absolutely no support once the price was ready to break this descending channel.

Pattern Start: 12/6/2007   Break Price: $6.15   Percentage Change: −68%
Pattern Break: 10/6/2008   Postbreak Price: $1.96

Louisiana-Pacific Corporation

There are countless instances in technical analysis where you can observe a given technical object change roles from support to resistance or vice versa. The chart of LPX shows a channel pattern that highlights this phenomenon.

Observe the higher trendline of the channel in Figure 5.7. For many months, it provided support to the prices above it. Although it is not drawn here, if there were a

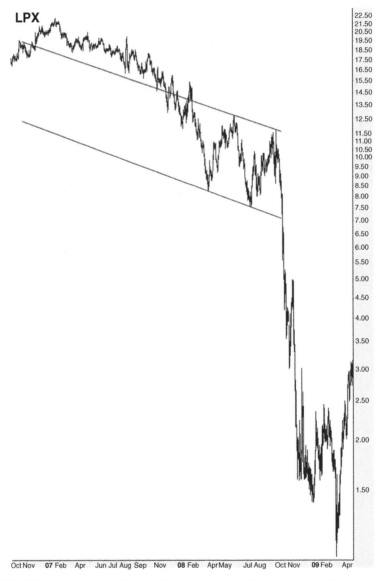

FIGURE 5.7 This channel is particularly interesting since the upper trendline served as support for many months before it changed roles and served as resistance for subsequent months.

Pattern Start: 2/4/2008   Break Price: $7.12   Percentage Change: −86%
Pattern Break: 10/7/2008   Postbreak Price: $1

third parallel line drawn above the present upper line, it would fit the price bars above it to show there was another descending channel (with a smaller range) preceding this one.

Nuveen Multi-Strategy Income and Growth Fund

The Nuveen Multi-Strategy security (symbol JPC) was in a gently descending channel for about a year before its prices fell steeply below the pattern. There are two interesting actions that took place following this break: (1) in spite of the sharp drop, a powerful recovery brought the stock back to the $6.60 price level from where the pattern had failed; and (2) the price lingered at this level for a surprisingly long time—two months—before it began to fall in earnest.

Of course, when trading without the benefit of knowing the nature of future price bars, it is impossible to know what is next. Whether a retracement takes place or doesn't, whether that retracement takes the price well into the pattern again, and whether a recaptured price will remain intact for many weeks (as it did here) are all speculative when you are actually trading. The important thing that can be known from a chart like this is that, provided a stop-loss order is in place and that the order is set to a sensible price level based on the chart, a trader can stay in position irrespective of the length of time a price may dawdle at a certain level.

Stocks maintain a state of equilibrium when neither buyers nor sellers are able to push it in their direction. The fact that JPC broke its pattern, recovered, and then was able to tread water for a number of weeks is rather unusual, but it is clear that owners of the stock were not spooked enough by the recent drop to sell in quantity (see Figure 5.8). The pattern break did signal something was wrong, however, and that signal's strength was finally known once the security took a 57 percent drop in the coming months.

FIGURE 5.8 This channel was exceptionally clean, but once it failed, there was no stopping the price's plunge.

Pattern Start: 8/17/2007   Break Price: $6.60   Percentage Change: −57%
Pattern Break: 7/10/2008   Postbreak Price: $2.86

Plug Power, Inc.

The final example of a channel, Plug Power (symbol PLUG), is shown in Figure 5.9. There are several things that can be learned from this chart, which is yet another example of a stock's weakness following the price break beneath its channel.

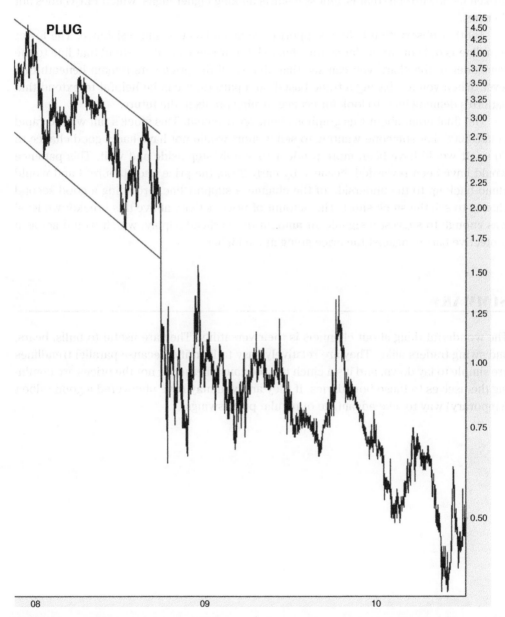

FIGURE 5.9 Although the lower trendline is drawn only the length of the channel, you can see that an extension of this trendline would act as strong resistance to prices all through 2009.

Pattern Start: 10/19/2007   Break Price: $1.59   Percentage Change: −77%
Pattern Break: 9/26/2008   Postbreak Price: $0.36

The first is that a stock whose price is falling doesn't necessarily have to fall as hard and fast as some of the other examples shown earlier. This stock takes its time—nearly two years—to finally reach its bottom. Unless the stock you are short pays a meaningful dividend, it is not costly to simply hold on to a position like this as long as it has not broken its downtrend (that is, unless it starts making higher highs, which PLUG does not do here).

Another observation is how support once again has become resistance. The lower trendline is only drawn as far as the channel, but if you mentally extend that line to the remainder of the chart, you can see that almost all the price bars remain beneath that level. When you are basing a trade based on a pattern, it can be helpful to extend that pattern's defining lines to look for crucial turning points in the future.

The final point about this graph is about retracement. This stock's fall was so rapid in late 2008 that someone wanting to sell it short would not have had a good chance to do so. It would have been more prudent to simply step aside and wait. This patience would have been rewarded, because by early 2009, the price had stabilized and would climb back up to the underside of the channel's support line, providing a good second chance to sell the stock short. The amount of price activity above this breakdown level was enough to suggest a significant amount of overhead supply, which would act as a protective barrier against the price going much higher.

SUMMARY

The wonderful thing about channels is their versatility. They are useful to bulls, bears, and swing traders alike. They are relatively easy to identify, because parallel trendlines are simple to lay down, and it's a cinch to ascertain whether or not the prices are confining themselves to those boundaries. If they are, you may have uncovered a good (albeit temporary) way to take advantage of regular price swings.

CHAPTER 6

Cup with Handle

T he cup-with-handle pattern is one of the most recognizable and popular patterns in technical analysis. As the name suggests, the pattern looks like a cup and handle as viewed from the side. That is, a rounded saucerlike shape is followed by a much smaller saucer (approximately even with the upper levels of the big saucer) and then is followed by a breakout to higher prices.

DEFINITION OF THE PATTERN

The criteria for this pattern are as follows:

- **Prior Uptrend:** Since this is often a continuation pattern, it is most desirable for there to be an uptrend preceding the pattern, although this is not a requirement, as examples in this chapter will show.
- **U-Shaped Cup:** The cup portion of the pattern should be relatively smooth and round, as opposed to a sharp V-shaped pattern.
- **Similar Highs:** The highs on the left and right sides of the cup should be roughly equal, and these highs in turn should be equal to the highs of the handle.
- **Partial Retracement by Handle:** The drop in price contained within the handle should be only a modest part of the range between the cup's high and low. In other words, if the cup spans a range of $10 to $16, the handle shouldn't dip very much below the high price of $16. A good rule of thumb is no more than one-third of the range, which in this example would suggest a handle no lower than $14 in price.
- **Breakout:** The price should break out above the top of the handle and continue on to its target price.

The target price is the value of the price range of the pattern added to the price level at the time of the breakout. For instance, if the pattern spans $25 to $30, then the target price would be $35 (that is, the high price of the pattern—$30—added to the range of prices in the saucer—$5—equaling $35).

Here in Figure 6.1 is an example of a cup-with-handle pattern with additional lines drawn for emphasis. Take note how the volume shrinks as the handle is being formed and then subsequently surges higher on the breakout—this is a good sign with such a pattern, as the strong volume affirms the importance of the breakout.

FIGURE 6.1 The resistance at the $9.25 price level was clearly broken late in September on this chart, with a substantial increase in volume, validating the pattern's power.

PSYCHOLOGY BEHIND THE PATTERN

Let us consider a stock that has already been climbing steadily. Let's assume it has risen from $20 to $30. Owners of the stock are very happy with the performance, and the stock peaks at $30. This is the left edge of the cup that will be formed.

Now the price starts to gently fall. Some owners of the stock get nervous and want to lock in profits, so they start selling. The stock descends to $29, $28, $27, and on down to $25. At this point, selling dries up, as does volume, and the price flattens out at about $25 for a while.

Now that the stock is stable, new buyers start to enter the market and slowly bid the price up. The price moves back up through $26, $27, $28, all the way back to $30. It has now matched its former high, and over the couple of months that the stock descended and ascended, there is a saucer-shaped pattern in the price that constitutes the cup of this pattern.

Now the price starts slipping again, and a small number of owners once again get nervous that the stock is unable to get above $30. They think perhaps a double top is in place, and they sell. This time, the stock's drop is more modest and shorter-lived. It falls to $28.50, stabilizes, and pushes up again to $30. Now the handle is complete, and the market has a decision to make—whether to push the stock up past $30 or give way to sellers and fall hard.

If the handle is not completely formed and the price simply keeps falling, a double top will indeed be in place, and more serious selling may ensue. In this example, however, there are more buyers than sellers, and the price finally cracks above the $30 level, having paused there for both sides of the saucer as well as the handle. Now that a new high is finally reached, buyers pile into the stock, soon pushing it to its target price of $35 (which is the sum of the former high, $30, plus the pattern's range, $5). The pattern and its target are now complete.

Figure 6.2 illustrates again an idealized experience with the cup-and-handle pattern. Note particularly the surge in volume once the breakout is underway.

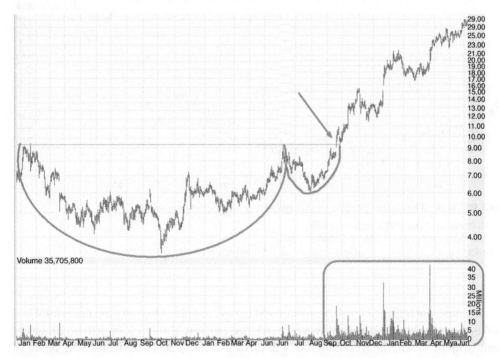

FIGURE 6.2 This is an extremely well-defined cup with handle, with the breakout marked by an arrow.

EXAMPLES

Here are some examples of the cup-with-handle pattern drawn from actual instances in the market. The first portion includes shorter-term patterns, followed by much longer-term patterns. Irrespective of the timeframe, the pattern itself (particularly the cleanliness and consistency of its form) is what counts the most.

SM Energy Company

In Figure 6.3 is a chart of SM Energy Company from the mid-1990s. You can see the especially smooth saucer pattern followed by a handle that retraced about 40 percent of the saucer. After the breakout, it met and exceeded its target price.

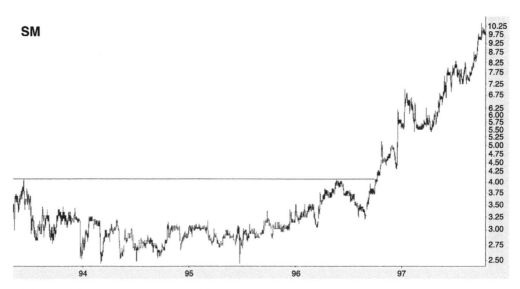

FIGURE 6.3 The saucer portion of this pattern is particularly smooth.
Cup Timespan: June 1993 to June 1996
Handle Timespan: June 1996 to October 1996
Price Range: $2.5 to $4, providing a target of 5.50, which was met December 1996

Because the high prices of the saucer and handle are close to even, the horizontal line tool is the most straightforward way to mark this pattern. If the prices instead tilt either slightly up or down, the trendline tool will provide a more accurate mark. Whichever of these two drawn objects you use, you will probably want to turn the Extend feature off, since there is no reason the line should extend infinitely into the future. You simply want to mark the high points of the saucer and its handle.

Schnitzer Steel Industries, Inc.

From 1998 to 2003, Schnitzer Steel (symbol SCHN) hammered out a saucer in a very wide $2 to $7 price range. Figure 6.4 shows the very modest drop that comprised the handle, followed by a multihundred percentage point surge.

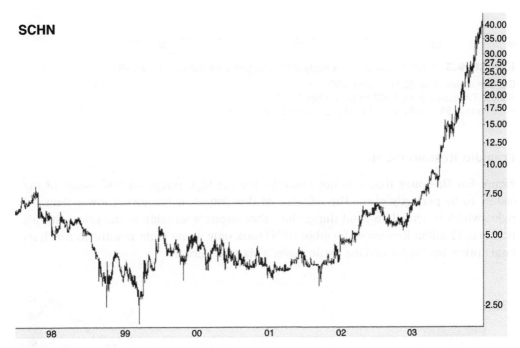

FIGURE 6.4 The saucer doesn't have to be perfectly smooth in order to be successful.
Cup Timespan: November 1997 to July 2002
Handle Timespan: July 2002 to January 2003
Price Range: $2 to $7 for a $12 target, reached June 2003

Peabody Energy Corporation

The example of Peabody Energy (symbol BTU), illustrated in Figure 6.5, is somewhat unusual in that the pattern actually began its formation starting with the company's initial public offering in 2001. Three years later, its pattern was complete, and it doubled in price shortly thereafter.

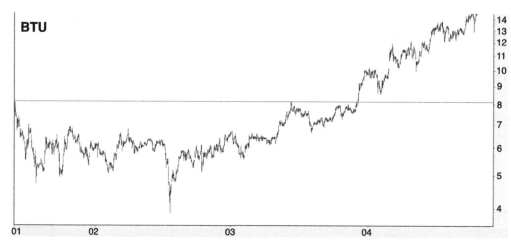

FIGURE 6.5 It is unusual to see a pattern that begins with the company's IPO.

Cup Timespan: May 2001 to June 2003
Handle Timespan: June 2003 to December 2003
Price Range: $4 to $8 for a $12 target, reached June 2004

Franklin Resources, Inc.

Figure 6.6 illustrates that it is not essential for the high prices on both sides of the saucer to be perfectly even. The left side of this pattern is somewhat lower than the right (which is actually a good thing, since that suggests strength in the price). In this instance, Franklin Resources (symbol BEN) took only about eight months to reach its target price, having formed the pattern over a six-year period .

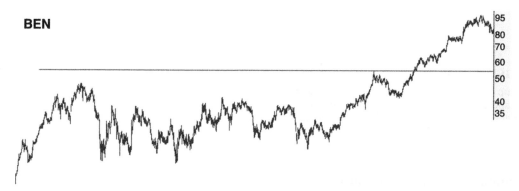

FIGURE 6.6 The left side of this pattern isn't quite as high as the rest, but this is close enough to be acceptable.

Cup Timespan: April 1998 to January 2004
Handle Timespan: January 2004 to November 2004
Price Range: $20 to $55 for a $70 target, reached July 2005

LONGER-TERM EXAMPLES

Some technical analysis books suggest that the cup-with-handle pattern shouldn't span more than a few months. However, plenty of chart examples illustrate that charts spanning longer than that—even as long as a decade—can still be useful harbingers of future price direction. Figure 6.7 illustrates a cup-with-handle pattern spanning more than a decade which preceded a multithousand percentage increase in price. The remaining examples in this chapter show similar long-term patterns.

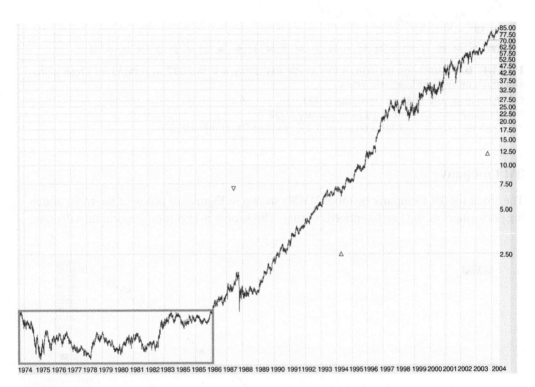

FIGURE 6.7 A chart illustrating a pattern spanning more than a decade.

Manitowoc Company, Inc.

Manitowoc Company (symbol MTW), illustrated in Figure 6.8, exhibits a 14-year cup-with-handle pattern. The target price was reached quickly—in under a year—and even though the price softened up somewhat years later, it went on to multihundred percent gains in the years that followed.

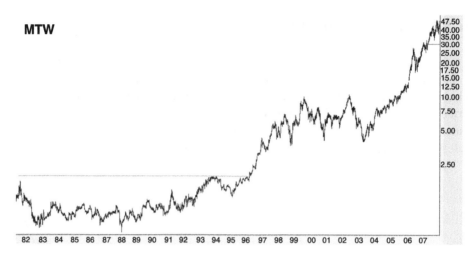

FIGURE 6.8 Although the rise in this stock was partly lost in 2002, it recaptured these gains, and much more, in subsequent years.

Cup Timespan: July 1981 to December 1993
Handle Timespan: December 1993 to January 1996
Price Range: 0.65 to 1.95 for a target of 3.25, reached December 1996

3M Company

The stock for 3M Company (symbol MMM) shown in Figure 6.9 is one of the most amazing performers of the late twentieth century. The saucer is enormous, spanning a decade,

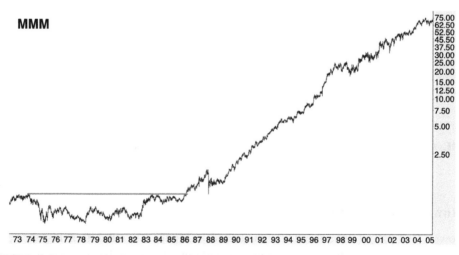

FIGURE 6.9 3M Corporation is one of the most consistent winners in the 1990s.

Cup Timespan: October 1973 to June 1983
Handle Timespan: June 1983 to December 1985
Price Range: 0.45 to 0.90 for a target of 1.35, reached January 1987

and the handle covered 1984 and 1985. What's interesting about this breakout is that the crash of 1987 hit this stock, but even with that severe a correction, the price did not descend beneath the horizontal line representing the breakout. After surviving the crash of 1987, the increase in MMM was nothing short of extraordinary, climbing thousands of percent.

Becton, Dickinson and Company

One of the cruder (that is, less smooth and well-defined) examples is shown in Figure 6.10 to illustrate that not all cup-with-handle patterns are as picture-perfect as the prior examples. The saucer, which also roughly resembles an inverted head-and-shoulders pattern, was followed by a handle that pierced rather deeply into the range of the saucer (approximately 50 percent). The slightly ascending trendline that defined the top of the pattern was finally penetrated early in 1986, and the stock enjoyed sensational gains for the rest of the decade and into the 1990s.

FIGURE 6.10 BDX's rise in the early 1990s was slow and steady and accelerated dramatically in the late 1990s.

Cup Timespan: December 1969 to December 1980
Handle Timespan: December 1980 to August 1985
Price Range: .75 to 2.00 for a target of 3.25, reached August 1986

Chevron Corporation

As with the prior example, Figure 6.11 features a handle that retraces deeply into the saucer's price range. Given the tremendous rise that took place afterward, you can see how important it is to not dismiss a pattern merely because the handle dipped more than the modest amount suggested by the parameters at the beginning of this chapter. Of course, if the price descends beneath the low price of the saucer's range, the cup-with-handle pattern is definitely invalidated.

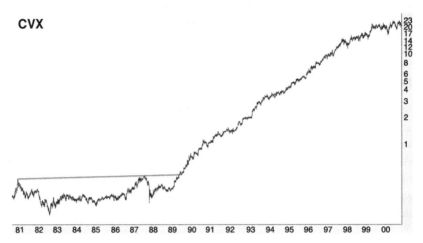

FIGURE 6.11 Chevron, like 3M, was a very steady performer in every year of the 1990s.

Cup Timespan: December 1980 to July 1987
Handle Timespan: July 1987 to April 1989
Price Range: .20 to .45 for a .70 target, reached December 1989

EMC Corporation

Finally, in Figure 6.12, we see EMC Corporation's stock price, which was one of the most dramatic and consistent of the 1990s tech boom. The pattern was somewhat long,

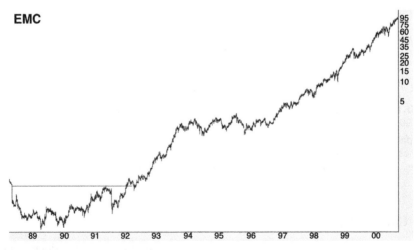

FIGURE 6.12 EMC's handle retraced more than typical—over 50 percent—but the pattern was still very successful

Cup Timespan: April 1988 to May 1991
Handle Timespan: May 1991 to December 1991
Price Range: 0.06 to 0.26 for a target of 0.46, reached November 1992

traversing four years, but the movement that was sustained after the completion of the pattern was many times this length.

SUMMARY

The illustrations in this chapter appear very similar because the rationale and psychology behind the price action of a cup-with-handle pattern is very consistent. Understand that this pattern can span anywhere from a few hours to many years, and that both the volume surge on the breakout and the length of the original pattern are both important indicators of how high the pattern will ultimately push the price.

CHAPTER 7

Descending Triangles

The rules that apply to the ascending triangle—covered elsewhere in this book—can simply be turned upside down in order to understand the nature and parameters of the descending triangle, its opposite. This pattern is defined as having a horizontal line, representing the supporting price level, and a descending trendline, which constitutes the top line of the triangle. As with its twin, the descending triangle is also known as a right-angle triangle, since a line connecting the leftmost points of the existing lines would complete the three sides, and a right angle would exist in the lower-left corner of the formation.

DEFINITION OF THE PATTERN

Las Vegas Sands, shown in Figure 7.1, experienced a breathtaking 98 percent drop in value after the completion of its descending triangle. There is a horizontal line (the lower one) at about $70, and there is a descending trendline, representing resistance, showing a series of lower lows in price. The horizontal line represents support, and after it is broken slightly, there is still enough strength from the buyers to push the price a little higher and back within the confines of the triangle.

A couple of weeks later, the stock starts falling hard, and then it regains its strength and ascends to just beneath its former support level (which is now resistance). When such an opportunity comes, this is the perfect time to short the stock, because the pattern has already failed, the weakness has already been illustrated, and the stop-loss price is well defined (in this instance, since the stock price has already taken a significant dip down, any price above the resistance level would be a suitable stop-loss basis).

After this retracement, the stock begins tumbling precipitously. Of course, not many stocks move down with this much vigor, but this illustrates how a descending triangle can be a harbinger of serious price weakness.

FIGURE 7.1 LVS lost virtually its entire value during the financial crisis of 2008 and early 2009.

As with the ascending triangle, the descending triangle is a continuation pattern, meaning that it is effective in a market that is already in a downtrend. It is a bearish pattern, so it must be used within the confines of a bearish trend. For the purposes of measuring a target, you can take the height of the triangle and subtract it from the lower line (which is the supporting horizontal line). Thus, a triangle ranging from $50 to $40 has a height of $10 and thus a target price of $30 (the horizontal line, $40, minus the triangle height, $10, yields the $30 target).

PSYCHOLOGY BEHIND THE PATTERN

As a continuation pattern, a stock forming a descending triangle is already in a down-trend and will have a relatively nervous and uncomfortable group of owners (excepting, of course, those already short the stock).

The stock descends, reaches a certain price level, and moves higher. The point where it stops falling is a support level, and it will be the first touch-point of the horizontal support line that will later become clear. The bounce higher is substantial, as buyers rush in to buy a stock that now seems cheap.

The buying dries up, and the stock starts selling off again, once again reaching the support level. Buyers once again enter the picture (or frustrated short sellers decide to cover), and the price again moves higher, but not as high as the last time. We have our first lower low of the descending resistance line. The stock is slowly weakening.

For a third time, the price drops to the support level. Owners of the stock are getting increasingly uncomfortable. Their stock is threatening to break support, and when it gathers its strength, it is doing so with diminishing gusto. The price pushes higher, going up only slightly this time, not even managing to reach the descending resistance line.

At last, the stock pierces support. A few bargain hunters jump in, pushing the price above the line for a few days, but the selling pressure overcomes these buyers, and the stock begins falling in earnest. The selling picks up speed, as frustrated owners throw in the towel and add to the selling pressure.

EXAMPLES

The following five examples provide more clarity as to what a descending triangle looks like and how to identify its potential.

GeoMet, Inc.

Another dramatic example of the descending triangle's bearish potential is revealed with Figure 7.2, which features symbol GMET forming a triangle between the prices of $6 and $10. The price drops quickly, recovers for several weeks, but then begins a waterfall decline into sub-$1 territory. As with the ascending triangle, just because a price reenters the triangle zone after a breakaway movement, that does not negate the pattern. In fact, it may provide an opportunity to increase the size of your position at even more attractive prices.

FIGURE 7.2 GMET took only half a year to drop over 90 percent in price.

Pattern Start: 3/26/2008   Break Price: $6   Percentage Change: −92%
Pattern Break: 9/8/2008   Lowest Price: $0.50

Novellus Systems, Inc.

Where a stock breaks away from its triangle varies; sometimes the price falls about halfway along the triangle's formation, and other times it may wait until the two lines converge into a point. It's normally best to see the breakdown take place between halfway and two-thirds of the way along the triangle's horizontal axis.

Figure 7.3 shows a price breakdown that took place earlier. It is also an interesting example since the upper line was briefly penetrated by an *overshoot*. Even if you want to be a stickler for never having a price cross above or below a line (except for the breakout), there are still two touch-points on the upper line that follow this overshoot.

The range of the triangle is from about $25 to about $31, suggesting a target price of $19. The stock falls to this target and then rises powerfully to nearly $24, so a trade based on this target would have been a clean, profitable one. The stock does weaken after that retracement, however, ultimately falling to nearly $10, representing an overall 60 percent diminishment in price after the pattern's completion.

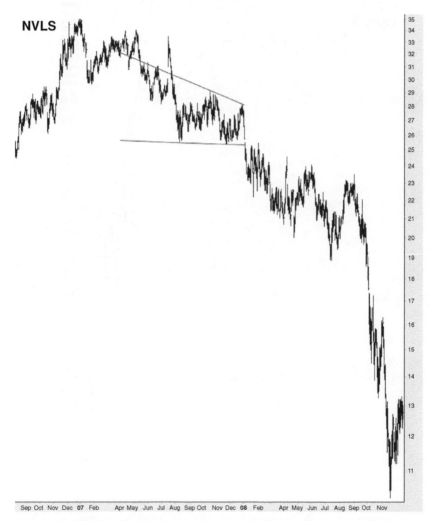

FIGURE 7.3 This chart of NVLS shows that the majority of a stock's drop might be delayed somewhat after the initial breakdown of the pattern.

Pattern Start: 7/25/2007   Break Price: $25   Percentage Change: −60%
Pattern Break: 1/4/2008   Lowest Price: $10

Genworth Financial, Inc.

Sometimes a stock will break a pattern and not react immediately. This is rather un-usual, because the entire logic behind a pattern's violation is that support is broken (or resistance is overcome), and the stock moves swiftly in a given direction. As shown in Figure 7.4, Genworth Financial (symbol GNW) broke its descending triangle, recovered, and then spent months meandering at about $23, plus or minus a few dimes. The pro-jected direction of the pattern was fulfilled magnificently, but it took a few months for the

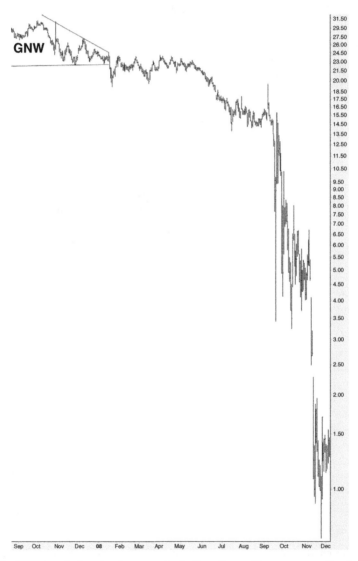

FIGURE 7.4 GNW treaded water for months before the selling pressure finally overcame its inertia.

Pattern Start: 10/26/2007   Break Price: $22.50   Percentage Change: −97%
Pattern Break: 1/17/2008   Lowest Price: $0.70

movement to actually kick in. It seems that on occasion, as with prayers, delay doesn't necessarily mean denial.

Ingersoll-Rand

Retracements may or may not happen after a pattern breakdown, but this example, Figure 7.5, shows how a retracement provided an exceptional opportunity for more

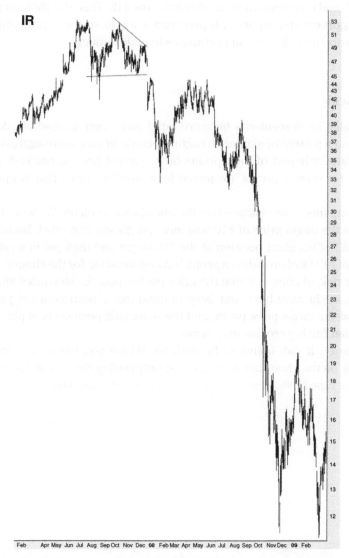

FIGURE 7.5 IR gave people a superb second opportunity to enter short positions, since the stock retraced back to its original breakdown point several months after initially falling away from the triangle.

Pattern Start: 8/17/2007   Break Price: $43   Percentage Change: −74%
Pattern Break: 12/17/2007   Lowest Price: $11.38

cautious traders, or latecomers, or those who wanted a second bite at the proverbial apple, to partake in a very profitable short sale.

The descending triangle pattern was broken and then swiftly retracted to just below the horizontal line. The stock fell from about $43 to about $33, giving bears some excellent profits. Then the stock began a multimonth recovery back to the lower 40s, recapturing for the second time the former support (now resistance) level.

The price fell again to just beneath the prior low, recovered somewhat again to approximately $40, and then began a swan dive to below $12. This triangle pattern not only preceded an important drop in price, it preceded a whole series of profitable plunges, giving nimble bears three discrete opportunities to make money.

Syneron Medical

When a price falls, its descent can be more rapid and larger in absolute dollar terms than ascents from a pattern of similar strength. Because of this, more aggressive traders might want to take only part of their profits once a target price is reached, leaving the rest in position for greater profits, protected by a stop-loss price that is updated on a regular basis.

A trader doing this in an instance like the one shown in Figure 7.6 would have been glad for it, since the target price of $10 was met and greatly exceeded. He or she might have covered half of his short position at the $10 target and then put in a rather liberal stop-loss order of $13 (still providing a profit, but also allowing for the chance of a further price drop). The risk, of course, is that the price pushes past the stop price and the profit isn't as big as it might have been, but keep in mind that a portion of the position was already closed at the target-price profit, and the remaining position is in place based on the possibility that further erosion may occur.

In this instance, it did, falling to beneath $5. Where you put your stop-loss price depends entirely on the chart, but sometimes simply setting the stop at the most recent lower low (in the case of short sales) is a crude but sensible method.

FIGURE 7.6 Instead of closing an entire position once a target price is reached, you can keep your stops up to date on your position as the price waterfalls lower in price.

Pattern Start: 2/12/2008   Break Price: $13.88   Percentage Change: −67%
Pattern Break: 9/18/2008   Lowest Price: $4.55

SUMMARY

One big difference between falling stocks and rising stocks is the speed at which they move. Stocks tend to fall much faster than they rise. Compare the examples in this chapter with the stocks shown in Chapter 3, "Ascending Triangles." The patterns are the same in construction (albeit upside down from one another), but the amount of time it takes for a stock to climb to its ultimate high is often several times longer than in the examples provided here. Also, for stocks that have ascended rapidly in price in the past, the levels of support that are available to slow down a plunging price may be few and far between.

CHAPTER 8

Descending Wedges

U sually when a person is watching a stock's price steadily sink, the assumption is that the stock must be in trouble. This is sometimes the case, but there are some instances in which the stock is in fact creating a very bullish pattern known as the descending wedge.

Just as an ascending wedge (see Chapter 4) is a bearish pattern, the descending wedge is a bullish pattern. It consists of two nonparallel lines that, if extended, will meet on their right side. As the price bounces up and down between the two extremes, the price action becomes more compressed as the bullish and bearish reactions draw the lines closer together. If and when the prices break the upper trendline, the descending wedge pattern is complete, and the stock should move higher in price.

DEFINITION OF THE PATTERN

The graph of FEI Company (symbol FEIC), shown in Figure 8.1, went up 56 percent after its breakout from the descending wedge pattern. The two trendlines look parallel, but the higher one is descending at a slightly faster rate than the lower one.

The descending wedge is bounded by these two lines. As long as the price bars between the lines are moving lower (*descending*) and the lines are angled such that they will eventually converge on their right side (wedge), the pattern is valid. Whether the stock is in a general uptrend or downtrend doesn't matter. If the stock is in a broad uptrend, the descending wedge is a continuation pattern; if the stock is in a broad downtrend, the descending wedge is a reversal pattern. In either case, a breakout from above the descending wedge is considered bullish.

FIGURE 8.1 The breakout was given extra credence by the gap up in price that happened about a month afterward.

PSYCHOLOGY BEHIND THE PATTERN

Whether the overall direction of the stock is bullish or bearish, the descending wedge behaves as a *clearing out* of the owners of the stock who are not inclined to hold on during a downturn. Those who remain are either more patient with the stock's downdraft or simply acquired the stock at a newer, lower price.

Each drop down to the supporting trendline acts to scare out the weaker hands of the security, and each push higher to the resisting trendline acts to give owners of the stock hope that things are going to turn out. With each successive dip and rise, holders of the stock are on a roller coaster that alternates between despair and hope, and the volume typically will dry up as fewer and fewer people are interested in hanging on to a stock that is going through these gyrations.

The big change takes place when the resisting trendline is at last broken. For those who bought during the most recent dip, they are suddenly in the happy position of having a profitable stock, and for longer-term purchasers, their losses have at least been trimmed down and they see that the stock may have finally changed from a downtrend to an uptrend. A big increase in volume is particularly encouraging here, since it accentuates the fact that the withering volume was a symptom of the stock's former weakness and not a persistent loss of interest in the stock by the market. Now that the security has found its footing, buyers are willing to participate on a broader basis.

If the stock moves higher and sinks back to approximately the breakout point, it is simply finding its new equilibrium point where those who are nervous about undergoing another hard dip down want to sell, balanced by those who believe the stock has fundamentally changed its overall direction. A successive push to a new recovery high validates the view of this latter group, and the stock then has the opportunity to truly make a big move higher.

EXAMPLES

The percentage changes that can take place with a descending wedge can be substantial, as the following examples help show.

Cytori Therapeutics

Figure 8.2 provides a good illustration of how a measured target on a pattern can be prescient and helpful. The descending wedge has a range of approximately $1.50 at its nadir and $7 at its apex, yielding a difference of $5.50. The stock breaks out at $4, meanders gently lower, and then finally finds strong support at about $3.

Adding the stock's breakout price, $4, to the height of the wedge, $5.50, produces a sum of $9.50, the target price. Late in 2009, once the stock's new base has firmed up, CYTX swiftly ascends to $9.50, yielding a percentage gain of 138 percent. It's worth noting that, as is often the case after breakouts, the stock didn't immediately move in its anticipated direction. Holders of the stock had to endure a lot of uncertainty and waiting before the potential was fulfilled, but their patience was awarded not long thereafter.

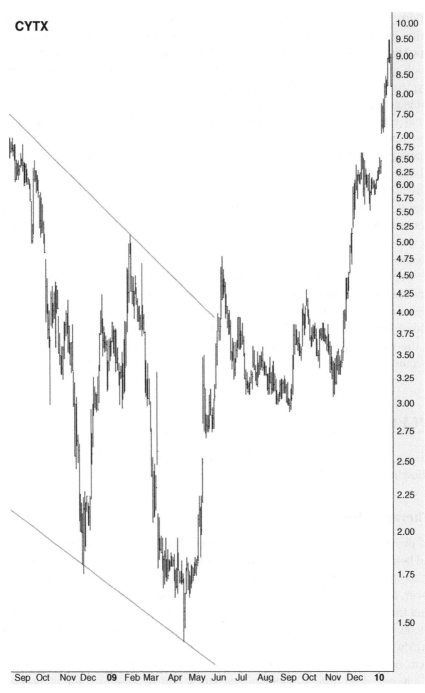

FIGURE 8.2 In percentage terms, this wedge is especially wide, which makes sense, given the substantial lift that the stock experienced after the breakout.

Pattern Start: 7/23/2008   Break Price: $4   Percentage Change: 138%
Pattern Break: 6/1/2009   Postbreak Price: $9.50

Intricon Corporation

Let's step through the price action of Intricon, shown in Figure 8.3, to understand the perception of the stock action while it is taking place. The stock is, during the early

FIGURE 8.3 The retracement here was a little stronger than normal, which may have caused some who bought during the breakout to dump their positions. It took a couple of months for the stock to become stable enough to rise sharply.

Pattern Start: 7/4/2007   Break Price: $11   Percentage Change: 64%
Pattern Break: 2/2/2008   Postbreak Price: $18

summer of 2007, moving smoothly from $16 to above $20. Although unknown at the time, this price establishes the first touch-point of the resistance trendline, and earlier, at $17, the first touch-point of the supporting trendline.

Now the stock starts dropping, falling back to $16 at first, wiping out recent profits, recovering partly to $18, and then moving much more swiftly into the single digits before finding any stability. The price double-bottoms and then manages to claw its way back to $13. The second touch-points of both trendlines have now been made, and remaining owners of the stock are scared and frustrated.

A new plunge begins, dropping the price from its recent $13 peak to half that price, and a great many holders of the stock have been cleared out since two-thirds of their equity's value has been destroyed between August 2007 and January 2008. At that point the stock begins a very strong rally—its third to take place within the pattern—and stops hard at the resistance trendline when $11 is reached.

Instead of resuming the fall, it begins hammering out some support at $10.50, and as the price continues at this level, it also penetrates the resistance trendline, thus completing the pattern. One last dip late in April takes about 10 percent off the stock's value, but the bullish potential for IIN is already in place, and it moves steadily to $18 by early summer, providing a 64 percent gain and, for longer-term holders, recovering almost all of the earlier losses.

Toro Company

The next instance, Figure 8.4, is similar in form to the prior example, although the percentage movement is more substantial. Take note of the high price of the wedge—about $45—and the low price of the wedge—about $20, indicating a range of $25. This stock fell steadily from nearly $60 to $20, two-thirds of its value, but then broke its descending wedge at $29, implying a target price of $54.

It achieved this target price superbly, although it took about a year to get there. But this length of time is insignificant considering both the size of the gain, 93 percent, and the steadiness of the price action. The post-breakout behavior of TTC was a steady series of higher highs and higher lows, and although there was a modest dip in early 2010, only a rather tight stop would have taken an owner out of that position, since it did not violate any recent lows.

FIGURE 8.4 This is an especially well-formed descending wedge.

Pattern Start: 7/15/2008 Break Price: $28 Percentage Change: 93%
Pattern Break: 4/24/2009 Postbreak Price: $54

Encore Wire Corporation

Although it is useful to measure a target price to calculate a place where you may decide to take all or part of your profits, there is of course no guarantee that a target price will be met, even if the direction of the stock is the same as the pattern predicts.

The measured move for Figure 8.5, for instance, should have taken the stock to about $39, but it stalled in the lower 30s. The 60 percent increase in value after its breakout is

FIGURE 8.5 Although the stock lost value during the financial crisis, it recaptured its high price by early 2010.

Pattern Start: 8/2/2008   Break Price: $20   Percentage Change: 60%
Pattern Break: 5/3/2009   Postbreak Price: $32

still a very handsome return, but it is unwise to hold on to a stock indefinitely until a particular target is achieved.

It is better to simply take note of the most recent major low and use that as your stop-loss value. In this instance, the stock made a series of higher lows at about the $24 level in late 2009 and early 2010, and that would have been a good stop-loss level. Once the stock moved higher, the stop might have been tightened to the reaction low just beneath $30, since sustaining a prospective drop from the lower $30s back to the mid-20s is probably too much of a sacrifice in profits.

Apollo Investment Corporation

Judging how much of a retracement to tolerate is an important part of maintaining a stock position after a breakout. You may find it helpful to extend the trendlines in your charting program and make sure that at least the price doesn't re-enter the pattern's internal area after it has clearly broken out.

It is easier—and less nerve-wracking—when a stock retraces only modestly after a breakout, and you can use that retracement low as a stop-loss level. In Figure 8.6, the stock for Apollo Investment breaks smartly above resistance at $4, pushes to $6, and then loses over half its recent gain. However, the drop to about $4.50 is well above the internal portion of the wedge, and a horizontal line (not shown here) at about $4.50 would indicate that the supporting line is holding up both the two post-breakout lows (in the summer of 2009) as well as the second touch-point of the supporting line that makes up the descending wedge. This is clearly a price level of importance, and a stop-loss just beneath that level would have provided a measure of security while still retaining ownership of a stock that ultimately went on to a 178 percent post-breakout gain.

FIGURE 8.6 The heavy trading between $6.00 and $11.50 during the downturn provided little in the way of resistance during the stock's recovery.

Pattern Start: 9/23/2008   Break Price: $4.50   Percentage Change: 178%
Pattern Break: 4/3/2009   Postbreak Price: $12.50

General Dynamics Corporation

The military contractor General Dynamics, whose chart is in Figure 8.7, offers another fine example of a retracement that is substantial, but not so significant that it would have taken a technician out of the position.

FIGURE 8.7 Although the initial breakout was terribly fast, the retracement in the summer of 2009 provided a good opportunity to establish the position for those who initially missed the breakout.

Pattern Start: 9/2/2008   Break Price: $47   Percentage Change: 64%
Pattern Break: 4/22/2009   Postbreak Price: $77

We see that, after the stock's bottom at $34, the price moves sharply to the resisting trendline at $47. It doesn't even pause there, instead breaking sharply above the line and reaching nearly $60. The stock loses about $10 in value, but the stock doesn't approach the inside of the now-broken descending wedge.

Also take note that the penultimate touch-point of the former supporting line, at about $46, happens to form a left shoulder of an inverted head-and-shoulders pattern (see Chapter 15). Indeed, the range from October 2008 to October 2009 establishes an outstanding inverted head-and-shoulders pattern, with the right shoulder being higher than the left, as it should be. The lowest point of this right shoulder, just below $50, represents a perfect stop-loss level, and GD moves steadily to nearly $80, providing a 64 percent gain to those who had bought at the breakout.

SUMMARY

The descending wedge pattern is flexible, because it is useful in both uptrends and downtrends. The percentage gains of this bullish formation may not be as gigantic as some of the other patterns found in this book, but they also don't take as long to reach their target prices. The most artful part about using this pattern effectively is knowing the difference between an acceptable retracement (one that is merely revealing weaker hands that are eager to take their recent profits off the table, since they have been frustrated by the stock's former inability to rise) and a false breakout (which, in spite of the price's agreeable direction, yields price movement that reenters the pattern and perhaps takes the stock to much lower prices).

The key to all of this is to have sensible stops once the position is in place. What defines *sensible* depends on the chart and relies heavily on both your experience and skill. Overly tight stops will take you out of positions that go on to produce outstanding gains, whereas overly liberal stops will keep you in positions that erode your equity based merely on the hope that the price will turn around and move where you want it to move.

CHAPTER 9

Diamonds

A s with the mineral found in the earth, diamonds are rare and precious, and instances of this pattern can be some of the most powerful predictors of price movement in the realm of technical analysis. This chapter is rather short, because there are not many good examples of diamond patterns to present, but the four bearish and two bullish charts shown will give you a good idea what to seek.

DEFINITION OF THE PATTERN

A diamond pattern is formed on the left side by a series of higher highs and lower lows and, once past the midpoint, a series of lower highs and higher lows. The security loses its ability to trend (becoming increasingly wide in its range) and then begins tightening its range up again, suggesting that it is losing its moorings. This inability to sustain a clear trend is why this kind of pattern often accompanies a reversal, and it is more common for the reversal to happen at a market top instead of a market bottom.

One way to think of a diamond pattern is as a head-and-shoulder pattern with a V-shaped neckline (for a top) or an inverted head and shoulder with an A-shaped neckline (for a bottom). Although most patterns require a discerning eye that has been trained by experience, diamonds require an even more skillful eye, since they are rather difficult to spot, particularly without the benefit of significant hindsight.

Diamonds that are sloppily formed generally aren't worth your attention. As with other patterns, the cleaner the pattern is and the wider a timespan it traverses, the more potent it is as a predictive tool. Measuring the price movement potential of a diamond consists of measuring the spread between its highest and lowest points and then adding that value to the price point where it breaks outside the diamond. Thus, if a diamond spans from $60 to $70, and it breaks down at $65, then you can target $55 for the price movement downward.

For diamond tops, volume usually increases substantially during the formation of the pattern, largely because the amount of churn increases as the bulls and bears struggle over the direction of the stock. One of the benefits of a diamond, as opposed to a head-and-shoulder (H&S) pattern (of either variety), is that the signal tends to come earlier. This is because of simple geometry: A price will break below an ascending line (or above a descending line, as the case may be) much sooner than a horizontal line, so the amount of move that you can capture is that much larger.

Studying the example in Figure 9.1, the pattern starts forming in May 2007. This chart, of Morgan Stanley Technology Index, is so strong that it hardly touches any points of

FIGURE 9.1 Diamond patterns can be broken to the upside or, as in this example, broken to the downside.

the lower trendline. The stock peaks and actually forms a very nice H&S pattern with a neckline beneath $600. The index falls hard, as might be expected with an H&S pattern, and then recovers strongly, climbing back over the neckline (which is not denoted here, as the focus is on the diamond pattern).

Volatility is strong in 2008, as the index dips down hard, recovers partially again, then resumes its weakness. It is at this point that the price level finally pierces the ascending trendline of the right half of the diamond. It does not take the index to lose over half its value, as the $MSH starts plunging with hardly any interruption.

PSYCHOLOGY BEHIND THE PATTERN

The psychology of a diamond pattern is best expressed with the idea of a changing of the guard. The broadening price action indicates that there is a loss of control by whoever formerly was in control, and the power struggle will either resolve itself as a continuation of the past trend (in which case the diamond will be distorted beyond usefulness) or will consolidate into a decision in the form of a break in one direction or another. The reason the fall from a diamond top is so dramatic is that so many parties have been involved in the maelstrom contained within the increasingly broad price action, and frustrated bulls will succumb *en masse* to the price failure.

EXAMPLES

The diamond pattern doesn't occur that frequently, and it can be a little difficult to spot until well after the fact. These examples will help train your eyes for what to seek.

Oil Services ETF

One of the most widely traded exchange-traded funds is Oil Services ETF (symbol OIH), which comprises oil service companies. The diamond shown in Figure 9.2 represents a top that marked the peak of the commodities crazy of the first half of 2008. Take special note that, once the diamond was broken, the price briefly regained strength and approached the underside of the violated trendline. This is common with patterns, although it only happens a portion of the time. As with other pattern examples, shorting on a retracement (or going long, if the breakout is to the upside) is a more conservative move than going all-in during the initial piercing.

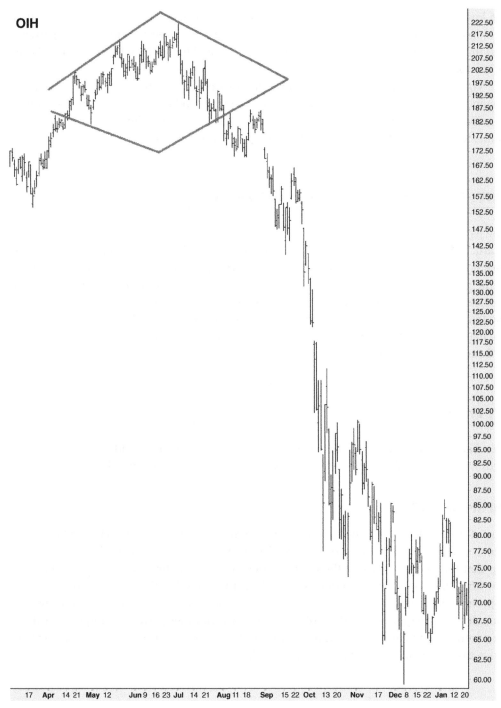

FIGURE 9.2 This reversal pattern preceded a huge move down in this widely traded ETF.

Diamond Start: April 2008   Break Price: $186   Percentage Change: −68%
Diamond Break: September 2008   Postbreak Price: $59

Alpha Natural Resources, Inc.

Figure 9.3 is remarkable for a couple of reasons: first, the depth of the plunge; and second, the consistency of the price drop. The descent in price takes place with virtually no interruption, making for some very happy bears and some very disconcerted bulls. It also is a poignant example of the importance of having stop-loss orders in place, since convincing yourself that the price is bound to come back is often a tempting bit of self-talk.

FIGURE 9.3 Many natural-resource stocks suffered in mid-2008, after a gigantic run-up in commodity prices.

Diamond Start: June 2008   Break Price: $103   Percentage Change: −86%
Diamond Break: August 2008   Postbreak Price: $14

MIPS Technologies, Inc.

Although many of the examples in this book are drawn from the period 2006–2010, this example predates this range by a year. The diamond shown in Figure 9.4 is unusually large and has a remarkable number of touch-points on the four defining trendlines. The diamond itself is tilted somewhat downward, which is not only acceptable but, in the case of a market top, somewhat agreeable, since the foundation of the stock price is deteriorating, thus providing worse footing for the right side of the diamond.

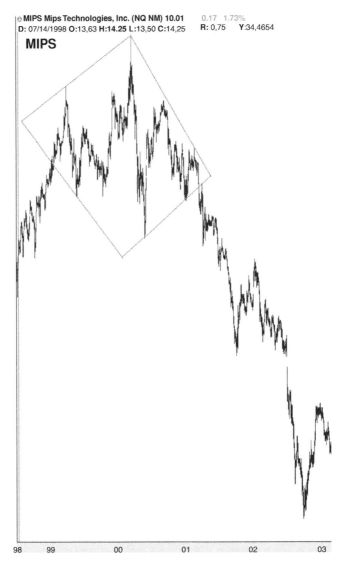

FIGURE 9.4 This diamond pattern signaled a failure in the stock's price that almost entirely wiped out shareholder equity.

Diamond Start: August 1998   Break Price: $33   Percentage Change: −96%
Diamond Break: May 2001   Postbreak Price: $1.33

Also take note that the price had a very clean retracement after the price break. Because of the length, height, and cleanness of the pattern, a person monitoring this chart would have had a very tempting opportunity to sell the stock short (or buy puts on it) at this retraced price level. This example also provides an especially clear demonstration of how the diamond pattern is a close cousin of the head-and-shoulders pattern, except with an angled neckline.

S&P500 Index

The other examples in this chapter are tradable securities, but Figure 9.5 instead shows an index, the always-important S&P500. Although divining the direction of a nontradable cash index can yield specific ideas that are in fact tradable (such as buying index options), knowing the likely direction of a broad direction is just as valuable for informing your general disposition.

In other words, if you ascertained, based on this chart, that the S&P500 was going to head higher, you might not even decide to trade the S&P at all. You instead might use

FIGURE 9.5 The diamond can be a powerful bullish indicator as well, if prices break to the upside.

Diamond Start: April 2009   Break Price: $1,105   Percentage Change: 10%
Diamond Break: October 2009   Postbreak Price: $1,220

this insight to construct a very bullish portfolio, since a broadly rising tide tends to lift all boats (and, for bears, the diminution of security prices makes for a more short-friendly environment). This is also an important example since it shows a diamond *bottom*, as opposed to the diamond top pattern of the prior four graphs.

Brigham Exploration Company

We close with another diamond bottom, Brigham Exploration, in Figure 9.6. The rise following the breakout above this diamond is an impressive 60 percent. The midline of the pattern—that is, the imaginary line separating the upper and lower halves—is almost perfectly flat, affirming the cleanness of the pattern, and although volume isn't shown here, the volume picks up appreciably during and after the breakout, confirming the influx of buying power.

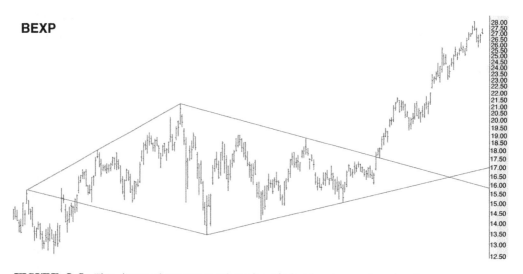

FIGURE 9.6   This diamond pattern is relatively wide but has a very clean break.

Diamond Start: January 2010   Break Price: $17.75   Percentage Change: 60%
Diamond Break: September 2010   Postbreak Price: $28.39

SUMMARY

The sample set of diamonds in the market is small, but these examples hopefully should be plain enough to make identifying your own patterns possible. The rareness of this pattern is important to keep in mind, since you don't want to misinterpret normal price fluctuations as a diamond that simply doesn't exist. The important thing to remember is that if you do indeed find a diamond pattern, pay very close attention to it, because its strength is a welcome counterbalance to its infrequency.

CHAPTER 10

Fibonacci Fans

T his chapter is somewhat different since Fibonacci studies—in this instance, the study of Fibonacci fans—are more about finding important support and resistance levels than about finding a projected target price. Fans are also somewhat challenging since it requires a good eye to find appropriate charts for their application. This skill comes with experience, but hopefully the many examples provided in this chapter will provide some training.

DEFINITION OF THE PATTERN

Setting down Fibonacci fans on a chart is the easy part: All you need to do is choose a high and a low point for the reference line. The charting program you use will draw the fan lines for you, and it is up to you to decide if those lines are useful to you in your trading or not. I sometimes use the term *Fibonacci-friendly* to state whether or not a given price chart happens to agree with a particular Fibonacci-drawn object.

The way the charting program draws these lines is useful to understand. Imagine a reference line being drawn on a chart with the low price at $10 and the high price at $20. Think of this as one line of a triangle. Now imagine a horizontal line projecting from the point at $10 off to the right; this is the second line of the triangle. Finally, imagine a vertical line being drawn straight down from the $20 point of the first line; this is the third line of the triangle.

The charting program draws lines, in this instance, from the $10 point to various points on that third line, the vertical line, based on certain Fibonacci numbers. One of the points on the vertical line will be at the 50 percent point (that is, $15); another will be at the 38.2 percent point; another will be at the 61.8 percent point. Most charting programs let you change these values, although it is best to use the default values.

As you are laying down the fan lines, take note whether or not those fan lines seem to have any meaning with respect to the historical price bars. If the prices repeatedly pierce the fan lines and seem to offer little in the way of support or resistance, then the fan lines are not useful to you; they will just be extra noise on the chart that makes your job harder. On the other hand, if you find the prices repeatedly bouncing between the fan lines, you are probably looking at a Fibonacci-friendly chart.

Whether your reference line is ascending or descending depends on the general trend of the chart. If you are working with a broad downtrend, you probably want to start your reference line at a high price and end it, later on the timeline, at a low price. The reverse applies with a stock in a general uptrend. You will see examples of both uptrends and downtrends in this chapter.

Figure 10.1 provides a good example of a very Fibonacci-friendly chart. This symbol, $CZH, is the China index, and as you can see from the many circled points, this index had a great amount of respect for the otherwise invisible fan lines. Over and over, in spite of wild fluctuations, the index stopped hard at various fan lines and reversed direction. The starting point for the reference line is much earlier than this graph shows, indicating how long-lived the impact of fan lines can be.

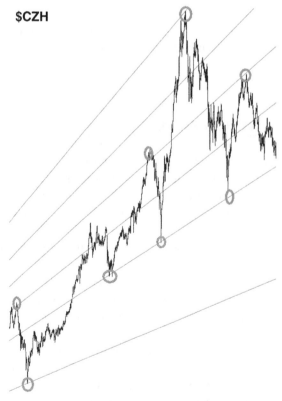

FIGURE 10.1 The China index shows eight instances of major turning points based on the fan lines, emphasizing the import of these lines on future price action.

PSYCHOLOGY BEHIND THE PATTERN

The psychology of the pattern is a difficult subject to address in a Fibonacci study. Some believe that numbers associated with Fibonacci, particularly the Golden Ratio, have significance in nature and in social dynamics, whether the individual participants are aware of it or not. Others believe that these studies are self-fulfilling prophecies, since enough traders are watching the same pattern that they may join together in creating the buying and selling pressure necessary for prices to obey the pattern. I personally dismiss this theory, since the percentage of traders in a particular security that are (a) using a Fibonacci pattern as the basis of their decision, (b) are using it properly, and (c) are using the same pattern as a large number of other traders is going to be minute and inconsequential to trading at large.

Whatever the basis, the fact is that it probably doesn't matter why it works when it works. The key is to be able to discern where the pattern has meaning and where it is simply cluttering up a chart that shouldn't have a fan drawn on it in the first place.

The examples in this chapter contain information on just the starting and ending dates for the high and low points, and nothing else. There are no price projections, percentage changes, or any other irrelevant data. The dates are provided simply so you have the option of drawing the same patterns on your own chart and interacting with the historical events on your own.

For clarity's sake, the highest line (in the case of ascending fan lines) or lowest line (for descending patterns) is called the reference line. The one next to it is called the second line, the next one is called the third, and so forth. Therefore, in an ascending fan line, the second-highest fan line is called the second, whereas in a descending pattern, the second-lowest line is called the second.

EXAMPLES

Proper placement of the starting and ending points for fan lines is crucial, and what follows are a large number of examples to illustrate how this is done.

Eurodollar

The chart of the euro (more specifically, the ratio of the euro to the U.S. dollar, which is the most widely followed and heavily traded of all the currency pairs) is shown in Figure 10.2, with its reference line spanning from late 2000 to early 2005. Although the price pierces the reference line (which is the highest one) several times, it reverts to the second-highest line repeatedly.

Take note of what happens in 2005 as the EUR/USD begins falling. Although it has been supported by the second line repeatedly, once it breaks that line, it moves rapidly to the third. At that point, it stabilizes, illustrating the value of this pattern (since it would

FIGURE 10.2 The prices of the euro remained bounded for years between the fan lines shown here.

Pattern Start: 7/5/2001
Pattern End: 12/29/2004

provide a signal for a person to go long). The price crawls along this third line but, a few weeks later, fails that line as well and drops to the fourth. At this point, EUR/USD starts a steady climb, moving to the highest levels of the chart.

Much later, by 2008, the euro is so strong that it manages to get above the third line again. It remains there for a couple of months and then dramatically plunges back through this line back to the fourth line.

The fascinating thing about this chart—and this happens frequently with good fan lines—is how the prices stay confined between lines. A person who went long the euro in early 2006, based on support at the fourth fan line, would have enjoyed a long bull market in this currency. Indeed, even with the big plunge at the right extreme of this chart, there was no real violation of the uptrend.

American Electric Power Company, Inc.

This is a close-up view of American Electric Power (symbol AEP), shown in Figure 10.3, showing the oft-seen behavior with fan lines of the prices clinging to each line before slipping to the next level. Fan lines can behave as support and resistance, but they can also behave like magnets to nearby prices.

FIGURE 10.3 Once prices break below a fan line, that line should then be regarded as resistance instead of support.

Pattern Start: 10/10/2002
Pattern End: 4/25/2007

Gold Bugs Index

Even during dramatic changes in price, fan lines can serve as important markers of turning points. In 2008, precious metals fell in value across the board, and the widely watched gold bugs index, shown in Figure 10.4, fell from 519 to 150 in a matter of months. As you can see with hindsight, the lowest point in this plunge was almost perfectly stopped at the lowest fan line. There were only three days—October 24, 27, and 28—in 2008 in which the price managed to get below that line even a little, and the amount it penetrated was so small as to be inconsequential.

What's particularly remarkable about this is that the starting point for this set of fan lines was nearly eight years before this free-fall even took place. The two price points in late 2001 and early 2008 (the low and high price extremes, respectively) were all that were required to establish these lines, which eerily confined the price plunge to the lowest fan line.

Added to this, although it is not shown in this graph, the fourth and fifth fan lines acted as solid boundaries for $HUI for years to come after the price recovered.

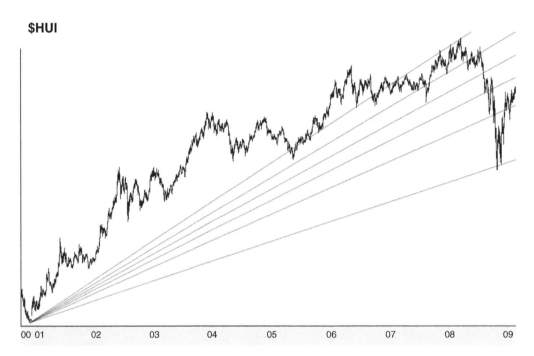

FIGURE 10.4   These fan lines were very helpful in determining the best buy point following gold's dramatic plunge.

Pattern Start: 11/13/2001
Pattern End: 3/17/2008

Dell, Inc.

Up to this point, the examples have been of ascending fan lines. Figure 10.5 shows instead a series of descending fan lines whose reference line ranges nearly a decade, from early 2000 to early 2009. This chart shows Dell in a very broad downtrend, and these lines would be useful to (a) bulls looking for an opportunity to escape the stock at a better price; (b) bears looking to short the stock upon its reach to the underside of any given fan line. Although it has not happened in this graph, it would also be a good way to watch for a fundamental shift in the stock's direction, in case the prices start piercing successively higher fan lines.

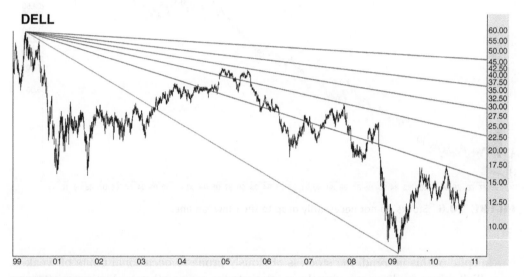

FIGURE 10.5 Descending fan lines can track major resistance and breakout points for a security whose prices has substantially diminished.

Pattern Start: 3/22/2000
Pattern End: 2/20/2009

Emerson Electric Company

There are a number of examples in this chapter which are shown in pairs—the first graph being a long-term view, and the second being a closer, shorter-term view.

Figure 10.6 shows Emerson Electric in a very long-term uptrend.

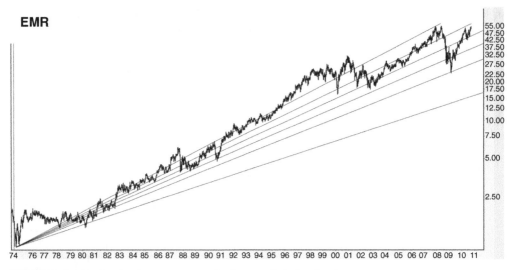

FIGURE 10.6   Stocks do not necessarily drop to their low fan line.

In spite of this uptrend, the stock is obviously prone to occasional bouts of weakness. Well-drawn fan lines can give those interested in owning the stock at more attractive prices an objective means to assess when the stock is relatively cheap. Notice in Figure 10.7 that the stock cuts through three fan lines before finally coming to rest at about $24, which marks an important low.

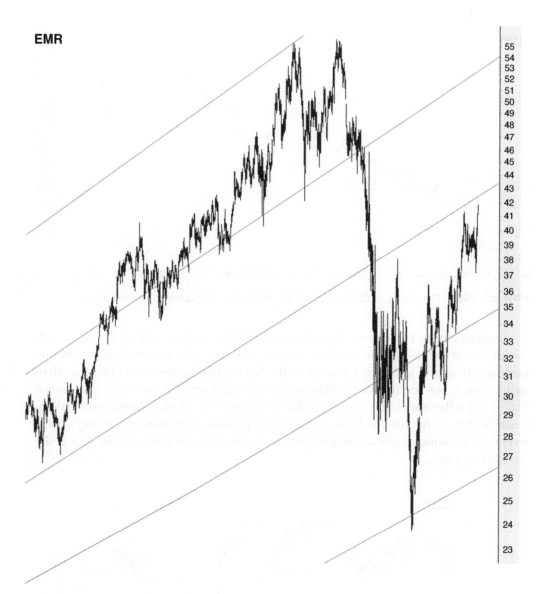

FIGURE 10.7 A close-up view shows the accuracy of the fan's projections.

Pattern Start: 10/4/1974
Pattern End: 12/4/2007

Caterpillar, Inc.

One of the challenges in using fan lines when trying to find buy and sell points is that you do not know which line, if any, will create enough support or resistance to stop the price. In EMR's case, it stopped short of the lowest fan line, whereas in Caterpillar's case, shown in Figure 10.8, it fell, for the first time, to this lowest level.

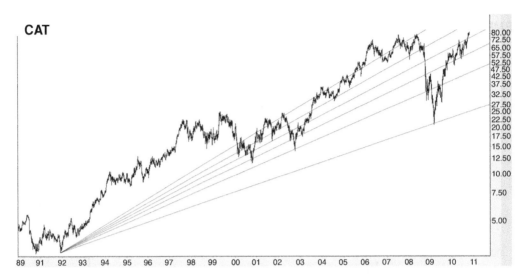

FIGURE 10.8 The selling of Caterpillar was so strong that it dropped to its lowest line.

Looking closer, you can see how Caterpillar did try to find support at the second-lowest line; it double-bottomed in this vicinity, climbed to the underside of the fan line immediately above, and then fell hard to the lowest line without even pausing. Here again, though, we see the remarkable sway these fan lines can have over prices (see Figure 10.9); there was only one day—March 3, 2009—in which prices descended beneath the lowest fan line, and that was by mere pennies. This marked the very lowest level for CAT, which made a V-shaped bottom and went on to a 350 percent gain in the coming two years.

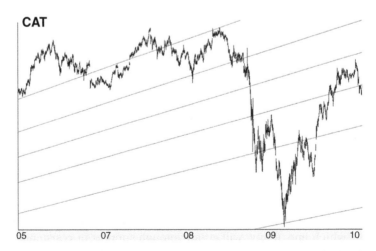

FIGURE 10.9 While recovering from its drop, Caterpillar paused at each higher line.

Pattern Start: 11/26/1991
Pattern End: 5/19/2008

Cubic Corporation

Whether a stock is moving up or down, its fan lines can offer you key support and resistance points irrespective of the stock's current direction. Figure 10.10 and 10.11 show the price chart for Cubic Corporation.

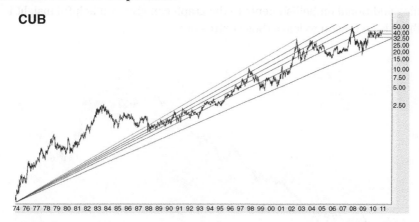

FIGURE 10.10 This is an especially long-term fan formation.

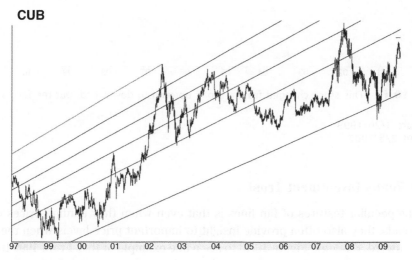

FIGURE 10.11 When viewed closer, it is easier to see how the major turning points were predicted by fan levels.

Pattern Start: 12/30/1974
Pattern End: 5/14/2002

The stock pushed strongly higher up to May 2002, then it began drifting sideways for many years. Upon drawing this fan line set, you would see the many instances of the prices bouncing off the lines (particularly the fifth line, which behaved as strong resistance from 1998 through 2001). As the stock moved sideways, this same line behaved in the role of support, and it was finally violated late in 2004. It's evident from a chart like this how indicative well-placed fan lines can be for traders.

Essex Property Trust, Inc.

Symbol ESS, in Figure 10.12, combines both fan lines and a descending trendline. There is, of course, no reason not to use multiple drawn objects on a chart to give you guidance as to where key levels of support and resistance will be. Simpler charts tend to be better, but if adding additional embellishments to the graph can give you helpful insight in your trading, there is no reason to leave those extras out.

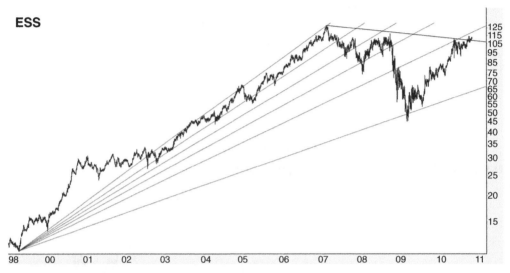

FIGURE 10.12 This stock changed from a broad uptrend to downtrend, but the fans still had meaning.

Pattern Start: 3/26/1999
Pattern End: 2/8/2007

Federal Realty Investment Trust

One of the peculiar features of fan lines is that even when they confine prices during long uptrends, they also often provide insight to important price levels when the stock turns downward. Examine Figure 10.13 to see a fine example of this. From 1999 to 2007, symbol FRT steadily moved higher, and in the final several years of its bull run, its price bounced magnificently between the reference line and the second line.

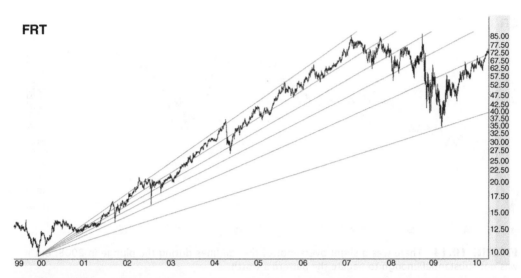

FIGURE 10.13 Likewise, this stock did a major turn from bullish to bearish, yet its lowest level was predicted by fan lines that were laid down during the bullish run.
Pattern Start: 12/15/1999
Pattern End: 2/7/2007

After February 2007, the stock began a steady downward path, and the fan lines (which would have been available to a trader at this time, since the starting and end points of the price extremes were already established) served as superb support levels, over and over again. It would have been hazardous to buy such a stock during a downtrend this long-lasting, but these support levels would have been helpful to bears in a couple of respects: (1) they would have suggested good prices at which the stock could be sold short, and (2) they could have provided important signals when the price movement was going to accelerate downward, as successive fan lines were violated.

Most important of all, once the lowest fan line was touched, the price had bottomed out and started moving smartly higher. Take a moment to consider how remarkable this is: fan lines, drawn on two points in 1999 and 2007, predicted almost to the penny where a stock would turn around two years later.

Goodrich Corporation

The tire manufacturer Goodrich bounced its way from a top to a bottom, as illustrated in Figure 10.14. From the peak in late 2007, the price swept down to its third fan line and then bounced up to the underside of its second; it then fell to its fifth fan line, bouncing to the underside of its fourth; it finally fell to the lowest fan line, bounced to the underside of the fifth, and fell again hard, dropping slightly beneath the lowest line. This illustrates that the stock price may not stop hard precisely at the line, but even if it does so, that suggests a situation so oversold that the price is almost certain to make a rebound soon, as it did here.

GR

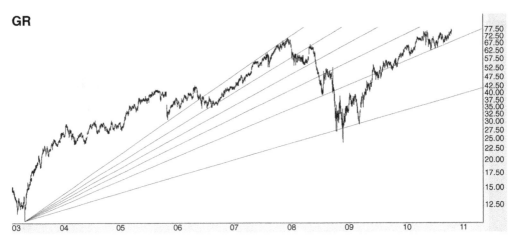

FIGURE 10.14 There was a slight overshoot of the fan lines during the plunge in 2008, but it was not substantial enough to negate the pattern's worth.

Pattern Start: 4/28/2003
Pattern End: 12/11/2007

Apple, Inc.

The turnaround of Apple's was one of the most remarkable in recent stock market history. From a low in April 2003, the stock produced a gain exceeding 5,000 percent over the next eight years, and during that entire time, the stock was remarkably well confined to its fan lines.

For those who felt they had missed out on an amazing opportunity by not buying it in 2003, the financial crisis gave them an excellent second chance, aided by fan lines. In March 2009, the price came within a dollar of the lowest fan line (see Figure 10.15). This was a strong signal that the price was probably about as low as it was going to go, and even if it did fail this lowest line, the prudent trader who had bought AAPL based on this low line would have known that something core had changed about the stock, and it was time to sell the long position at a modest loss. He would not have faced this, however, as the price ascended hundreds of percent once that line had been threatened.

FIGURE 10.15 Apple's fan lines were in place for a decade.
Pattern Start: 4/17/2003
Pattern End: 12/27/2007

Alexandria Real Estate Equities, Inc.

There have been a number of examples of prices bouncing hard off low fan lines, but this surely is not always the case. Alexandria Real Estate's stock, Figure 10.16, spent nearly a full two years (with the exception of one unusual spike higher) meandering around its lowest fan line. Buyers accumulating at this level must have had to practice a lot of patience in order to stay with the position. The fan line, however, did act as a very strong magnet, even though month after month of frustrating price inaction was taking place.

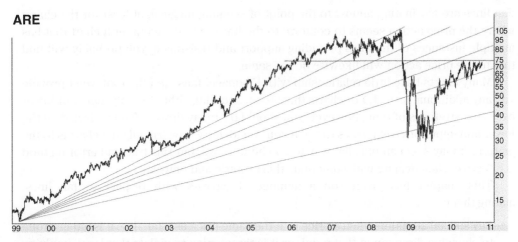

FIGURE 10.16 This shows a combination of objects—both fan lines and a horizontal line representing the division between support and resistance.

The good news for those owners was that at least the price never fell away from this line, and finally by July 2009 it was on its way higher, as shown in Figure 10.17.

FIGURE 10.17   The horizontal line shows the resistance was so strong that the prices could not manage their way back to the fan line above it.

Pattern Start: 3/26/1999
Pattern End: 9/19/2008

SUMMARY

Fan lines are fascinating almost to the point of seeming magical, at least for the charts where the price action seems to conform to the lines. If you encounter a chart that has multiple instances of the lines providing support and resistance, you probably will find that future price action will likewise do the same.

Many charts have little relationship with Fibonacci fans, and the tool won't provide you any additional insight. For charts that are meandering either broadly higher or lower over long stretches of time, however, you should try to lay down a fan line based on the lower and upper price extremes to see if you can identify how friendly the chart is to the pattern. It may seem an unusual way to go about things, but this trial-and-error method is effective when dealing with something this esoteric and unusual.

This chapter has given you a number of caveats with respect to fan lines, among them:

- Pay special attention when a price is at the same price as a fan line: it is either prone to changing direction at that point, or it is threatening to violate that level, implying a strong move in that direction.

- Don't hesitate to try two or three fan patterns on a chart, using different extremes of highs and lows; you may find some interesting relationships among these patterns.
- When the price action violates the fan lines too often—in other words, if prices seem to pay no heed to the lines—it may be time to delete the object, simply because it has lost its meaning and effectiveness on the chart.

Not many people are able to use fan lines effectively, but by carefully studying the examples in this chapter (and, if you have a charting tool equipped with this object, by trying out these examples on your own), you will help train your eyes and your mind to discover new instances in your own trading.

CHAPTER 11

Fibonacci
Retracements

L eonardo of Pisa lived from 1170 to 1250, and he is regarded as perhaps the greatest mathematician of the Middle Ages. His father William had the nickname "Bonaccio," which means good-natured, so Leonardo was subsequently known by the nickname of "Fibonacci" (short for filius Bonacci, or the son of Bonaccio).

William worked in North Africa at a trading post, and even though his home country of Italy had used the Roman numeral system for centuries, he came into contact with traders who instead used the Arabic method of numbers (which is what we use today—1, 2, 3, 4, and so forth, as opposed to numbers such as XI and MMC). Leonardo helped his father with his work, and in the course of doing so, he became acquainted with and enamored by the Arabic style of numbering, which seemed far more sensible and efficient than the Roman style. The world owes Leonardo a debt of gratitude for helping to popularize this system of numbers, since it's doubtful anyone today would appreciate having to use Roman numerals in everyday life.

Another great contribution Leonardo made was with respect to his writings related to what we today call Fibonacci numbers. This is a sequence of numbers which begins like this: 0, 1, 1, 2, 3, 5, 8, 13, 21, 34, 55, 89, 144, 233, 377, 610, 987, 1597. Each number is the sum of the two preceding numbers. These numbers have a variety of interesting properties, including the fact that, as the sequence progresses, each number divided by its preceding number approaches the mathematical figure phi (approximately 1.618033989), known as the golden ratio, which has a wide variety of expressions in nature.

In the world of stock charts, the concepts put forth by Fibonacci are manifested in drawn objects—retracements, time zones, arcs, and fans. Fibonacci retracements, the topic of this chapter, are created by connecting the highest and lowest extremes of price, at which point the charting program lays down horizontal lines at Fibonacci-specific percentage levels between those points. With some charts, these levels have great significance with respect to providing support and resistance.

DEFINITION OF THE PATTERN

By far the most popular and easiest-to-interpret Fibonacci study is the retracement. The retracement study is performed by drawing a line between two extreme points on a graph (a significant high point and low point), which then creates the drawing of a series of horizontal lines set at key Fibonacci ratios (23.6 percent, 38.2 percent, 50 percent, 61.8 percent, and 100 percent). These ratios represent a certain proportion of the vertical distance between the extreme high and low you have identified.

The impact of these levels on a financial chart can be profound, since they represent significant areas of support and resistance. In many instances, you will see a stock price bounce off these lines until it penetrates one of them, only to behave the same way with the next line. The predictive power of retracements is that you can anticipate levels of support and resistance where prices will tend to cling.

It should be stated early on that not all charts are *Fibonacci-friendly*. Some charts perform better with Fibonacci studies than others. Luckily, there is a fairly easy way to determine whether a stock is Fibonacci-friendly or not, and that is to lay down the study and examine whether past price behavior seems to comply with the study or not. If it does, chances are that it will continue to do so.

In order to make this assessment, it's valuable to understand the reference line and its relationship to time on the chart. The reference line is the line drawn between two extremes. Whichever of those two points is more recent creates a division between the *before* and *after* of the retracement. For instance, if you drew a line from January 1998 to March 2001, then the point at March 2001 is the more recent one, and the part of the chart prior to March 2001 would be before the study and the part after March 2001 would be after the study.

Figure 11.1 shows a very Fibonacci-friendly chart of the New Zealand dollar's ratio to the U.S. dollar (known as the NZD/USD cross-rate). Again and again, the price hits a retracement line and reverses direction. This behavior indicates that future price behavior will likely act in a similar fashion.

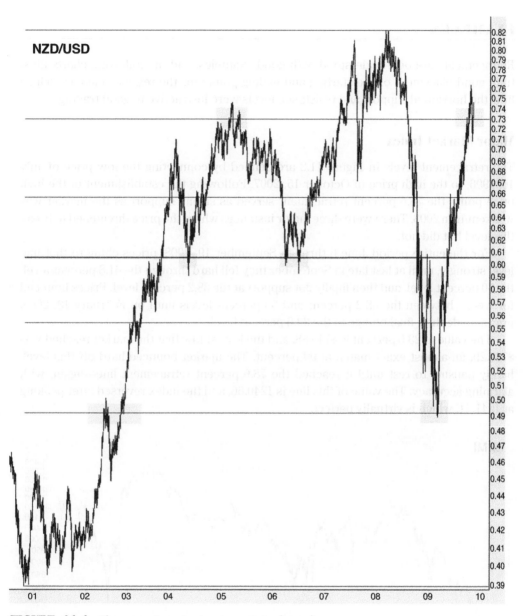

FIGURE 11.1 There are six major turning points shown here.

EXAMPLES

Retracements are best understood with good examples, and the following charts illustrate good placement of the starting and ending points for the retracements as well as how the horizontal support and resistance levels were instructive to good trading.

Major Market Index

The retracement levels in Figure 11.2 are defined by connecting the low price of July 16, 1996, to the high price of October 15, 2007. Following the establishment of the high price point, the 78.6 percent retracement served as strong support as the market was weakening in 2008. There were three major instances where the price threatened to break this level but did not.

For the entire period June 6 through September 19, 2008, prices clung to that line level strongly, until at last late in September they fell hard through the 61.8 percent level, the 50 percent level, and then finally got support at the 38.2 percent level. Prices bounced for weeks between the 38.2 percent and 50 percent levels until on February 13, 2009, prices made their final plunge to the 23.6 percent level.

The value at 23.6 percent is $748.88, and the lowest low that the market reached was $739.29, an almost exact match at 99 percent. The market bounced hard off this level, barely pausing to rest until it reached the 78.6 percent retracement line—again, with alarming accuracy. The value of this line is 1240.66, and the index reversed after peaking at 1241.41, which is virtually perfect.

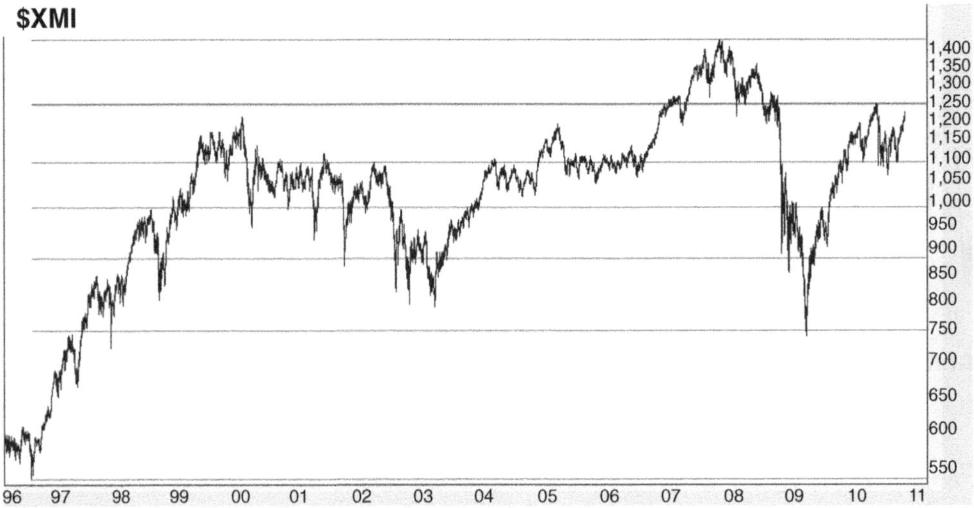

FIGURE 11.2 The low price in 2009 was anticipated by a fraction of 1 percent by the Fibonacci retracements of the Major Market Index.
Date of Low Price: 7/16/1996
Date of High Price: 10/15/2007

As you can see, the value of retracement levels is to anticipate major turning points. Sometimes the price data pauses (or stops hard) at each level, and other times it will sail through to a subsequent level if the price is too strong or weak to rest at the current station.

Nordstrom, Inc.

A close-up view of retailer Nordstrom's chart is shown in Figure 11.3. In any of these examples, the thing to focus on before the second date point is how many instances of bounces there are between the first and second dates, and the thing to focus on after the second data point is how you might have made use of the retracement levels in your own trading.

In other words, the retracement levels did not exist until such time as the second date. It is interesting to look backwards and notice how and when different bounces off support and resistance took place, but the reality is that the retracement levels would not have been there. However, once the Fibonacci retracement is laid down, examining these touch-points is useful, because it indicates just how reliable these lines are with respect to the price movement.

If there are many touch-points, and the lines do seem to have an important relationship with the price movement, then you can have a certain degree of confidence that there will be value forthcoming from these same lines, and in the course of examining these examples, you should reflect on how you would have made use of such lines in your trading.

Turning our attention back to Nordstrom, you can see the price shot up to the first retracement level, paused briefly, continued its ascent to the second level, eased back down to the first, blasted higher to the third level, eased back to the second, and then shot higher to the fourth level. In other words, the classic tendency of a stock to go through a series of backing and filling movements with respect to price is shown here, but it is doing so with a special respect for the levels established by that Fibonacci retracement value.

Therefore, in your own trading, you would have found the best buying opportunities at the points where the price retraced back to a lower price level, and, if you wanted to be conservative and take smaller profits, you would have done well to have taken those profits at the points where the price was at the underside of a retracement level. Based on this chart, you would have something that followed a pattern like this:

April 2, 2009—buy
May 7—sell
June 23—buy
July 23—sell
August 19—buy
September 16—sell

And all of these decisions would have been based on nothing more than the simple horizontal lines on your screen.

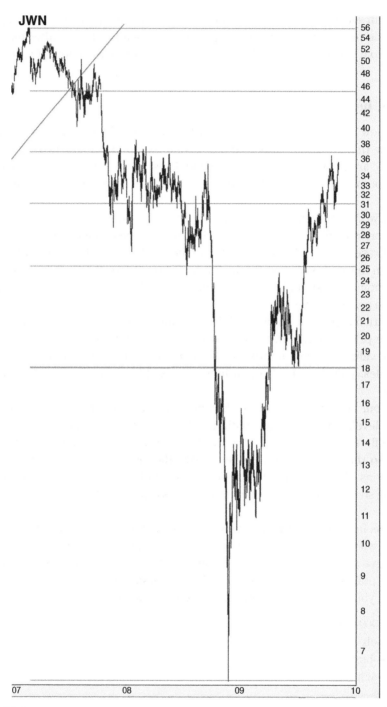

FIGURE 11.3 Clusters of activity spanning weeks are confined between the retracement levels.

Date of Low Price: 2/22/2007
Date of High Price: 11/21/2008

American Express Company

Similar to the Nordstrom example, Figure 11.4 shows American Express performing the same backing and filling, moving toward, and then away from, each of the retracement levels.

FIGURE 11.4 The price recovery of 2009 followed a steady path, ascending to one retracement level, backing away to the one just below, and then repeating the process.

Date of Low Price: 7/19/2007
Date of High Price: 3/6/2009

General Electric Company

The importance of these horizontal lines can even be seen with retracements that span a very long period (in some cases, even as long as a century). General Electric, charted in Figure 11.5, is enhanced with a Fibonacci retracement of about nine years. After GE fell from its peak in 2007 of $36.70 to $5.40 in March 2009—an astonishing 86 percent drop from one of the largest corporations in the world—it began to climb back.

What is remarkable is that the price rose in 2011 to $20.74, which is circled, and the retracement level at this point was $20.61, a difference of merely thirteen cents. Prices are certainly not guaranteed to stop hard at the exactly point where a line is, but they certainly can come very close with charts that are conforming to the support and resistance levels suggested by these retracements.

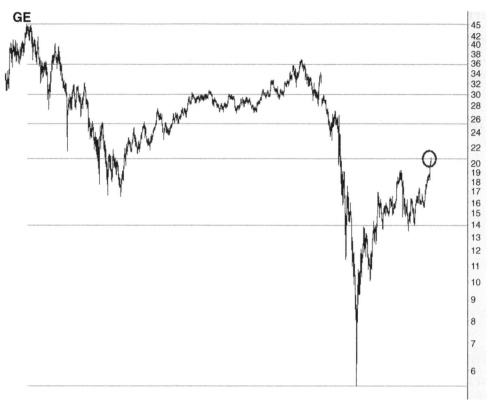

FIGURE 11.5 The peak price in 2011 seems to have been anticipated in advance by the retracement levels defined by the 2000 and 2009 price extremes.

Date of Low Price: 8/25/2000
Date of High Price: 3/4/2009

Dow Jones Industrials

The Dow Jones Industrial Average has exhibited some very interesting behavior with respect to Fibonacci retracements, only one of which is shown in Figure 11.6. Even very large price ranges—for example, from December 9, 1974, to October 11, 2007—provide remarkable instances in which the price is bound (for years at a time in some cases) between two price levels or, conversely, clings tightly to a single price level before shifting to another.

It is worthwhile to experiment with multiple retracements, particularly with an index as long-lived as the Dow 30, to see what kinds of major turning points were pinpointed by certain retracements. Once you have found these, then you can leave those retracements in place to anticipate future significant price levels.

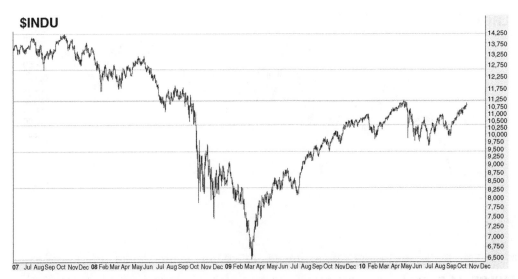

FIGURE 11.6 The Dow Industrials, the most famous stock index in the world, has exhibited surprisingly reliable behavior toward its retracement levels.

Date of Low Price: 5/7/1996
Date of High Price: 3/6/2009

Lam Research Corporation

Figures 11.7 and 11.8 show the same stock, Lam Research, but the latter chart shows a close-up view so you can see the price behavior more clearly as it nears various retracement levels.

The time span for the reference line is large—from 1990 to 2007—and what happens after the July 2007 data point is interesting and would have been terribly helpful to a person trading this stock from that point forward.

The stock starts selling off, and it pauses at the 38.2 percent level. It continuously bounces at that level from January 9 through July 2, 2008, before falling next, almost to the penny, to the 50 percent level. It bounces back up to the 38.2 percent level and then falls hard down to almost the 78.6 percent level, at which time it begins a steady ascent, pausing each time it reaches the next lever higher.

When you are looking at a stock chart against these lines, it seems almost predictable and easy, but temporarily remove these lines (which you can do in ProphetCharts by pressing Ctrl-D) and see what a difference it makes. Once a trader becomes accustomed to the guidance Fibonacci retracements can provide, he or she may feel that they are flying blind once those lines disappear, because without them, there's rarely any clear indication as to where a price may stop rising or falling (see Figure 11.8).

FIGURE 11.7 The broad, multidecade view shows many bounces off retracement levels.

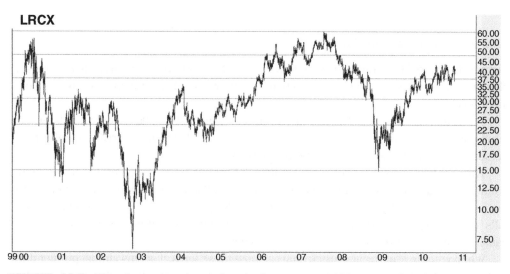

FIGURE 11.8 This closer view shows that the low price in 2008 was predicted almost to the penny with retracement levels.

Date of Low Price: 8/24/1990
Date of High Price: 7/17/2007

SUMMARY

Retracements are easy to use, because you can focus your attention on a stock only when its price approaches one of those levels. A given level might compel you to buy a stock, short a stock, or take profits on an existing position.

The real challenge comes in identifying the charts that are the best candidates for these retracement levels, and in taking the right action when those levels are reached (or breached). Given the choice, though, of trading with Fibonacci retracements or without them, you will probably find it much easier (and hopefully more profitable) to have them in your trading arsenal. Used properly, they can be the trader's equivalent of X-ray vision into the market's next move.

CHAPTER 12

Flags

S ome of the patterns in this book can become established for the long term, spanning years or even decades. The flag pattern is nothing of the sort. It is, instead, a fleeting, short-term pattern, typically lasting just a few weeks, and it is a continuation pattern, allowing a security to take a breath before moving in its dominant direction.

DEFINITION OF THE PATTERN

The first requirement for a flag pattern is that it be preceded by a strong move in the first place. That move can be up or down, but it must be strong and sharp, since the entire basis for a flag pattern is that it represents a brief pause in the action of an overall powerful move. Even though prices may form flag patterns in the midst of markets that are meandering, the fact that they aren't in the context of a strong move negates their import.

Next, the flag should be countertrend to the general trend. Because of its countertrend nature, the flag should be downward-sloping for a bullish move and upward-sloping for a bearish move. After all, the buying or selling action is supposed to abate during the formation of the flag—often on dwindling volume—and it makes sense that the dominant direction would be opposed while the flag is being formed.

The flag itself is defined as a group of prices that are cleanly bounded by a pair of parallel trendlines. If the lines are converging, the pattern is a pennant, which is covered in a different section. The flag itself shouldn't be terribly lengthy; a length of three months is probably the longest acceptable timeframe, and a more typical age will be a month or less.

Finally, when the price breaks out of the flag pattern, that breakout should be accompanied with an increase in volume. The trend is eager to resume itself, and after weeks of waiting, buyers (or sellers, as the case may be) should push the equity back into its longer-term trend with an abundance of activity.

Even though flags aren't particularly big patterns, the moves they portend can be substantial. The distance from the beginning of the broad trend (whether up or down) to the beginning of the flag is sometimes known as the flagpole, and its height is the figure you want to use to compute the measured move. That move is calculated by adding (or, in a downtrend, subtracting) the price value from the end of the flag pattern.

For instance, if a stock was trading at between $10 and $12 for a long time, and then it suddenly made a rapid ascent from $12 to $20 before starting its flag pattern, the flagpole would be $8 in height (that is, $20 minus $12, since $12 is the value when the stock changed from trading in a tight range to soaring sharply higher). Let us assume the flag was formed by a gentle down-sloping pattern lasting three weeks that took the price back down, but then the bulls stepped in again on big volume and broke out of the flag at $18. The measured target would therefore be $26, since $18 (the breakout level) plus $8 (the flagpole's height) equals $26.

PSYCHOLOGY BEHIND THE PATTERN

Let's look at a real-life example of a flag pattern to understand the thinking behind the crowd trading it. Figure 12.1 shows PNM Resources, a stock that until early March was in a very sharp downtrend. The stock bottomed and began an extremely rapid climb. The participants in such a climb would be a combination of those who had bought the stock much earlier and were relieved to see their losses diminishing and new owners who bought at nearly the bottom and were delighted at their quick profits. The stock moved from about $5.50 to about $8.50, a flagpole with a height of $3. At this point, most people are extremely happy with what has been happening to PNM.

After such a dizzying ascent, selling starts to overcome buying, and the stock begins to ease back. There is no panic selling, however, as the angle of the descent is modest and suggests an orderly taking of profits. There are enough people satisfied with (or uncomfortable with) a 50 percent increase in price in such a short amount of time that they would rather exit all or part of their position rather than hold out for even bigger gains. Fear briefly overcomes greed, but there is enough sustained interest in the stock to avoid any kind of rapid selloff.

After about a month of moving between $8.50 and $7.25, the weak hands have been cleared out of the stock, and it's ready to resume its strong move higher. It pushes above the flag pattern, and it's evident to those trading the stock that the consolidation is now over and there is an opportunity for greater gains. Existing owners buy more, and bystanders who don't yet own the stock finally decide to do so. Once the price exceeds its former recovery high of $8.50, which takes place almost immediately after the breakout, greed overcomes fear once more, and the stock can work its way to its target price.

That target price, $11.25, is the sum of the price at the breakout ($8.25) and the flagpole height of $3. This target is met by July, and there is enough buying to even exceed that target. In the end, this turns out to be an almost perfect illustration of the flag pattern, both in its form and its targeted price.

FIGURE 12.1 This example makes it easy to see how the second flagpole height equaled the first.

EXAMPLES

Here are seven examples of the flag pattern, its breakout price, and the percentage change that was enjoyed after the pattern was completed.

Sunstone Hotel Investors, Inc.

Although it isn't shown in Figure 12.2, the flagpole of this flag started at the low price of $4.87, and the value of SHO moved very fast. The downward angle of this flag is more

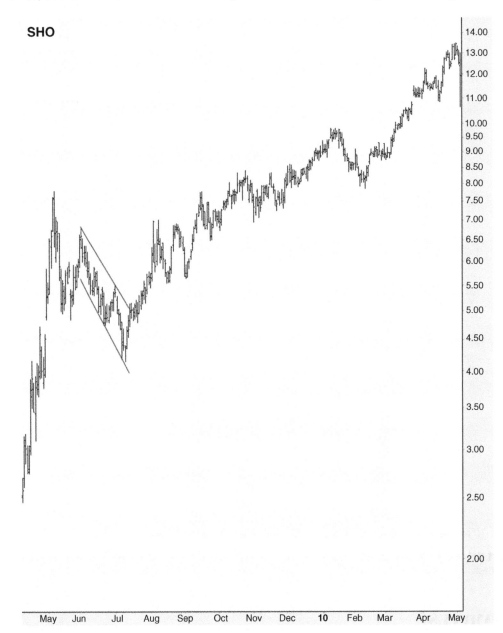

FIGURE 12.2 The bullish move continued after this flag pattern, but at a more leisurely pace.

Pattern Start: 6/1/2009   Breakout Price: $5   Percentage Change: 169%
Pattern End: 7/15/2009   Postbreakout Price: $13.47

extreme, but that is not surprising considering how fast the stock moved from $1.87 to $7.81.

The takeaway from this chart is that the move preceding a flag may be more dramatic than the moving following it, particularly during upward trends. Stocks climb the proverbial wall of worry, and it can sometimes take months or even years for a bullish move to complete, even if it begins with an exhilarating jump. The target price of approximately $11 was indeed achieved, but it took about eight months to get there after the flag, whereas the price increase prior to the flag took one-quarter of that time.

Waddell & Reed Financial, Inc.

There will be occasions in your charting career when you see a series of flags that happen in succession. This is logical, since a long-term trend might need more than one opportunity to pause and backfill before continuing. It is also valuable to be able to distinguish between distinct flags since it will help you more accurately measure the target move.

Figure 12.3 has one flag marked, but by looking at the area preceding this flag, you can see another larger, more sharply angled flag that formed during February and March of 2009. If you were to look at this chart and assume that the entire span from November 2008 to July 2009 was the flagpole, the target price would be far too high.

Instead, the first flagpole is from about $8 to $17 (a height of $9) which, when added to the first flag's breakout of $13, gives a target of $22. When the second flag begins forming (and this is the flag that is marked on the graph), the flagpole ranges from $11 to $22, a height of $11, which, when added to the breakout price of $25, produces a target of $36, which was met by April of 2010.

Discerning these two flags gives you two benefits: First, it lets you have accurate target prices to know when a move has reached its likely potential, and second, it helps you avoid severely overstating where a price might move. These two might sound the same, but the first is a matter of knowing when to exit, and the second is a matter of avoiding a severe misjudgment of a pattern's potential.

FIGURE 12.3 Although the angle of the ascent was less sharp after the flag, the target was still met.

Pattern Start: 6/10/2009   Breakout Price: $25   Percentage Change: 52%
Pattern End: 7/23/2009   Postbreakout Price: $38

Carnival PLC

Most stocks making big moves higher in price will have plenty of times in which the price softens and then ascends again. Not every one of these times represents a flag pattern. In your mind's eye—and then, with your charting tools—you need to discern the difference between a group of prices that is bounded by parallel lines and a group of prices that is simply going down in an ill-defined fashion.

The price chart for Carnival, Figure 12.4, has four distinct areas in which the price drops substantially, but only the second of these is a flag pattern, and it is marked as such. Although some charting programs, such as ProphetCharts, have built-in tools to automatically find patterns such as flags, you will also find that, over the years, your eyes will get better at distinguishing what is a true pattern and what is simply noise.

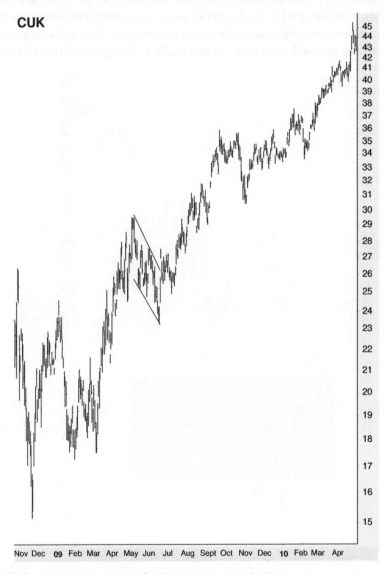

FIGURE 12.4 The measured move for this pattern was ideal.

Pattern Start: 5/7/2009   Breakout Price: $25   Percentage Change: 44%
Pattern End: 6/19/2009   Postbreakout Price: $36

DreamWorks Animation SKG, Inc.

The animation house DreamWorks experienced a very strong rally for most of 2009, and there were at least four big gaps up in price during this rally (gaps are a charting event covered in a different section of this book). Between the first and second gaps, a steeply descending flag pattern was formed.

Even though the gaps are open, they are still included in the calculation of the flag-pole. Using Figure 12.5, DreamWorks's chart, as our example, the first flagpole ranges from $18 to $29, a height of $11. The breakout point is at about $28, offering a target of $39. The price was bested by the end of 2009, and interestingly, that is also approximately the level where the upward movement began stalling. The gaps were an encouraging

FIGURE 12.5 This stock had a series of huge gaps higher in price during its uptrend.

Pattern Start: 6/1/2009   Breakout Price: $28   Percentage Change: 36%
Pattern End: 7/16/2009   Postbreakout Price: $38

affirmation of the stock's rally, but the flag allowed us to anticipate when to take our profits.

Sysco Corporation

Although having a target price is a good way to take profits at a nonarbitrary level, the price that a stock might reach could far exceed this target. That is why you may find it prudent to take partial profits at your target price and leave a portion of the position in place with a tight stop, just in case you have the good fortune to enjoy even larger profits.

A fitting example of this is Sysco, shown in Figure 12.6. The price moved from $19 to $23.50, then the flag began forming. After the breakout at $21.50, a target price of $26

FIGURE 12.6 The move higher greatly exceeded the target.

Pattern Start: 6/2/2009　　Breakout Price: $21.50　　Percentage Change: 45%
Pattern End: 7/15/2009　　Postbreakout Price: $31.17

was implied. It reached this price, but then it continued into the lower $30s. Keeping, for instance, half of your position even after the $26 target was reached would have permitted you to tack on another $5/share in gains before the move was finally exhausted.

DTE Energy Company

Flags can be continuation patterns for stocks that are falling as well. Figure 12.7 offers an example of this with symbol DTE, and the same rules that apply to flags for bullish stocks apply in reverse to flags for bearish stocks.

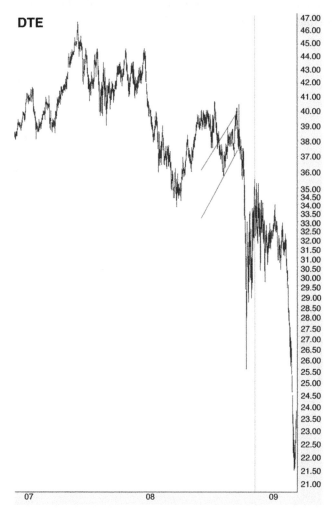

FIGURE 12.7 This equity looked like it might be recovering in mid-2008, but the failure of the flag confirmed that the general downtrend was still on.

Pattern Start: 7/23/2008   Breakout Price: $36   Percentage Change: −31%
Pattern End: 9/19/2008   Postbreakout Price: $25

The flag highlighted in this chart is at the half-mast point between the extremes of the graph. In other words, the flagpoles on each side of the flag are both about the same height, as you would expect from this pattern. The stock's fall started at about $47, and the flag started forming at $38, a price $9 lower. The flag pattern finished about a month later at $36, suggesting a target low of $27, which was reached and exceeded.

Take note how the flag itself is slanted upward versus the downward-slanting flags of the bullish charts in this chapter. This agrees with the concept that the flag is a countertrend resting period within the context of the larger move. The stock price briefly fights its way higher, but the pattern eventually succumbs to the overall selling pressure of the trend and the price decline resumes as before.

Sinclair Broadcast Group, Inc.

The time-length of the flags in both Figure 12.7 and Figure 12.8 illustrates how much shorter bearish flags can be when compared to bullish flags.

The stock's fall began on October 5, 2007, at a high price of $11.38. When the flag pattern started on August 6, 2008, the price was $6.31, suggesting a flagpole height of a little more than $5. The flag pattern was complete on September 25, 2008, at a breakout price of $5.60, suggesting the bottom of the rightmost flagpole would be an alarming 60 cents.

Amazingly, the price got very close to this target. The price bottomed at 83 cents on March 17, 2009, and then commenced a huge reversal in price of greater than a thousand percentage points. As small as the flag was, particularly in the context of a multiyear drop in price, its ability to serve as a measuring tool for the ultimate low was remarkable.

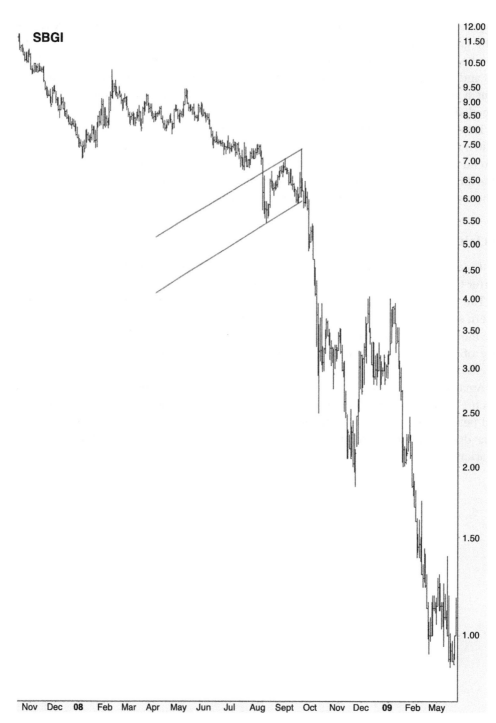

FIGURE 12.8 This flag was very short-lived, because the selling pressure was so intense that it did not take long for it to resume with full force.

Pattern Start: 8/6/2008   Breakout Price: $5.60   Percentage Change: −82%
Pattern End: 9/25/2008   Postbreakout Price: $1

SUMMARY

The flag's power is in its ability to predict a target price. Flags can be difficult to spot when they are being formed, but when you are tracking a stock that has just completed a very large move up or down, you should be on the look-out for a flag, which serves not only as a stopping point but also as a projection method.

Remember, flags can appear in either up or down markets, but they need to run contrary to the broader trend. They also need to enclose the price action between parallel lines lasting not more than three months. If your observations match these parameters, you will have a valuable ally with respect to determining the next important price for your security.

CHAPTER 13

Gaps

A gap in the price of a security takes place when there is a large amount of empty vertical space between price bars, representing a sudden (and usually unexpected) rise or fall in price. Many things can cause a price gap, such as surprisingly good earnings, surprisingly bad earnings, FDA approval (or disapproval) of an important drug at a pharmaceutical company, a takeover of a company, and so on. Usually, something has taken place between market sessions that compels much more buying and selling pressure than would be experienced by the same stock on an ordinary day.

This is one reason that, while stop-loss prices are very helpful, they are not a guarantee of safety. If you are long a stock you bought at $10, and you have a stop-loss at $9.99, you are not assured that, no matter what happens, any loss you experience will be miniscule. The company might announce that it has been fabricating its accounting for the past five years, and it opens the next day at a bid of $2, which is the price you'll probably get (if you're lucky). Such a shock-event would be a gap.

DEFINITION OF THE PATTERN

The simplest definition of a gap is a positive difference in price between one day's maximum value and the next day's minimum value (or vice versa). If Monday's highest price is $15 and Tuesday's low price is $16, that would be a gap. If Thursday's lowest price was $14 and Friday's highest price was $13.75, that would also be a gap (albeit a small one).

The gaps that concern us are usually more dramatic than 25 cents; they are usually very easy to spot in a chart, and plenty of free scanning services on the Internet will provide you with a list of the day's up-gaps and down-gaps so far. If you have read about gaps, you have probably encountered various terms for different flavors, such as exhaustion gaps, common gaps, runaway gaps, and so forth. In my experience, these assignations aren't valuable, and we shall content ourselves with focusing on meaningful price gaps and how we may exploit them.

Figure 13.1 shows the company Equifax, which gapped higher on April 25, 2003, on strong volume. You will often see a substantial increase in volume on gap days because of the buying excitement (on up-gaps) or stop-loss orders being executed in large numbers (on down-gaps). The stock continued higher, buoyed by the excitement of the gap-up, then—as is often the case—it started selling off. It closed the gap, which is precisely the kind of action we want to see as a buy-signal, and then began a more sustained ascent, nearly doubling in price before its next meaningful correction.

FIGURE 13.1 Although the chart doesn't show the continued climb, this stock nearly doubled in price before enduring any meaningful correction after the gap took place.

The four stages described here—(1) a gap; (2) a push in the gap's direction; (3) a retracement; (4) a more powerful move in the original direction—form a pattern that is shown again and again in this chapter. Our job as traders is to spot these gaps and enter these positions at the safest time. In addition, you will want to look for gaps that break out in the same general direction as the stock. The up-gaps you are going to see in this chapter are for stocks that are already climbing, and the down-gaps you are going to see are for stocks that are already falling.

PSYCHOLOGY BEHIND THE PATTERN

Let's consider a hypothetical stock that has been steadily climbing in price from $10 to $20 over a period of a few years. It's a decent performer, and the shareholders are generally happy with the gently rising value of their holdings.

On a given Tuesday, after the close, the company announces surprisingly good earnings. The company's new product line is selling better than expected, and their margins have improved substantially. The analysts following the company up their recommendations from "buy" to "strong buy," and even though the stock closed at $20 during the regular trading session, it's already evident from the after-market quotes that there is a lot of buying interest in the stock, thanks to all the good news.

On Wednesday morning, the stock opens at $22, 10 percent higher than its close, and the stock appears automatically on various Top Gainers lists, Hot Stocks lists, and so on. The front pages of finance-oriented web sites mention the good day the stock is having, and more buyers pile in.

Over the coming three weeks, more analysts start following the company, offering glowing reviews of the firm's prospects, and the stock pushes up to $25, a 25 percent gain in just a few weeks. Now the price starts cooling off as owners of the stock decide that a 25 percent gain in a few weeks is plenty, and they would rather take money off the table rather than put their gains at risk. Those who are long the stock, both old-timers and newcomers, watch somewhat uncomfortably as the price ticks down to $24.50, $24, $23.50, and lower. Selling increases as stop-loss orders get hit, weak hands decide to click the Sell button, and those who jumped into the security at $25 are regretting their decision and decide to take their loss now rather than risk worse losses.

The stock is now getting close to the $20 price it was at before the good news was even announced. Those newcomers who bought between $22 and $25 have either dumped their position or have decided to wait it out. Long-term holders who bought between $10 and $20 are content to stay put, since they are still looking at a profitable position and the company's positive prospects haven't changed. Selling dries up, and slowly the buyers begin to get the upper hand on sellers once more. After all, the stock is now at about $20, which was its value before all the positive announcements from the company were factored in, so some people recognize a terrific bargain since they are able to get the stock without paying the premium that the gap demanded.

So the stock starts rising again, and the reality is that the company's fortunes have indeed improved, irrespective of the stock price's machinations. The products they sell are popular, the margins are good, and the earnings are going to continue to improve. Now that the excitement—and brief disillusionment—with the stock price are over, more normalized buying and selling return, and overall there is more buying interest than selling interest, pushing the stock far behind its prior peak of $25.

This scenario is, in broad terms, what happens with a gap-up, and the converse can be applied to gaps-down in price. There is excitement (or fear); a strong push up (or down); a retracement back toward the gap; and then finally a more sustained continuation in the direction that the gap established in the first place. This is why you can take advantage of long or short positions with gap-fills. Of course, a stock doesn't necessarily have to fill its gap, but when it does, it represents a lower-risk opportunity to enter into a position since the market has tipped its hand with respect to the security's likely next move.

EXAMPLES

Gaps are quite common in the market, so there are an abundance of examples to see in this chapter, including the post-gap percentage change.

CBS Corporation

The chart of CBS, Figure 13.2, makes the decision for a trader easier, because the gap fill also coincidentally marks the completion of an extremely clean inverted head-and-shoulders pattern. The gap was filled a mere ten days later, which also, by definition, was the retracement to the neckline.

It must be pointed out that a gap fill doesn't necessarily mean that the stock price will go back, to the penny, to where the gap took place. Indeed, the price may gap up (or down) and never look back. In those instances where the price is retracing, the closer the price gets back to the original gap, the lower the risk is. If a trader waits until the gap is totally closed, however, he may never get an opportunity to enter the position. In this case, the lower price of the gap was at $8.97, and the lowest price that CBS sank to afterward was $9.40, still about 5 percent above the gap. There is no predefined rule that states when a trade is safe to enter, but a good rule of thumb is to *leg in* to a position during the retracement.

In other words, if a person intends to take on a $10,000 position, he might buy $2,500 at one price, and the stock might sink a bit further, then buy another $2,500, and perhaps the stock sinks further still, buy another $2,500, and then suddenly the stock rockets higher, suggesting that the retracement is over, at which point he buys the final $2,500. Because he cannot know how low the price will go, he spreads his risk. The price will, by definition, be somewhat higher than the lowest possible price, but it is simply not realistic to expect to pay the best possible price for a position. At least by legging in one does not sit idly by as the stock quietly makes a bottom, rockets higher, and then makes the risk/reward much less attractive.

CBS

FIGURE 13.2 We can see here that the gap also represented the completion of an inverted head-and-shoulders pattern.

Gap Date: 8/7/2009   Gap Price: $9.40   Percentage Change: 79%
Retrace Date: 8/17/2009   Postgap Price: $16.87

Atheros Communications, Inc.

If a stock retraces back close to its gap, that is a relatively low-risk entry point, but the stock might revisit that gap in the near future. The key to holding on to such a position is to set the stop-loss price at a logical level. Some people choose a price just beneath the gap, although this opens up the risk that the price will move a few pennies beneath the gap before reversing, taking you out of an otherwise good position. If you want to be very conservative in your gap trading, you might want to set your stop-loss at just a small amount—perhaps half a percentage point—beneath the gap.

Figure 13.3 offers an illustration of a stock that revisited its gap once soon after, and then a second time some months later. Importantly, the second visitation did not violate the gap, and indeed its low price was a little higher than the first retracement. This was the kind of higher low that is constructive to positive movement in a stock's price.

FIGURE 13.3 This gap was partly retraced twice, but the window remained open.

Gap Date: 7/22/2009   Gap Price: $24.18   Percentage Change: 82%
Retrace Date: 11/3/2009   Postgap Price: $43.90

Darden Restaurants, Inc.

After a gap, a retracement may or may not take place, and if it does take place, it may happen quickly or it may take an uncomfortably long time for it to complete. This is another reason why patience—and legging in to a position—can make waiting for a full retracement more bearable.

A fitting example, which also is illustrative of the risk of jumping into a hot stock after it has initially taken off, is shown in Figure 13.4. Darden Restaurants leaped higher on

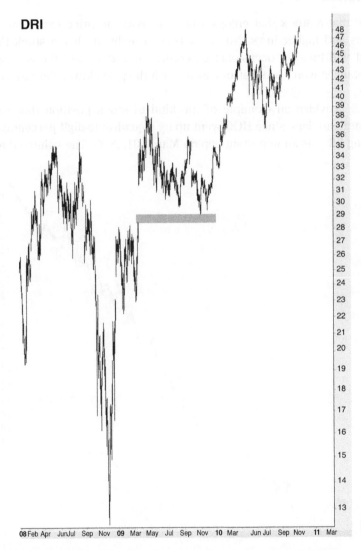

FIGURE 13.4 Those who bought after the gap had to endure a nearly 25 percent drop in price before the real move higher got underway.

Gap Date: 3/18/2009   Gap Price: $28.89   Percentage Change: 66%
Retrace Date: 11/2/2009   Postgap Price: $47.91

March 18 and it peaked soon thereafter on April 22. It then meandered slowly downward to a loss of about 25 percent by November 2. You can imagine how exasperating it was for buyers of this ostensibly hot stock to see their equity value wither away.

More prudent observers could use the gap as their guide, using a price of about $28.50 as their magnet to leg in to a position. The point is that a retracement can take a while, and patience can be profitable.

Holly Corporation

It is axiomatic that a stock that enjoys a large increase in price experiences a series of higher highs and higher lows. No stock goes straight up, but a stock that is in a broad uptrend will take its occasional downturns in stride, and the selling pressure from these instances won't be so strong as to push the price lower than its most recent important low.

Figure 13.5 provides an example of the kind of stock position that can be life-changing for large holders, since HOC went up by a quadruple-digit percentage. Preceding this amazing lift was an important gap on March 31, 2003. The volume that day was

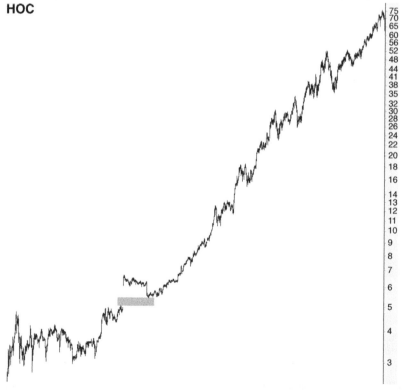

FIGURE 13.5 This astonishingly steady rise in Holly's price was signaled by a very strong up-gap and a retracement that offered a superb buying opportunity.

Gap Date: 3/31/2003   Gap Price: $5.37   Percentage Change: 133%
Retrace Date: 9/2/2003   Postgap Price: $12.52

also a strong signal, since there were 5,316,800 shares traded, versus only 120,800 the day before. Almost the entire gain the stock was going to see that year was experienced on that one day, and it fell from then on for almost the entire balance of the year.

Importantly, the retracement didn't sink beneath the gap, and an entry late in the year would have offered a superb price for a stock that had already demonstrated its ability to climb much, much higher.

Krispy Kreme Doughnuts, Inc.

We now turn our attention to some examples of stocks that gapped down in price during their own broad downtrends.

As a public company, Krispy Kreme has had an interesting history. It came public in the midst of a brutal bear market, but it was one of the very few stocks that actually went up during 2001. Indeed, on the week after the 9/11 terror attacks on America, Krispy Kreme actually closed higher for the week, which surely made it a rarity.

The stock made its ultimate peak on August 13, 2003, at nearly $50 and began to slide downward. By the time the gap in Figure 13.6 took place, the stock had already lost nearly 90 percent of its peak value.

FIGURE 13.6 The sudden drop with Krispy Kreme was followed by months of weakness, but nearly a year later, the gap was filled better than their jelly doughnuts.

Gap Date: 9/7/2007   Gap Price: $5.65   Percentage Change: −82%
Retrace Date: 6/19/2008   Postgap Price: $1.01

Dish Network Corporation

Now we see in Figure 13.7 a sudden drop in the Dish Network's stock on January 2, 2008. For those who are selling a stock short, it is especially important to time your short well, because you may have the added burden of dividends. In other words, if you buy into a long position too soon and have to wait a year for things to turn higher, you at least

FIGURE 13.7 When this stock got back to about $33, it represented an ideal opportunity for a short sale.

Gap Date: 1/2/2008   Gap Price: $32.85   Percentage Change: −77%
Retrace Date: 5/20/2008   Postgap Price: $7.59

will receive dividends while you wait (assuming the stock pays dividends). With a short position, the opposite is true; you not only have the uncomfortable uncertainty of dealing with a stock that may be moving higher, but you've got to pay dividends for the privilege (and, in many cases, interest for borrowing the stock in the first place). So minimizing your waiting period on short sales is key.

By May 20, 2008, the stock was back up to 32.85, only 45 cents beneath the gap. The stock had already visited $23.40 during its dip, so obviously waiting for the closure of the gap would have been very beneficial for a person waiting to enter a short position (or, alternately, would have offered a very good opportunity for an unhappy bull to get out of their long position). From that point, the stock fell hard, getting as low as $7.59 before finally turning around.

Agilent Technologies, Inc.

The electronics firm Agilent came public on November 22, 1999, and although it had a nice run higher initially, the bear market of 2000–2002 took its toll and sent the stock heading down beginning on March 7, 2000. As part of this downtrend, on July 21 the stock gapped down on volume more than ten times greater than the prior day.

The stock provided two opportunities for bears to get in at good prices; the first was not long after the gap, on August 29, and the next was on January 18 the following year. In each of these cases, the price approached—but did not exceed—the top of the gap. A person entering a short position on August 29 could be forgiven for entering somewhat too soon, since the price was still excellent.

The retracement on January 18 was a bit higher than the prior one, and afterward the price plunged 85 percent. It is evident with examples like this, in Figure 13.8, what a powerful risk/reward ratio can be found with short positions based on gaps. A person entering a short at, for instance, $63 with a stop-loss at $72 would be risking about 14 percent on the trade, but in light of the 85 percent profit that was enjoyed, it was well worth the risk.

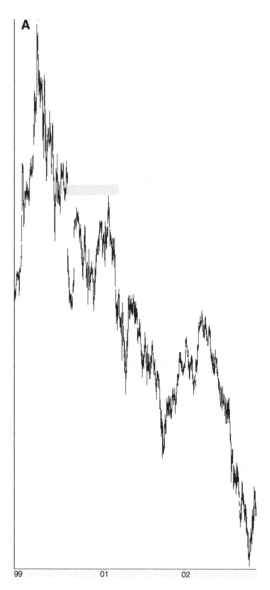

FIGURE 13.8 This is an outstanding gap-fill in which an earlier attempt to fill the gap failed but was bested somewhat later by a heartier push higher.

Gap Date: 7/21/2000   Gap Price: $67.77   Percentage Change: −85%
Retrace Date: 1/18/2001   Postgap Price: $10.46

Bemis Company

The next example, Figure 13.9, is a fascinating one, because it illustrates what is known as an island reversal. This kind of reversal is based on not one but two gaps. Island reversals are quite rare and are extremely potent as either bullish or bearish reversal patterns.

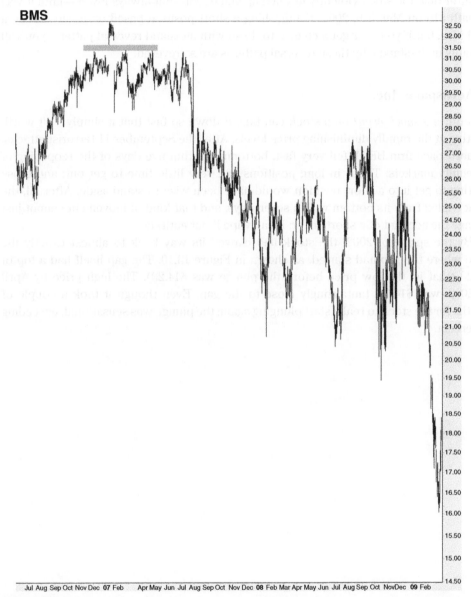

FIGURE 13.9 Island reversals that are this well defined are unusual and often quite potent.

Gap Date: 1/25/2007   Gap Price: $31.11   Percentage Change: −34%
Retrace Date: 7/9/2007   Postgap Price: $20.56

In this instance, the stock gapped up on January 11, 2007, to what was then a lifetime high. It then gapped down hard on January 25 on very strong volume. The trading activity between January 11 and January 24 was the island that was left behind by means of the two gaps, and this was an extremely bearish pattern for the stock.

By February 22, the price had retraced to within less than a dollar of the prior gap, and after that, the stock violently lurched up and down—but always lower—until it was beneath $16 on March 6, 2009. Establishing a short position based on a gap can be a good idea, but if you ever get a chance to do so with an island reversal pattern, you will probably understand why these reversal patterns are so revered.

Be Aerospace, Inc.

Sometimes a *shock event* on a stock can take it down so fast that it simply isn't worth shorting at the rapidly diminishing price levels. After the September 11 terrorist attacks, the aerospace firm BEAV fell very fast, bottoming within five days of the reopening of the equity markets. Those in long positions had very little time to get out, and those wanting to get into a short position would have been wise to stand aside. After all, the stock tripled from its bottom within seven days, and that kind of movement cannot just damage the account of a short-seller; it can wipe it out entirely.

By the spring of 2002, the stock had clawed its way back to almost exactly the place where the gap had started, as shown in Figure 13.10. The gap itself had a top of $14.23 (that is, the low price before the plunge was $14.23). The high price by April 11, 2002, was $14.05, tantalizingly close to the gap. Even though it took a couple of months for the stock to really start plunging again, the plunge was sensational, exceeding 90 percent.

FIGURE 13.10 The shock-event this stock suffered in late 2001 likely caused many losses among those holding long positions, but those that held on got a second chance to get out at much better prices the next year.

Gap Date: 9/17/2001   Gap Price: $14.05   Percentage Change: −91%
Retrace Date: 4/11/2002   Postgap Price: $1.23

Affymetrix, Inc.

There are instances in the market in which a stock experiences multiple price gaps within a reasonably short period of time. Some stock are *gappy* by their very nature, such as Google (symbol GOOG), which can often surprise investors with up-gaps and down-gaps based on earnings.

Figure 13.11 shows a stock, symbol AFFX, with three large gaps in a four-year period. The first gap takes place on July 22, 2005, and is retracted by November 22 of that year. The stock goes on to lose 64 percent of its value. A person with a long-term short in this

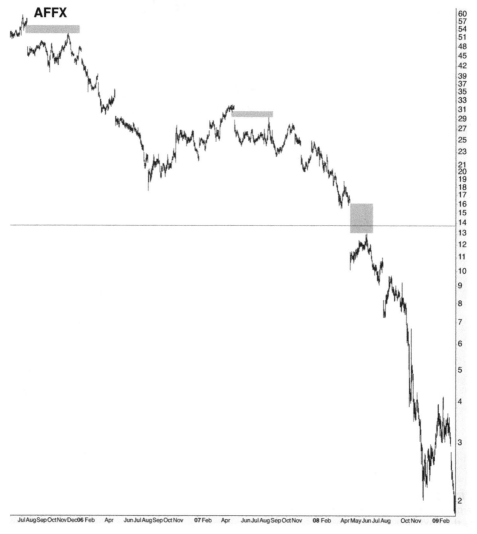

FIGURE 13.11 Here we see an unusual instance of three consecutive down-gaps.

Gap Date: 7/22/2005   Gap Price: $52.44   Percentage Change: −64%
Retrace Date: 11/23/2005   Postgap Price: $18.72

position might have been stopped out at a more modest profit since the stock picked up a lot of strength between August 2006 and April 2007.

However, the stock gapped down hard again on April 26, 2007, which was retraced by August 8, and the stock began its waterfall decline again falling from about $25 to $17. Before that was over, however, the stock gapped down once more on April 15, 2008, and it kept falling to $1.78 on March 9, 2009 (a date when just about all stocks seemed to pivot around and move much higher).

For a person holding a short position, multiple gaps down are nothing but good news. A stock gapping down is going to cause despair and frustration among the stocks' bulls and is going to egg on the bears. But a stock can only go so low, of course, so a plunge from $52 to less than $2 is probably—as in this case—going to turn around unless the company is headed for outright bankruptcy.

First Marblehead

Another example of multiple gaps down is shown in Figure 13.12. One interesting aspect of these two gaps is how different their behavior is. The first gap, which occurred on April 16, 2007, on very strong volume, retraced by July 11, and the stock spent seven months meandering around a relatively tight price range between about $30 and $40. So in spite of the very large selloff on big volume, the stock was not shocked into a general downtrend. It simply lost some value and tried to build some kind of base afterward.

The attempts at base construction failed in late November 2007, and finally the stock started falling quickly. In the midst of this downfall, on April 8, 2008, the stock gapped down hard again, retracing its drop by August 18 of the same year. The stock was so battered at this point, and the holders were probably so frustrated, there was no meaningful attempt to consolidate at any price level. Instead, the stock lurched lower, made a modest attempt at a retracement, and then finally reached its nadir of 58 cents on November 20, 2008.

With the first gap, there were plenty of opportunities for bulls to escape and bears to get on board. With the second gap, unless you were already out (or on board), it was too late. The entire nature of the stock's behavior had changed, and most days following the second gap were greeted with nothing but selling.

FMD

FIGURE 13.12 This stock was weak on such a sustained basis that it suffered two large down-gaps.

Gap Date: 4/8/2008   Gap Price: $5.14   Percentage Change: −89%
Retrace Date: 8/18/2008   Postgap Price: $0.58

eBay, Inc.

It is unusual to see a stock engage in a gap-based countertrend rally after a gap down, but eBay, shown in Figure 13.13, gives us an instance of this peculiar event. It also shows that there are opportunities to make money in both directions, if one is nimble enough.

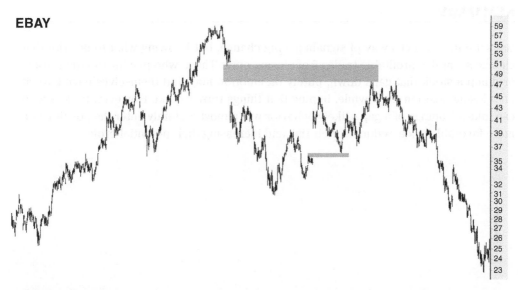

EBAY

FIGURE 13.13 There are two opportunities shown here: a bearish one, with the large gap, and a bullish one, with the smaller gap.

Gap Date: 1/20/2005   Gap Price: $47.46   Percentage Change: −52%
Retrace Date: 1/19/2006   Postgap Price: $22.83

The stock gapped down on January 20, 2005. There really was no retracement to speak of until a year later. But before that happened, while the stock was crawling down in price, the stock gapped up on July 21, 2005. You can imagine how perplexing this situation must have been. For someone short the stock, it would have been a disconcertingly strong countertrend; for someone long the stock, it would have provided encouragement that maybe the worst was behind him or her.

What's fascinating is that both events did retrace. The gap-up was retraced by September 21, offering a good short-term opportunity to be long eBay in the midst of an overall downtrend. More important, by January 19, 2006, the stock had retraced back to the gap-down, although the severity of the gap still left about a $3 spread between the high price of January 19 and the low price of January 20 the prior year.

From that point, the stock was in such a strong downtrend that it didn't stop falling until it was in the single digits. Whether or not a person took advantage of both these gaps depends on their timeframe. A longer-term trader probably would have simply waited for the down-gap to retrace, which required a year of waiting but was, in the end, an excellent trade. Someone more aggressive who could afford to watch the markets very closely might have been adept enough to short the stock on the gap-down and reverse the position on the gap-up, reversing the position yet again once the price had clawed its way back up to the $47 level.

SUMMARY

Gaps are the market's way of signaling a big change, but knowing what to do with that change separates profitable trades from losing ones. Those who pile into a rising stock, or dump a stock that gaps down, purely on emotion may find themselves having to sit on a losing position for a while, hoping that things turn around. However, traders who can take advantage of a gap's likely behavior will almost certainly enter the position at a more favorable price, reducing their risk and increasing their potential profit.

CHAPTER 14

Head and Shoulders

The head-and-shoulders (H&S) pattern has a funny name but a powerful purpose: to indicate the possible reversal of the security you are charting. It is one of the best known, most easy to recognize, and yet most widely misidentified patterns in technical analysis. As the name suggests, the H&S pattern looks like a head in between two shoulders, and a completion of this pattern indicates that the security is probably going to head down in price.

DEFINITION OF THE PATTERN

The criteria for this pattern are as follows:

- **Left shoulder:** An ascent in price (ideally following a long, major ascent in the stock's value), a leveling, and then a weakening back to a certain support level known as the *neckline*.
- **Head:** A further ascent in price, surpassing the high set by the left shoulder, once again leveling off and descending back to the neckline.
- **Right shoulder:** A final ascent in price, ideally not going as high as the left shoulder (and certainly not going as high as the head), a leveling off, and a descent back to the neckline, which it breaks beneath on strong volume.

The target price is the value of the price range of the pattern subtracted from the neckline. For example, if a neckline is at $20, and the top of the head is $25, the difference is $5. Therefore, $20 (the neckline) minus the range ($5), equals the target price ($15). This setup anticipates a 25 percent decrease in stock price.

Figure 14.1 shows an example of a very good H&S pattern exhibited by the now-defunct stock Technical Olympia (symbol TOA). Lines have been drawn on top of the chart to clearly show the shoulders, the head, and the neckline. The circled part indicates where the price broke beneath the neckline, completing the pattern and sending the price sharply downward, as expected.

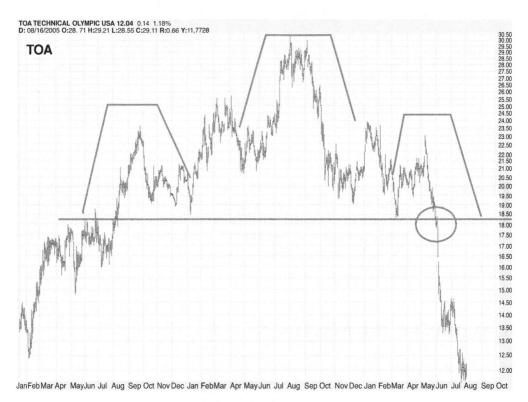

FIGURE 14.1 The circle indicates the point at which the neckline was broken, and the stock quickly descended immediately afterward.

PSYCHOLOGY BEHIND THE PATTERN

We return to the basic notion that bulls want to see a steady progression of higher highs and higher lows. During the formation of the left shoulder, assuming the stock has been enjoying a consistent run-up in price, the bulls are still satisfied that all is well. The peak of the left shoulder marks yet another high price in the stock.

As the head begins to form, the bulls remain satisfied, because once again they are seeing a higher high in the stock. But something is going wrong, because as the price eases back again, it returns to the same level that the left shoulder was at before (in other words, the neckline). So we no longer have a series of higher highs and higher lows. The lowers are matching one another. But at least, from the bullish point of view, there is still strong support at a given price level (again, the neckline).

When the right shoulder begins to form, the bulls want to see a new high made, exceeding the price just made by the head price. (Keep in mind the vast majority of individuals watching the stock aren't looking at a chart, let alone thinking in terms of heads and shoulders.) But not only does the price not exceed that of the head, it doesn't even match the price made by the left shoulder. So the stock is actually seen as weakening now, and the buying volume dries up as the price comes to rest, once again, at the neckline.

At this point, the market has a decision to make. It can continue to support the price at the equilibrium level it has found. Or the sellers can overcome the buyers, and the neckline will be broken. In the latter case, the H&S pattern is complete, and the stock price is probably in trouble (for the bulls, at least).

There is one more element to this story, however, and that is the retracement. Just as there are retracements with saucer-like patterns, the H&S pattern sometimes sports a retracement as well. In this case, after a brief, quick drop in price, bargain hunters come out and temporarily provide support for the stock. If the H&S pattern holds, the price will make its way back up to the equilibrium point (the neckline), but no further. This provides a golden opportunity in the form of a second chance for those wanting to sell the stock short, because it is likely that once the retracement is complete, the price will begin falling again, and it will fall far past the point where it originally paused.

THE IMPORTANCE OF THE NECKLINE

There is no more important feature to the H&S pattern than its neckline, because the neckline defines whether or not the pattern is complete and, therefore, has any meaning. As with other lines in technical analysis, the neckline represents a line in the sand dividing bulls from bears. Along the line itself is a sort of equilibrium between buyers and sellers. Trading above the line represents strength and hope. Trading beneath the line represents weakness and fear.

With an ideal H&S pattern, the neckline has five unique touch-points. The *first* is on the left side of the left shoulder; the *second* is at the right side of the left shoulder (which is also the left side of the head); the *third* is at the right side of the head; the *fourth* is at the right side of the right shoulder, at which point the price breaks beneath the neckline; and the *fifth* point (which is optional, in a sense) is when the price retraces back up to the neckline before falling hard once again.

Ideally, the neckline should be horizontal, since price equilibrium should concentrate in a tight, consistent price range. You may allow some leeway for a tilted neckline, however, perhaps as much as ten degrees either upward or downward sloping. Those newer to charting often look at any trio of price humps and assume they've discovered an H&S pattern, no matter how distorted the pattern or how sharply ascending the neckline. The higher quality the pattern, the more reliable it is as a predictive guide.

Once the price has broken beneath the neckline, the H&S pattern has validity only if the price remains *below* the neckline. (When the price retraces, you may want to allow for a few pennies of violation before dismissing the pattern altogether.) Just because the price goes above the neckline doesn't absolutely mean the stock will not fall, but it does indicate strength that is normally not a part of a good, strong H&S breakdown. A pattern with noise such as this should be viewed with more skepticism than a pattern absent such noise.

EXAMPLES

Let's examine some instances of this important technical pattern.

Hutchinson Technology, Inc.

We begin with an imperfect example, since the chart in Figure 14.2 has a somewhat roughly defined neckline at a little under $18. The three elements of this pattern are highlighted with triangle tops, and the range of the pattern—from $17.30 to $43—is extremely wide. Indeed, the range is so large that the measured move upon pattern completion is a negative number, which is an obvious impossibility. What it does make clear, however, is that a neckline failure suggests a very dramatic move downward, and that prediction was fulfilled with a 93 percent drop in price.

Although the neckline isn't perfectly formed, the retracement in this example is excellent. Once the neckline is broken, the price falls to about $12 before recovering to approximately $17. This would make a superb shorting opportunity, since the neckline has already failed, the ability of the stock to fall swiftly has been proven, and you would have a relatively safe stop-loss level of a price just above the neckline. In other words, if you shorted at this level, and the stock pushed up to, say, $19, the pattern would be so compromised that you would have been stopped out of the position.

In retrospect, we can instead see that nothing of the sort took place. After a brief stint pushing back toward the failed neckline, the price plunged rapidly lower. This illustrates one of the great appeals of bear markets (or selling stocks short)—the moves can be terribly fast. You have probably heard the maxim that stocks climb a wall of worry and slide down a slope of hope. Climbing a wall of worry takes time, because there will always be plenty of doubters to dampen the ascent of a stock's rise in price. When a stock starts crumbling, however, sellers rush toward the exits, and the selling tends to feed on itself. As with this example, it took only weeks to make a price move that, were the stock going up instead of down, might have instead taken months or years.

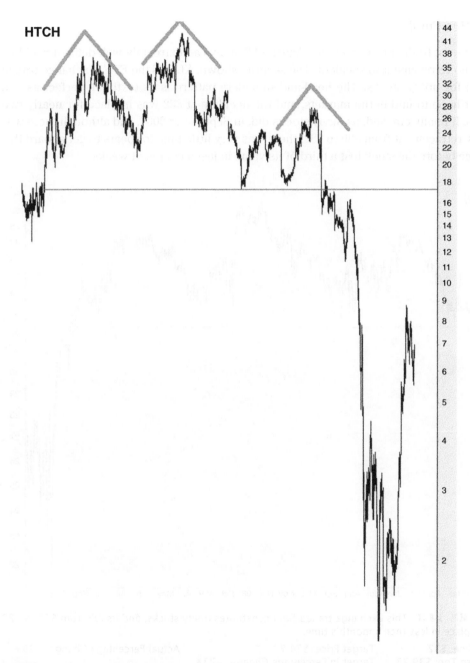

FIGURE 14.2 Although the neckline is somewhat rough in this example, the retracement and subsequent plunge are picture-perfect.

Neckline: $17.30   Target Price: n/a (negative value)   Actual Percentage Change: −93%
Pattern Top: $43.00   Target in Percentage Change: n/a

Utilities Fund

In contrast to the prior example, Figure 14.3 shows an extremely well-defined neckline with no retracement to speak of. The security shown, XLU, is the ETF (exchange-traded fund) for utility stocks. The head-and-shoulders pattern is as textbook-perfect as you might hope to find in the markets, and the neckline at $32 was in place for nearly two years. It finally cracked, as many stocks did, in September 2008, and although there was a tiny retracement from $30 to $32, there was very little time for bears to get aboard this plunge before the stock lost a third of its value in just a couple of weeks.

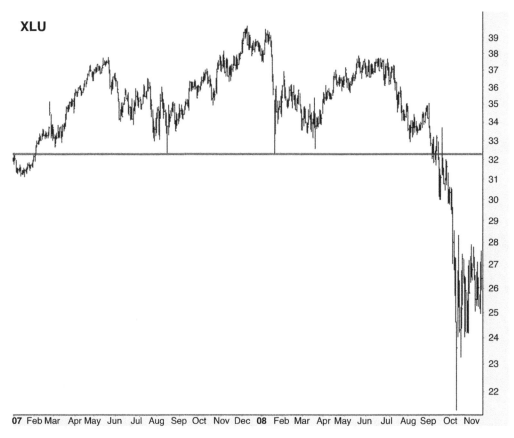

FIGURE 14.3 This exchange-traded fund constitutes utility stocks, and its fall from $32 to $22 took place in less than a month's time.

Neckline: $32   Target Price: $24.77   Actual Percentage Change: −36%
Pattern Top: $39.23   Target in Percentage Change: −23%

One note to make about stocks like XLU is that a trader should take into account the dividend component. When you are long a stock that pays a good dividend, you benefit. When you are short such a stock, you are responsible for paying the dividend out of your own pocket, since the owner of that stock is being denied the dividend that they would normally receive. In the case of XLU, even if the stock price stayed stagnant for a long period of time, you would still lose money, because you would be responsible for the dividend. Those short during the autumn of 2008 need not have worried about such matters, since the collapse in price dwarfed whatever the dividend loss would have been.

ProLogis

The next chart, Figure 14.4, gives us an opportunity to see a more complex pattern in action with extremely dramatic results. First take note of the left shoulder (again, triangle tops denote the three elements of this formation). The left shoulder, at the time, might have been considered an H&S pattern in its own right. It isn't perfectly formed, but it isn't bad, and some might have shorted ProLogis in 2007 with disappointing results. The stock did fall from about $60 to $45, but it regained its strength and went on to new lifetime highs.

The security went on to form a head, stabilize again at $40.75, formed a right shoulder, and then stalled at the neckline for a couple of weeks. You can see how much noise there was in the chart pattern around the neckline, as the stock fluctuated between +5 percent and –5 percent around the neckline. This neckline, established over a period of years, represented a critical equilibrium between buyers and sellers, and the furious tug-of-war that was taking place in September 2008 showed that the integrity of the neckline was fracturing but not yet failing.

Because of the prolonged tension around this neckline, once the selling began, there was almost no stopping it. The stock plunged from $40.75 to less than $3, virtually wiping out all shareholder equity, and then began a furious ascent back above $15. Keep percentages in mind here, since that quick spike higher offered a rare opportunity for over 400 percent in gains in just a couple of months. Obviously a stock moving like this, however, is loaded with risk.

Imagine, for instance, being on the sidelines and watching PLD at $3, thinking it might be a great buy. Of course, you stand the risk that the stock goes to $0 (or close to it), so that keeps you from buying. The stock moves up to $4, $5, $7.50, $10. . . all the way back to $15. You can't stand watching your hot pick go up in price anymore—after all, it was three times this high in price just recently, and it might get back up to that level, so you finally take the plunge and buy. At that point, the stock reverses and falls back down to $5, wiping out two-thirds of your position.

This is an overly dramatized example, of course, but the point is that playing either the short or long side of a stock after it has already been thrown into wild gyrations is little better than gambling. Those who recognize the move before it takes place are taking much less risk. If you are short PLD at $45, and it falls to $3, you have plenty of time to make reasonable decisions with very little risk, since it is virtually impossible at that point that you will emerge from the trade with anything but a profit.

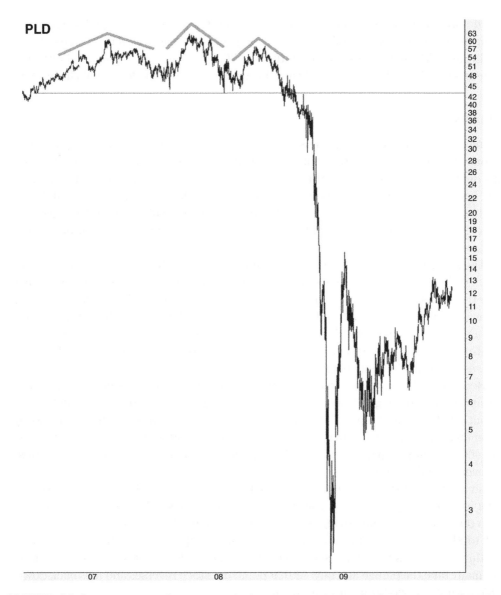

FIGURE 14.4 Not many stocks were as volatile as ProLogis during the financial crisis of 2008.

Neckline: $40.75   Target Price: $22.19   Actual Percentage Change: −95%
Pattern Top: $59.31   Target in Percentage Change: −46%

Russell 2000 Index

Traders have a universe of financial instruments from which they can choose to trade. One of them, of course, is index options, and this example of an H&S pattern in the Russell 2000 index (Figure 14.5) illustrates how an insight about an index's likely next move can be very profitable.

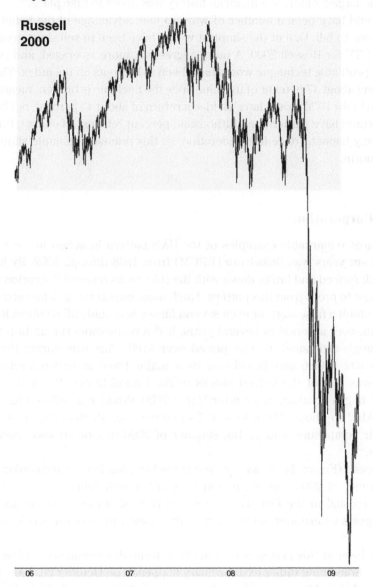

FIGURE 14.5 Being long put options during the Russell's plunge would have yielded astonishing returns.

| Neckline: $643 | Target Price: $430 | Actual Percentage Change: −47% |
| Pattern Top: $856 | Target in Percentage Change: −33% | |

What's impressive about this pattern is its uniformity and its length. For three years—2006, 2007, and 2008—the Russell 2000 index of small capitalization stocks hammered out a fantastic H&S pattern. Added to this, if you examine the head independently, this portion comprised a cruder head and shoulders pattern in its own upper half. It is far easier to see these patterns in retrospect, but it is no surprise, given the massive pattern, that one of the largest plunges in financial history was about to take place.

There would have been a number of ways to take advantage of the belief that this index was about to fall. One of the simplest would have been to sell short symbol IWM, which is the ETF for Russell 2000. A more aggressive, more leveraged, and (in this instance) more profitable technique would have been to buy puts on the index. The Russell winds up losing about 47 percent of its value once the neckline is broken, meaning that a short position in the IWM would have yielded a return of about 47 percent, but being long put options would have garnered multithousand percent returns. Of course, this kind of excitement only happens once in a generation, so this dramatic example should not be taken as the norm.

Broadcom Corporation

One of the most remarkable examples of the H&S pattern in action in the U.S. stock market in recent years was Broadcom (BRCM) from 1998 through 2002. By looking at how this stock formed and broke down with the H&S as its reversal formation will yield insight into how to profit from this pattern. Much more important, it demonstrates that a pattern can exhibit a false start, or even several false starts, and still manifest itself fully.

Broadcom, over a period of several years, had a remarkable run-up in price, moving from a single-digit stock to one priced over $180. This was during the Internet boom of the late 1990s, and Broadcom, as a major force in network-related semiconductors, was one of the hottest stocks in the United States. When the NASDAQ stock market began breaking down after March 2000, Broadcom suffered badly, falling from about $160 to about $80, a loss of 50 percent. But stocks related to networks regained their composure, and by the summer of 2000 Broadcom was reaching new lifetime highs.

In retrospect (Figure 14.6), we can see something fascinating happening between July and October of 2000—the formation of a rather well-defined H&S pattern. This one is a bit unusual in the fact that it has two right shoulders. This is not unheard of, but it suggests a hesitation on the part of the market to push the stock beneath its neckline.

Looking closer at this period where the H&S formed, you can see a clear neckline at about $130. Something rather extraordinary happened on October 26, 2000: the stock pushed below the neckline on strong volume . . . and then returned above the neckline again! You can imagine how frustrating this was to the bears on this stock, since the widely anticipated breakout of BRCM had finally started taking place, only to be canceled out the very same day.

Eight sessions later, the stock gapped down beneath the neckline, but this time there was no turning back. Even more important, the breakdown in the stock was accompanied by a gigantic rise in the volume as owners of the stock rushed for the exit doors. Even though there had been a false breakdown that had fooled many investors, it seemed this second breakdown was authentic.

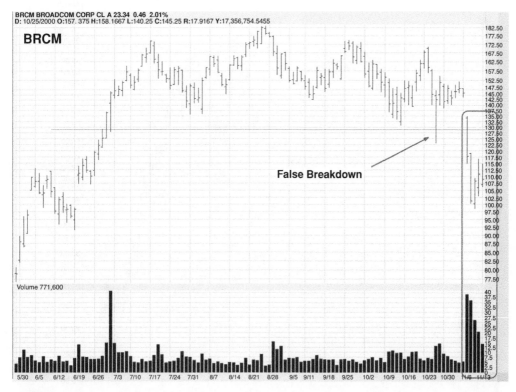

FIGURE 14.6 Notice how the volume multiplied severalfold once the genuine break began taking place.

What happened following this breakdown was extraordinary. From November 7, 2000, through April 4, 2001, Broadcom lost about 90 percent of its value, all in a span of about five months. And it did so on extremely high volume. The H&S pattern, in spite of its false start, provided an astonishingly prescient prediction of this stock's direction (Figure 14.7).

After the stock reached its bottom on April 4, 2000, it spent about the next fourteen months bouncing in a huge trading range between $12 and $36. Clearly the investing public had been caught in a horrible tailspin and was trying to establish an appropriate value for the stock. After all this churning, the stock starting losing support again, and it ultimately bottomed at a little over $6 (a little over 3 percent of its peak price) in October of 2002.

FIGURE 14.7 As large as this plunge is, it doesn't even capture the final move, which wiped out virtually the entire capitalization of Broadcom at its nadir.

Neckline: $134.75   Target Price: $88.00   Actual Percentage Change: −66%
Pattern Top: $181.50   Target in Percentage Change: −35%

Mela Sciences, Inc.

As was mentioned earlier, the neckline of a pattern doesn't have to be absolutely flat in order to be valid. Figure 14.8 shows ticker symbol MELA, whose neckline was tilted slightly downward. One could argue that this is actually a positive aspect for this pattern, since it only emphasizes the weakness of the security in question. In ProphetCharts, instead of using the Price Level horizontal line tool, you would use the Trendline tool, since it is important that the touchpoints on the neckline be accurate, even if it is not perfectly level.

FIGURE 14.8 The slightly downward-sloping neckline on this stock belied the underlying weakness of the security.

Neckline: $5.65   Target Price: $1.31   Actual Percentage Change: −59%
Pattern Top: $9.99   Target in Percentage Change: −77%

iShares MSCI Index Fund

Similar to the example of the Russell 2000 in Figure 14.6, the MSCI Index Fund illustrates how uniformly the broad market fell during the financial crisis of late 2008. The formation of the pattern itself in Figure 14.9 is textbook perfect; notice how the right shoulder is noticeably lower than the left shoulder, which agrees with the premise that the security is weakening with age. Even though this index represents many hundreds of individual stocks, it lost fully half its value once the neckline was broken.

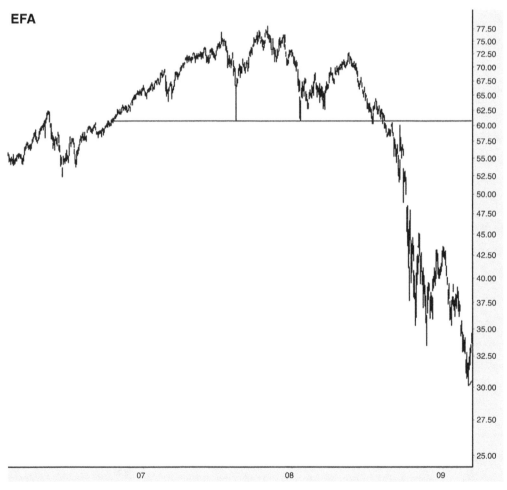

FIGURE 14.9 The introduction of widely traded, popular ETFs such as this make taking advantage of trading opportunities much easier for present-day traders.

Neckline: $60   Target Price: $42.78   Actual Percentage Change: −50%
Pattern Top: $77.22   Target in Percentage Change: −29%

Darden Restaurants, Inc.

The example displayed in Figure 14.10 is unique to this chapter since it shows the stock with not just one but two retracements. The stock sported an ascending neckline, and once it broke the neckline, the price dropped swiftly from about $35 to $20. It turned around almost immediately, zooming back to about $35, giving bears another opportunity to sell the stock short. The stock fell, not as hard this time, and then pushed yet again to approximately the $35 level. Nimble bears got many bites at the proverbial apple, and the stock's most dramatic plunge commenced after this second retracement.

FIGURE 14.10 Darden's behavior was somewhat unusual, since it recovered fully not just once but twice, giving bears multiple opportunities to benefit from the stock's drop.

Neckline: $35	Target Price: $26.86	Actual Percentage Change: −65%
Pattern Top: $43.14	Target in Percentage Change: −23%	

Allegheny Energy, Inc.

A trader may wonder: When is the best time to short a head-and-shoulders pattern—
before it breaks its neckline or after it retraces? There is no clear answer, but it is
almost certainly safer to short a stock when it retraces rather than simply anticipate
a neckline break. Indeed, anticipating what might happen with a stock is quite hazardous, since fake-out patterns are in great abundance in the markets. Instead, a trader
should wait until the neckline is actually broken, even if that guarantees smaller profits, rather than short a stock before the pattern is completed in the hope that it will
ultimately break.

As for retracements, those are not guaranteed to happen. A stock may start falling
and never look back. The instance in Figure 14.11 illustrates this, since AYE fell from

FIGURE 14.11 The only thing resembling a retracement for this stock took place many months
after the neckline break, and even then it only recovered about half of the drop from the neckline.

Neckline: $42.95   Target Price: $24.21   Actual Percentage Change: −54%
Pattern Top: $61.69   Target in Percentage Change: −44%

$44 to $24 without interruption. It began to partly fight its way back, getting as high as the low 30s, but a trader waiting for the price to reclaim the $44 level before shorting would simply never have had the opportunity.

Isle of Capri Casinos, Inc.

Just to drive home the point that the retracement is not guaranteed, examine Figure 14.12, a casino stock. The neckline was broken at about $17, and a nimble trader

FIGURE 14.12 Many other casino stocks, such as Las Vegas Sands (LVS), took tumbles similar to Isle of Capri's.

Neckline: $17.25	Target Price: $0.20	Actual Percentage Change: −88%
Pattern Top: $34.30	Target in Percentage Change: −99%	

could have shorted at a little lower than this level and still enjoyed plenty of profit. The stock tumbled to nearly $4, recovered partly to about $10, and then resumed its fall, completing with an 88 percent loss in price. The selling pressure simply didn't permit a complete retracement to the neckline.

Morgan Stanley

The investment bank Morgan Stanley had a very dramatic time in 2008, as you can well imagine, but what led up to this movement was equally as interesting. Even though the financial crisis didn't reach wide recognition until the autumn of 2008, Morgan Stanley spent most of 2007 forming a downward-tilting H&S pattern. Late in the year, it broke beneath its neckline, and it then gently retraced back to the underside of this neckline a number of times. Those long this stock might have imagined the price was stabilizing, but those charting the security knew that something big was likely to happen on the downside.

The stock fell much harder in March 2008 with the Bear Stearns crisis, but since Morgan Stanley isn't Bear Stearns, the selling abated and the stock recovered to approximately the level of the extended, tilted neckline. The selling continued in relatively gentle up-and-down waves, always tilted down, until September arrived. Once hard selling started, the stock plunged into the single digits (an absolutely unthinkable notion several months prior), and the stock fell over three times more than the projected target price of the H&S pattern. See Figure 14.13.

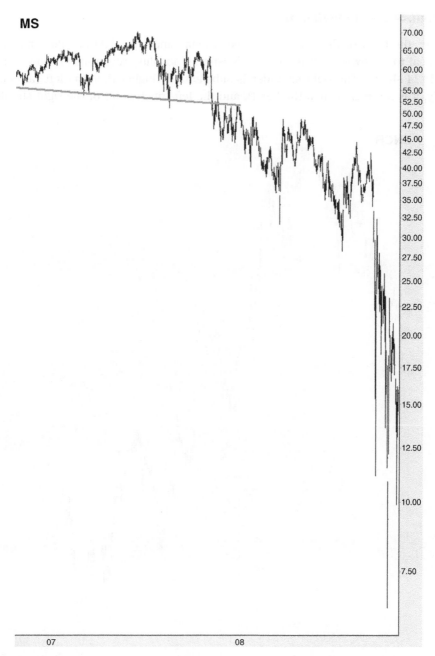

FIGURE 14.13 Morgan Stanley spent the first three-quarters of 2008 stumbling its way lower, but the real plunge didn't take place until late September and early October of that year.

Neckline: $55.00   Target Price: $40.09   Actual Percentage Change: −88%

Pattern Top: $69.91   Target in Percentage Change: −27%

Synchronoss Technologies, Inc.

Until now, the form of the patterns has been ideal since the right shoulder has been either equal to or lower than the left. This isn't an absolute requirement, however, as Figure 14.14 shows. The right shoulder is substantially higher than the left (although, critically, it is not higher than the head), and the left touch-point of the right shoulder

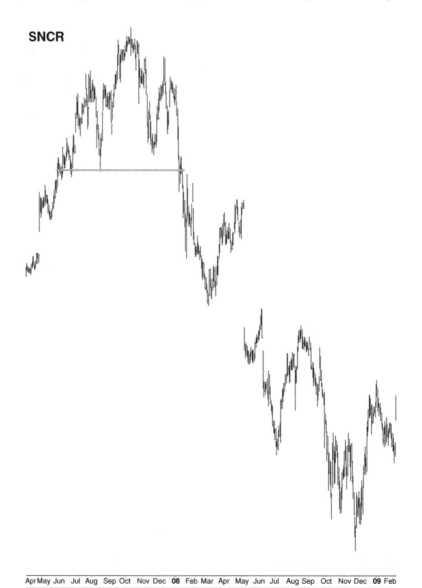

AprMay Jun Jul Aug Sep Oct Nov Dec **08** Feb Mar Apr May Jun Jul Aug Sep Oct Nov Dec **09** Feb

FIGURE 14.14 This chart features an unusually large gap after its retracement.

Neckline: $25.89   Target Price: $3.75   Actual Percentage Change: −79%
Pattern Top: $48.03   Target in Percentage Change: −86%

doesn't even come close to touching the neckline. This indicates there is more strength to this security than someone wanting to short this stock might want to see, so it would be especially prudent to wait for a very clear violation of the neckline before entering a short position.

This chart is interesting for another reason, which is that after a fairly robust retracement, the stock gapped substantially lower at the opening bell of one session. Those who had waited to short the stock until this retracement took place surely were thrilled at the nearly instantaneous gratification of seeing the stock drop to new lows without even having to wait for it.

Hovnanian Enterprises, Inc.

Our final example, Figure 14.15, is superb in both its form and its power. Both shoulders are well below the head, and the right shoulder is significantly lower than the left. Once the neckline was violated, the price fell quickly and was only partially retraced. Perhaps most remarkable of all was the movement in price, since this stock lost over 99 percent of its value from its peak before it finally recovered from its post-crash nadir.

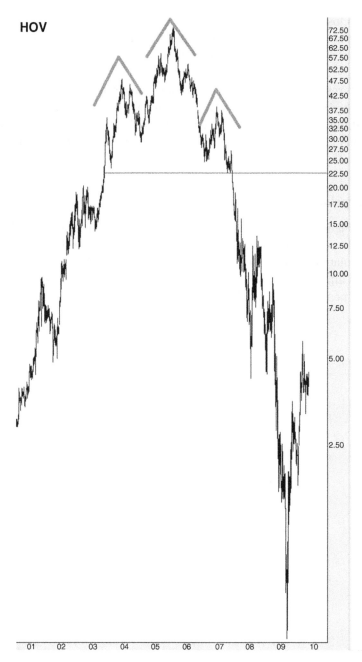

FIGURE 14.15 The bursting of the housing bubble led to a loss of nearly 100 percent of HOV's peak value.

Neckline: $22.59   Target Price: n/a   Actual Percentage Change: −99%

Pattern Top: $73.4   Target in Percentage Change: n/a

SUMMARY

Because it is fairly easy to recognize, the H&S pattern is well known to even beginning traders. What separates the amateurs from the professionals is being able to distinguish between a legitimate pattern and a distorted one, and understanding the appropriate balance of risk with opportunity. You have seen many examples in this chapter that capture the various nuances among the patterns, including neckline tilt, false breakdowns, and the nature of retracements. Refer to these examples any time you believe there is an H&S pattern present in your own trading, and learn to discern whether or not what you are observing merits your attention and capital.

CHAPTER 15

Inverted Head and Shoulders

Something very unusual about the head-and-shoulders pattern is that it has a doppelganger called the *inverted* head-and-shoulders (IH&S) pattern. While the H&S pattern ideally precedes a top, the IH&S precedes a bottom. This bottoming pattern quite literally turns everything about the H&S pattern on its head, since the direction is the opposite, but all the other rules are the same.

DEFINITION OF THE PATTERN

The criteria for this pattern are as follows:

- **Left shoulder:** A descent in price (perhaps following a long, major drop in the stock's value), a leveling, and then a strengthening back to a certain support level known as the *neckline*. The trading volume during this period should ideally increase notably.
- **Head:** A further descent in price, dropping beneath the low set by the left shoulder, once again leveling off and ascending back to the neckline.
- **Right shoulder:** A final descent in price but on lower volume, ideally not going as low as the left shoulder (and certainly not going as low as the head), a leveling off, and an ascent back to the neckline, which it finally breaks above on strong volume.

The *target* price is the value of the price range of the pattern added to the neckline. For example, if a neckline is at $20, and the bottom of the head is $15, the difference is $5. Therefore, $20 (the neckline) plus the range of $5, equals the target price ($20 + $5 = $25). This hypothetical setup therefore anticipates a 25 percent increase in stock price.

Figure 15.1 shows Alcatel-Lucent with a neckline at $2.93 and a bottom at $1.09, implying a target price of $4.77, which is a 63 percent rise in price. Once the neckline

FIGURE 15.1 The V-shaped lines highlight the three elements of this pattern.

was broken, the price did indeed ascend 69 percent, slightly surpassing the measured target. In some of these examples, the price ultimately goes much, much higher, but here we are using the highest price it attains prior to a meaningful drop.

PSYCHOLOGY BEHIND THE PATTERN

Let's reuse the example of Figure 15.1 to explore the psychology behind this pattern. We will put ourselves in the shoes of owners of Alcatel in the summer of 2007. The stock is at about $14.50, and it starts falling. A little more than a year later, which is the left shoulder of this pattern, the stock is down 80 percent (as a side note, this was an $82 stock in the year 2000, so some poor souls actually were looking at a 96 percent loss by this point).

ALU falls below $3, then below $2, and tries to find a base. It struggles around the $2 price point into the new year. Long-term owners of the stock are disgusted enough to either throw in the towel or simply hold on, hoping one day to have less severe losses. New buyers enter the picture, thinking that a stock that is 96 percent cheaper than its peak might be a good gamble. The left shoulder illustrates the struggle between buyers and sellers to find an appropriate price for the stock, now that it has ceased its free fall.

However, an eight-week span of time from early January to early March sees the stock resuming its free fall, and the only clear floor for the stock which no one questions is $0/share. The stock hits $1.06 on both March 6, 2009, and March 9, 2009, and on March 13 it gaps higher. Between March 6 and May 6, the stock more than doubles in price, providing risk-takers with triple-digit gains (for longer-term holders, such a mover might simply provide a 96 percent loss instead of a 97 percent loss). Thus, the plunge from January 8 down to March 6, and its subsequent rise to May 6, creates the head, as the ultimate low for the stock is found and all the selling is exhausted.

The next three months are more discouraging for those who own the stock. With each element of the pattern—the left shoulder, the head, and the right shoulder—we continue to see these brief periods of equilibrium where the stock isn't moving dramatically higher or lower, but is instead churning between buyers and sellers. Even though ALU manages to get as high as $2.93 on June 11, it loses its footing, and it drops about one-third of its value.

Between July 8 and July 31, the stock fights its way back to the neckline and, finally, on August 3, it gaps above the neckline on volume, which is about 65 percent higher than the prior day's, completing the pattern and providing a target. This entire process has cleared out the selling pressure, established some very happy new buyers, and finally launched the stock into a meaningful recovery.

As an interesting side note, this exact same scenario with the same pattern played out years earlier, between July 2002 and January 2003, with Alcatel. And, as with 2002–2003, the inverted H&S pattern of 2008–2009 preceded a hearty recovery only to see the stock stumble later to newfound weakness down the road.

THE IMPORTANCE OF THE NECKLINE

As with the H&S pattern, the neckline defines whether or not the pattern is complete and, therefore, has any meaning. As with other lines in technical analysis, the neckline represents a line in the sand that divides bulls from bears. Along the line itself is a sort of equilibrium between buyers and sellers. Trading above the line represents strength and hope. Trading beneath the line represents weakness and fear.

With an ideal H&S pattern, the neckline has five unique touch-points. The *first* is on the left side of the left shoulder; the *second* is at the right side of the left shoulder (which is also the left side of the head); the *third* is at the right side of the head; the *fourth* is at the right side of the right shoulder, at which point the price breaks beneath the neckline; and the *fifth* point (which is optional, in a sense) is when the price retraces back up to the neckline before falling hard once again.

Ideally, the neckline should be horizontal, since price equilibrium should concentrate in a tight, consistent price range. You may allow some leeway for a tilted neckline, however, perhaps as much as ten degrees either upward- or downward-sloping. Those newer to charting often look at any trio of price humps and assume they've discovered an H&S pattern, no matter how distorted the pattern or how sharply ascending the neckline. The higher-quality the pattern, the more reliable it is as a predictive guide.

Once the price has broken above the neckline, the pattern has validity only if the price remains *above* the neckline. (If the price retraces, you may want to allow for a few pennies worth of violation before dismissing the pattern altogether.) Just because the price goes below the neckline doesn't absolutely mean the stock will not rise, but it does indicate weakness that is normally not a part of a good, strong breakout. A pattern with noise such as this should be viewed with more skepticism than a pattern absent such noise.

EXAMPLES

Let's examine some examples of this important reversal pattern.

Newport Corporation

Newport, shown in Figure 15.2, is an exceptionally good example of an IH&S pattern. It features very well-defined components, a right shoulder higher than its left, an extremely clean neckline, and a retracement on November 30 that was an ideal low-risk entry point for a long position.

The retracement is of particular interest here, because it took a full four months from the initial breakout for the stock to retrace. This shows that you don't always have to be watching every tick of a stock price to get into a good opportunity. There was ample opportunity to discover this pattern, determine the neckline, get into the position, and

FIGURE 15.2 Newport more than doubled after pushing above $6.80.

Neckline: $6.80   Target Price: $10.67   Actual Percentage Change: 113%

Pattern Bottom: $2.93   Target in Percentage Change: 57%

know the appropriate level for your stop-loss order. Those entering the trade soon after the neckline might have found themselves frustrated at the meandering behavior of the price, particularly as it threatened the neckline. All buyers, however, were rewarded in the end, since the stock more than doubled in price from its breakout point.

Mylan, Inc.

Mylan, shown in Figure 15.3, is one of the uglier examples, since its left shoulder isn't terribly clean and doesn't even reach the neckline. However, a right shoulder substantially

FIGURE 15.3 It's always better to have a right shoulder whose base is higher than the left shoulder.

Neckline: $14.94   Target Price: $24.13   Actual Percentage Change: 58%
Pattern Bottom: $5.75   Target in Percentage Change: 62%

higher than the left only amplifies the possibility that the stock is gaining strength, and an upward-tilting neckline is acceptable.

Mattson Technology

Here again, in Figure 15.4, we have a nice example of a retracement. Keep in mind that these are not guaranteed to take place. Some breakouts never look back, whereas others

FIGURE 15.4 This retracement encroached slightly on the neckline, but a little leeway would have allowed the position to stay in place.

Neckline: $1.89	Target Price: $3.48	Actual Percentage Change: 192%
Pattern Bottom: $0.30	Target in Percentage Change: 84%	

give people a second opportunity (and sometimes even a third) to get on board the long position. The breakout took place on September 4 and, almost exactly two months later on November 3, the stock had retraced back to its neckline after a 65 percent run-up in price. You can appreciate how it would be more comfortable getting into the stock back at its neckline without having to pay this 65 percent premium, even though all buyers were eventually rewarded with a 192 percent gain.

Brigham Exploration Company

Although it is safer to wait for a retracement before entering into a position, it may also foreclose you from getting into a position at all, should the retracement never take place. Examine the breakout in Figure 15.5, which began with a strong volume day on July 27, 2009. The stock gained 70 percent in just a couple of weeks, paused briefly, and then continued the climb. No serious pause took place until Brigham had soared over 350 percent. One risk-reducing strategy that still avails you to such runaway moves is to enter half your intended position at the breakout and the other half at the retracement (should one occur). This way, even if the price never gives you another opportunity to get it near the neckline price, you at least will have some profit to show for your efforts.

FIGURE 15.5 Some breakouts are more powerful than others, and this was a particularly strong one, pushing the stock into triple-digit gains within just a few months.

Neckline: $4.68	Target Price: $8.32	Actual Percentage Change: 352%
Pattern Bottom: $1.04	Target in Percentage Change: 78%	

Masco Corporation

Sometimes a stock's retracement will take it a little underneath the neckline. If your stop-loss is too loose, you run the risk of letting a profitable position turn into a loss (or, even worse, subjecting yourself to a gap-down in price, resulting in a substantial loss). On the other hand, if your stop is too tight, you run the risk of blowing yourself out of a position just because of a very minor pattern violation and then missing out on what, in the end, turned out to be a very good trade.

An example of this latter possibility is shown in Figure 15.6, in which the price dipped just a few pennies beneath the neckline on November 7. It is impossible to know at the

FIGURE 15.6 The anticipated rise for this pattern, 69 percent, was almost perfectly nailed with a 66 percent ascent in value.

Neckline: $11.11   Target Price: $18.77   Actual Percentage Change: 66%
Pattern Bottom: $3.45   Target in Percentage Change: 69%

time, of course, whether this violation of the neckline is a warning that the pattern is invalid, and that much lower prices are forthcoming. After all, those who based their purchase on this bottoming pattern will be eager to get out, and prudent traders with stop-losses in place at the neckline will flood the market with sell orders.

There is no hard-and-fast rule for this situation. If you tend to be more conservative, you may want to play things strictly by the book and have the stop-loss set precisely one penny below the neckline. On the other hand, if you'd rather give the stock permission to dip beneath its neckline by some amount you consider reasonable (1 percent, 2 percent, or whatever figure is comfortable for you), you will reduce your chances of getting unnecessarily stopped-out but, at the same time, open up the possibility that you are being too liberal with the chart and could experience losses that could otherwise have easily been avoided.

Ship Finance International

Ship Finance suffered a very deep plunge. In the course of doing so, it formed a left shoulder (ranging from about $13 to $7), a head (ranging from about $12 to as low as $3.50), and a right shoulder (spanning $9 to $13).

What's somewhat unusual about this chart, shown in Figure 15.7, is just how deep it is. The depth of a chart refers to the distance from its neckline to its most extreme point (in this case, the bottom of the inverted head). With the neckline at $13, the bottom of the head is very far away at $3.50, which suggests a very powerful upward move if the price manages to push above the neckline (which it did). Several studies in the field of technical analysis have affirmed that inverted head-and-shoulder patterns that are deep, such as this one, tend to be more reliable than wider, shallower ones.

FIGURE 15.7 Past research in technical analysis suggests that tall formations such as this one are more reliable than wide, shallow ones.

Neckline: $12.60   Target Price: $21.71   Actual Percentage Change: 83%
Pattern Bottom: $3.49   Target in Percentage Change: 72%

PolyOne Corporation

Typically the stocks that make the most dramatic percentage moves are lower-priced instruments. After all, if a stock like Google, at $600 per share, has surprisingly good news, it might move the stock up 5 percent or 10 percent, but you are unlikely to find that, a year later, GOOG is trading for $3,000 per share. An inexpensive stock, however, being especially attractive to a large number of retail traders, can offer far more substantial percentage rewards (and, naturally, risks).

Ticker symbol POL, whose chart is in Figure 15.8, hammered out a bottom between November 2008 and July 2009. Even after more than doubling in price from its spring

FIGURE 15.8 The move for this stock was not only powerful but long-lasting, resulting in a severalfold increase in value.

Neckline: $3.56   Target Price: $5.80   Actual Percentage Change: 231%
Pattern Bottom: $1.32   Target in Percentage Change: 63%

bottom, the stock was still only about $3.50 per share and, importantly, its volume picked up noticeably in its early July price breakout. The stock had a projected move of 63 percent, but it actually wound up soaring 231 percent before settling back (it went on, months later, to even more significant gains).

This may beg the question: Does one dump out of a position the moment the price objective is met? For conservative traders, the answer would be yes. If you are more aggressive (or greedy), there are a couple of techniques you might employ. One would be simply to keep your stop-loss price tight and, if you are fortunate enough for the stock to keep pushing higher, so be it—because your entry point is so far away, there is virtually no chance that the trade will result in anything but a profit, no matter what. Another method would be to sell half the position once your profit target is met and, as before, simply keep your stop-loss price fresh and up-to-date for the remaining portion, perhaps padding your already handsome gains.

SM Energy Company

The chart in Figure 15.9 is perhaps the cleanest example of a retracement among any of those shown in this chapter. The neckline, at $24.43, is pierced on August 3, 2009. The stock pushes up for a couple of weeks and then, having lost the initial strength from breakout buyers, sinks softly for another couple of weeks, finding a low at $25.07, only about half a dollar higher than the neckline. Chartists watching SM at this time would have been wise to jump on board, because the risk of loss was modest.

For instance, if the most conservative of traders had bought the stock at $25.10 and had placed their stop-loss just beneath the neckline at $24.42, their risk is less than 3 percent. The pattern is already very clean, the breakout took the stock up about 15 percent in price, and the stock is actively traded in the millions of shares each day. A purchase around this area would have had an excellent risk/reward ratio, and owners were rewarded with a doubling of the stock's price by June of the following year.

FIGURE 15.9 Here is a textbook-perfect example of a retracement hitting the neckline.

Neckline: $24.43 Target Price: $37.73 Actual Percentage Change: 101%
Pattern Bottom: $11.13 Target in Percentage Change: 54%

Industrial Sector ETF

The historic example provider in Figure 15.10 doesn't have the gigantic gains of some of the other examples, because it is an ETF comprised of many individual securities. The gain is still handsome, however, at 40 percent within a period of about nine months, and

FIGURE 15.10 This upswing had a few meaningful dips along the way, but nothing substantial enough to break the general uptrend in price that was in place for over a year.

Neckline: $23.62   Target Price: $32.79   Actual Percentage Change: 40%
Pattern Bottom: $14.45   Target in Percentage Change: 39%

it illustrates that there are opportunities to be had with nontraditional instruments such as ETFs along with common stocks. There is no reason not to examine popular ETFs on a regular basis for instances of such patterns, since they are typically highly liquid, have narrow bid/ask spreads, and lack the element of surprise that common stocks have. (In other words, you will not be shocked one morning to find a highly diverse ETF has suddenly lost half of its value due to terrible earnings news.)

SUMMARY

The IH&S pattern is one of the easiest patterns to identify and exploit, because the parameters for the trade are so clean. Pay close attention to the volume, particularly during the breakout, since you want to see a lot of strong buying interest once the neckline is breached. As always, take care not to jump into the security before the neckline is actually overcome, because the stock market is packed with instances of patterns that are 95 percent complete before they simply roll over and fail to fully blossom.

CHAPTER 16

Multiple Bottoms

S tocks that enter long bullish runs do not do so by suddenly reversing from a downtrend. They almost always need to establish some kind of base first, and the form this base takes varies from stock to stock.

One of the most common and easy-to-understand bases is that of a multiple bottom. You will often see references to *double bottoms* and, less frequently, *triple bottoms*, but the fact is that stocks might hit a certain low level four, five, six, or more times before finally gathering up the buying power to push much higher. This chapter examines instances of stocks hitting multiple bottoms and then moving on to very substantial gains to the upside.

DEFINITION OF THE PATTERN

The first requirement of a multiple bottom is that the stock has to have experienced a meaningful drop in price. After all, you cannot have a bottom if you are in the middle or top of a formation. The premise of a multiple bottom is that the stock has already suffered a serious decline, and a buying opportunity has been forming for a while at a lower price.

Just because a stock drops to a certain level a number of times doesn't mean it is forming a bottom. Those instances should:

- Have significant amounts of time between them.
- Experience failed attempts at rising before falling back again.
- Ideally, exhibit diminishing amounts of volume with each instance of hitting the low.

The amount of time between lows might be many weeks, several months, or even several years. If you look at a daily chart of a stock, you will want to see large gaps between these lows as the stock tries—and fails—to push its way higher at least a couple of instances. The market refers to stocks that are trying to consolidate at a certain low price as *hammering out a bottom*, and this hammering-out process doesn't happen in a week or two. It takes months or years, because what is hopefully happening is that the stock is preparing itself for a completely different change in direction.

As the pattern is forming, what you ideally want to see is a generally consistent lower price and—less importantly—a generally consistent higher price that represents resistance as the price attempts to move higher. This range, if there is one, will give you a target price. For instance, if over a span of two years the price keeps falling to $10, pushing up to $15, falling to $10, trying again to hit $15, and so on, then you have a $5 range and can comfortably set $20 as a target price if the price ever manages to assert its way past the $15 resistance level.

This upper-level price is sometimes referred to as the confirmation point, and it is at this point that you will want to see the price break above on high volume. The more times a stock hits a low price, and the more times it tries and fails to get past the confirmation point, then the more meaningful it is when the stock finally does burst above this level, because there will be a lot of pent-up energy driving it higher.

Our first example of a multiple bottom is shown with Figure 16.1, which experienced a marvelous 190 percent rise once the pattern was complete. You can see the circled

FIGURE 16.1   DST Systems went up 190 percent after establishing a low at about $26.

areas indicate that on four different occasions the selling drove the stock to about $26, but there was enough buying interest at that point to push the price back to the low 30s. Finally, on its fourth attempt, the stock was able to muster past this resistance area and create a new trend of higher highs and higher lows without succumbing to meaningful selling pressure anymore.

PSYCHOLOGY BEHIND THE PATTERN

As was mentioned in the definition of the pattern, the hypothetical stock about to experience a multiple bottom has already experienced a significant loss in price. Almost everyone who has bought the stock in recent memory is holding on to a losing position, and even those who bought recently at a bargain price watched the stock move lower still.

At some point, buyers and sellers reach equilibrium, and the stock makes a bottom. The stock price is low enough to attract buying interest, and bargain-hunters bid the stock price up by, let us say, 15 percent. For a while, the buying excitement feeds on itself, but the mass of overhead supply—that is, those many people who bought at prices equal to or higher than the already-improved price—weighs down the stock, and sellers take control again. The stock resumes its fall.

However, it does not fall farther than its prior low. Now that some recent buying interest has shown itself, the stock falls not quite so far as the last low, although it comes very close. Traders recognize this as a potential double bottom, and they regard the current low price as an important level of support, so buyers emerge again to bid the stock higher. Once more, it climbs over the next couple of months by 15 percent before stalling and then turning back down another time.

For a third instance, the stock finds support at the prior two low prices, and the company announces some important new products coming out that are well-received by the market. Buyers emerge this time based partly on the stock being attractively priced, but also based on the news from the firm that will probably improve earnings in the future. Over the next several months, the stock meets—and then exceeds—its recent high price, and volume swells as resistance is finally overcome. The company's earnings over the next several years steadily improve, and alongside that, the stock enters into a general uptrend, having established a solid base over a period of about a year.

So we see with this example that there was indeed a price where there was enough buying pressure to overcome whatever distressing news had compelled others to sell. The stock took about a year to heal itself, aided by three instances of the market setting a base price—that is, a supporting price level—and demonstrating that it could push higher, even though its first two attempts to mount a comeback were repelled by resistance. This final period of ups and downs cleared out the final weak holders and allowed a mass of new buyers to accumulate at better prices. These recent buyers will be more inclined to hold on to the stock, since their purchases are, on the whole, at least somewhat profitable.

EXAMPLES

Some of the most incredible gains can be made from stocks that have made multiple bottoms. The following examples will help show you.

Avon Products, Inc.

A base made of multiple bottoms might take several months or several years. For very large movements in price, long-term bases in price are the most probable predecessors, and the cosmetics giant Avon, whose chart is in Figure 16.2, gives us a good case of this.

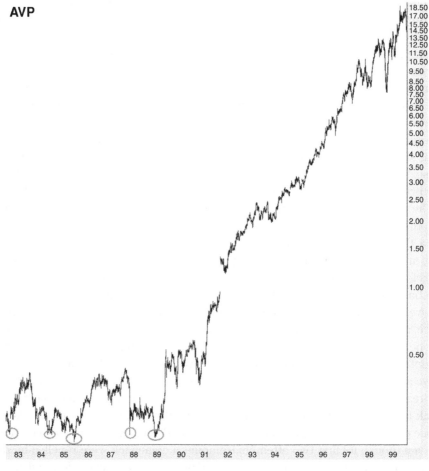

FIGURE 16.2 It took about seven years for this base to form, but after it did, Avon went on to a quadruple-point percentage gain.

First Instance: 8/17/1982   Bottom Price: $0.20   Percentage Change: 1,105%
Last Instance: 11/28/1988   Postbottom Price: $2.41

In 1982, Avon had already lost nearly two-thirds of its value over the past four years, and its stock sank to a split-adjusted level of about 22 cents per share. You can see that, over the next seven years, it dropped to this level on five different occasions. It had approximately doubled in price between 1982 and 1983, only to fall to its same low. It had a smaller rise, then another fall in 1985, at which point it sustained a nearly two-year rally, again doubling its price. The crash of 1987 almost instantly erased this rally, and AVP found itself yet again hovering at about 22 cents.

It made another attempt at a lift higher, fell once more, and then—at long last—began a rally in 1989 that carried it to a phenomenal 1,105 percent ascent, virtually uninterrupted by any selling over the next decade. The frustrating grind that had lasted for almost all of the 1980s was answered with an eye-popping period of hypergrowth in the stock for the entirety of the following decade.

Dow Jones Transportation Index

Those who take a top-down approach to investing first determine what they believe the major indexes are going to do, then move to sectors, and then move to individual stocks. If your trading is even partly based on index analysis, you can still apply the same pattern methods in this book to those, as illustrated in Figure 16.3, the Dow Jones Transportation Index.

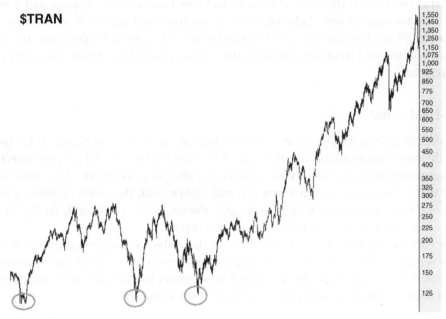

FIGURE 16.3 Many investors watch the major indexes to establish their general trading direction. The Dow Jones Transportation Index provided ample reason for bullishness when it broke out of its very long-term base.

First Instance: 7/3/1962   Bottom Price: $147   Percentage Change: 197%
Last Instance: 10/7/1974   Postbottom Price: $437

This historical perspective is of a particularly long-term call, since the multiple bottoms spanned a dozen years. This lengthy timeframe was appropriate, however, considering the longest and most meaningful bull market in modern history was about to take place.

The first low was made way back in 1962. The market rallied for most of the 1960s and then fell hard in 1970, getting almost as low as 1962's price. It then began to climb again, but it fell victim to the brutal 1972–1974 bear market, dropping again to a low in October of 1974. This is astonishing, since quite a bit of inflation had taken place in the dozen years between 1962 and 1974.

Take note of what was happening during this time—the Transportation index was enjoying hearty, multiyear rallies (up to resistance) and then suffering severe downturns (down to support), with the lows separated by years. Three times, the index hit about 130 (plus or minus several percent), but as the circled areas on the chart show, the low price was always about the same.

This index rallied a third time, and it struggled for a few years as it worked its way toward and through resistance. Finally, in 1980, it blasted through resistance; its first attempt in February was short-lived, but its second attempt in July took hold, and the market was off to the races.

Notice what happened in the two years that followed, however. This index pushed much higher by mid-1981, but then it started falling, and by late 1982, it was back at its former resistance level. However, resistance had now changed into support, and it was crucial that this support level hold, since it had asserted itself with such strength for so many years before. This low price in 1982 was the first of a series of higher lows that the Transports made, and from 1982 forward, the market enjoyed an almost uninterrupted bull run higher.

Harte-Hanks, Inc.

For a much simpler and shorter-term example, look at the example in Figure 16.4, which shows the most simple multiple bottom possible: a double bottom. All the prerequisites were met with this chart: There was a substantial slide in price (from $15 to less than a third that value); there was a sharp reversal higher, with the stock climbing about 30 percent; there was another drop to roughly the same low price; and, finally, there was an ascent up to and beyond the confirmation point.

The second bottom is slightly higher than the first, which is usually a good sign if you want to see higher stock prices. It indicates that the buyers have slightly more strength than the sellers, even in the midst of a sell-off into another bottom, and that strength will come in handy when the stock is trying to create a sustained rally.

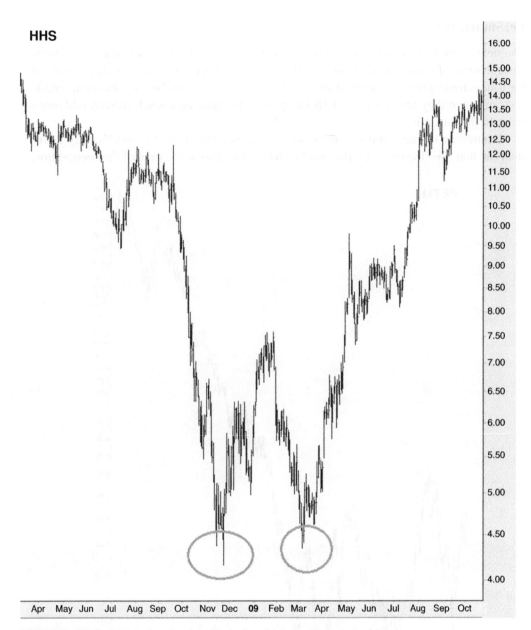

HHS

FIGURE 16.4 This is the simplest kind of multiple bottom—a double.

First Instance: 11/13/2008   Bottom Price: $4.32   Percentage Change: 219%

Last Instance: 3/6/2009   Postbottom Price: $13.76

PetSmart, Inc.

The next instance is a little more complex, not only because there are more low prices (four instead of two), but also because those prices aren't nearly as closely aligned. Of the four prices circled, the second and third could be most plausibly considered a double bottom, since they are almost exactly the same. The flanking lows, however, add some color to the formation.

Examining the first and second lows, we can see the second is significantly lower than the first (see Figure 16.5); this implies weakness, and at the time of the second low,

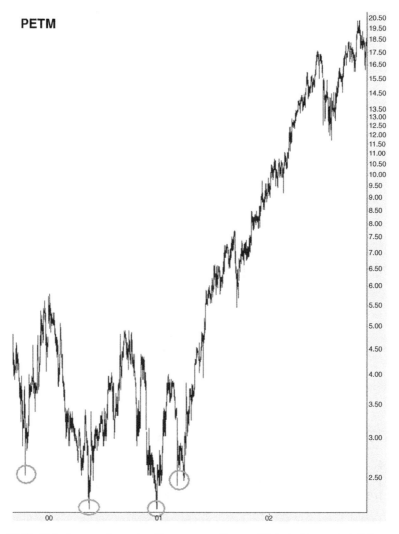

FIGURE 16.5 This is more irregular than some other multiple bottoms, but it is worth noting that the second and third bottoms were almost identical, and the final bottom was somewhat higher.

First Instance: 5/12/2000   Bottom Price: $2.17   Percentage Change: 257%
Last Instance: 12/21/2000   Postbottom Price: $7.74

it would be unclear if more lower lows were on their way or not. By the time the third low was made, the buying has strengthened to the point that the price is no longer dropping lower, and by the fourth nominal low, the price is actually higher. In other words, a higher low has been made, implying that perhaps a new trend is forthcoming.

After this, a sharp rally took place, and once serious selling began much later, it didn't take the price lower than the confirmation point at about $5.50. We see once again that resistance has now become support, and the multiple bottom has confirmed its presence and its power since the stock has rallied far above the lows past its former resistance level.

Regal-Beloit Corporation

How does one determine the confirmation level during a multiple bottom? The simple answer is that the confirmation level is the price at which attempts for a stock rally keep failing in between similar price bottoms. In other words, if a stock keeps hitting $12, rallies to $18, falls to $12, rallies to $18, and so on, it's evident that there is a $6 range and that $18 is the confirmation point.

Reality is rarely quite as clean as this, since the rally point might be very ragged. Figure 16.6 provides a simple example of this, since it wasn't entirely clear when the price would confirm a base had finally been made. After the first bottom, the stock rallied to 38.08 and started falling, reaching just a few pennies above its prior low. It started rallying again, and it exceeded 38.08, pushing to 42.31.

Does the fact that it went higher than its first high mean the bottom was in? At the time, it wouldn't be clear. After all, you are only working with one data point: the first high price. The stock might start sliding a third time to the $25 area. Indeed, it did start sliding, falling under the 38.08 point, suggesting that no confirmation was in place.

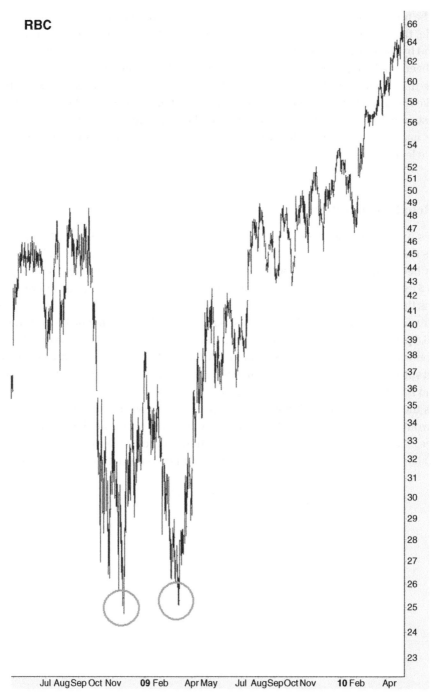

FIGURE 16.6 It is a positive sign when progressive bottoms are higher than their predecessors.

First Instance: 11/21/2008   Bottom Price: $25.66   Percentage Change: 160%
Last Instance: 3/10/2009   Postbottom Price: $66.77

The price did not fall much farther, however—it certainly didn't approach its prior low in the $25 vicinity—and after a few weeks it moved above 38.08 again, finally gapping up in price on July 15, 2009. So in this case, one formation—a double bottom—was confirmed by another—a gap up in price (covered elsewhere in this book). The gap held, and the price at that point moved robustly higher.

The more lows and highs you have in place, the more confident you can be in assessing a range. You would have had very little to work with in this instance, since only one high point had been made, so a separate confirming event (the gap) finally provided the sufficient weight of evidence to go long the stock.

Home Depot

Some of the examples in this chapter show bottoms that are many years apart, but how close can bottoms be together to be valid? One month is probably the bare minimum, with several months being a more reliable amount.

Home Depot, for instance, fell hard in late 2008 and made several similar bottoms on October 10, October 24, and November 21 of that year. It would be somewhat encouraging to see that the stock is resisting falling any further than this level, but such tightly grouped lows don't mean very much. The stock could simply be encountering some very mild support before plunging far lower; not enough time has passed for a large number of market participants to assess and decide what their next move is going to be.

After rallying about 30 percent, the stock resumed its fall, but—importantly—it didn't reach the low price of the prior autumn until March 9, a full five months later. That was plenty enough time to provide a plausible second bottom. The stock rallied into April, fell somewhat, and then rallied even more into September, created enough higher highs and higher lows to affirm that the multiple bottom was passed and the stock was again in an uptrend. See Figure 16.7.

FIGURE 16.7 Home Depot experienced several bouts of heavy selling, but it had enough buying support at $17 to stop any further erosion.

First Instance: 10/10/2008   Bottom Price: $16.58   Percentage Change: 57%
Last Instance: 3/9/2009   Postbottom Price: $25.98

DTE Energy Company

A good rule of thumb when it comes to patterns is that the longer the pattern is, the more potent it can be. With the prior example, Home Depot, the double bottoms occurred in just over five months, and the 57 percent increase in price that followed was a testament to the value of the base.

The next example, Figure 16.8, is over a much longer timeframe, and the percentage change, 717 percent, is correspondingly higher. The bottoms take place on December 1980, April 1984, and May 1988, about four years apart each and with an eight-year total time span. On a split-adjusted basis, the lows were all within pennies of one another,

FIGURE 16.8 DTE Energy's triple bottom had three successively higher prices.

First Instance: 12/15/1980   Bottom Price: $0.71   Percentage Change: 717%
Last Instance: 5/11/1988   Postbottom Price: $5.80

and the combination of proximal lows with great expanses of time demonstrate that, no matter what the circumstance, the stock has found a very solid base.

There was, of course, no assurance that the stock would ever launch from this base. It might meander in this range for years more, as far as a person in 1988 could know. However, in May 1989, the stock gapped higher above its confirmation point, and a true bull market in this stock was ready to take place. The base was set, and the buying finally could commence with certainty.

SUMMARY

The multiple bottom formation can be seductive in its simplicity, since it is so easy to spot. False positives abound, however, because naturally any stock is prone to bouncing along a certain level more than once.

The way to separate the wheat (valid multiple bottoms that precede big price rises) from the chaff (meaningless noise) is to mentally insist on plenty of space between the bottoms, a substantial rise (and subsequent fall) between bottoms, and a preceding large drop in price. Finally, and most important, make sure the stock has pushed high enough above the confirmation point to assure you that you are not about to experience another plunge to create another low price, since the distance between the high and low points of such ranges could make such a drop upsetting.

The longer the time span, the wider the gap between bottoms; and the greater the price range between the bottoms and resistance, the better likelihood you have of acquiring a security that is about to enjoy a substantial increase in value.

CHAPTER 17

Multiple Tops

When a stock has been steadily climbing but can't seem to get past a certain level, it stands a risk of experiencing a multiple top, which can precede a meaningful drop in price. The top can range from just two similar, widely spaced high prices (a double top) up to many similar price levels. When those subsequent high price levels become a little lower each time, it suggests even more strongly that the stock is about to change direction, since the buying strength is waning.

DEFINITION OF THE PATTERN

The first requirement of a multiple top is that the stock has to have experienced a sustained increase in price. The premise of a multiple top is that the stock has already enjoyed a healthy inflation in price, and a selling (or shorting) opportunity has been forming for a while at current lofty levels.

Just because a stock ascends to a certain level a number of times doesn't mean it is forming a top. Those instances should:

- Have significant amounts of time between them.
- Experience failed attempts at dropping before rising back again.
- Ideally, exhibit diminishing amounts of volume with each instance of hitting the high.

The amount of time between highs might be many weeks, several months, or even several years. If you look at a daily chart of a stock, you will want to see large gaps between these high prices as the stock tries—and fails—to push its way higher at least a couple of instances.

As the pattern is forming, what you ideally want to see is a generally consistent higher price and—less important—a generally consistent lower price that represents support as the price attempts to move lower. This range, if there is one, will give you a target price.

This lower level price is sometimes referred to as the confirmation point, and it is at this point that you will want to see the price break beneath on high volume. The more times a stock hits this supporting price, and the more times it tries and fails to get past the confirmation point, then the more meaningful it is when the stock finally does break through this level, because there will be a lot of nervous owners of the stock who recognize that it's time to get out.

An example of a multiple top is found in the example of Agilent, Figure 17.1, which lost 68 percent of its value after it broke support. You can see here that over a period of two and a half years the stock tried four different times, each circled, to get past approximately $40. The third proximal high was lower than the second, and the fourth in turn was lower than the third. During each of the stock's sell-offs, there seemed to be a base of support at the $30 level. When that level was violated in late September 2008, the stock fell hard.

FIGURE 17.1 The trading action from 2006 to 2008 was very irregular, but it was evident that resistance at $40 was formidable.

PSYCHOLOGY BEHIND THE PATTERN

The buying public wants stocks to go up, and they would like to see them do so in a fairly regular, steady pattern. When a stock's price seems unable to get past a certain price point—that is, when selling strength is strong enough to match buying strength—owners of the stock become frustrated, nervous, and skeptical.

Consider a stock that has steadily risen from $20 to $30 over a period of a year. Clearly the owners of this stock are going to be pleased with a 50 percent increase in their stock's value, but as the saying goes, stocks climb a wall of worry, and the possibility of a decline is always going to be present in the minds of those holding the security.

The stock now encounters profit taking and drops to $27.50, erasing a quarter of the year's gains in the span of a month. Latecomers to the stock are more interested in buying, since the price is more attractive, so they begin accumulating it over the next month, and the longer-term owners are relieved to see the stock's unusual drop in price change course and resume the behavior to which they are accustomed: rising.

Instead of pushing to a new lifetime high, the stock stalls again. Now people begin to wonder if the stock is fully valued at $30 and simply can't go any higher. The stock sells off to $27.45, stabilizes, and climbs a third time, this time getting to $29.50 a couple of months later. People looking at the chart can see that a possible triple top exists, and the third top couldn't even manage to get back up to the $30 level. In addition, buying interest seems to be dropping off, because on each of these price ascents, the volume is lighter.

The stock starts dropping again, and those who are long this security are growing weary of this roller coaster. They decide to sell, and they do so in large enough numbers that the buyers can't sustain the price at $27.50 anymore. The stock breaks hard under $27, and the stop-orders being hit and the nervous longs that want to get out while they still have good profits create a steady flow of sell orders over the next several months. The stock doesn't steady itself until it gets to about $22, turning a former 50 percent profit for those who bought at $20 to merely a 10 percent profit.

The events that can cause such a reversal can range from a stock getting so far ahead of itself that it is overvalued, to a company's prospects and earnings turning for the worse, to the market in general encountering a broad sell-off. Whatever the reason, a stock going through a series of multiple tops cannot muster the energy to go any higher, and the patience and nerves of the stock's owners can eventually create a substantial change in price direction and velocity.

EXAMPLES

The following are a few examples of this important topping pattern.

Acadia Realty Trust

When comparing multiple tops and multiple bottoms, there is a fairly important difference: It's more important with multiple bottoms that the price be very consistent, since the stock needs to demonstrate a good, solid base from which to ascend. As for tops, if the high prices are relatively close (within about 5 percent) but exhibit a subtle downtrend, the pattern is still valid. Indeed, weakening tops only amplify the stock's prospects for a drop.

Acadia Realty Trust (symbol AKR), shown in Figure 17.2, illustrates this nicely. In five different instances, the price tried to move higher but was unable to do so. There were two sharp sell-offs to the $19 level, and the final three proximal high prices were progressively weaker. With hindsight, we can see that the bull market in this stock ended on June 4, 2007, and all the trading action over the next fifteen months was little more than the stock marking time, with the prudent shareholders distributing their stock to new buyers.

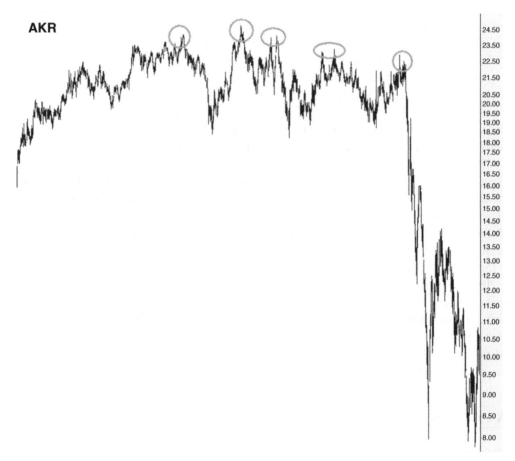

FIGURE 17.2 Here are a series of gently descending lower highs.

First Top Date: 2/14/2007   Top Price: $22.67   Percentage Loss: −66%
Last Top Date: 9/19/2008   Posttop Price: $7.74

Diodes, Inc.

By keeping track of a stock's highs, perhaps by marking them on your chart with a circle, you can keep track of the general trend, no matter how subtle, and watch for a trend shift. Figure 17.3 shows that the first three tops formed a series of higher highs, even

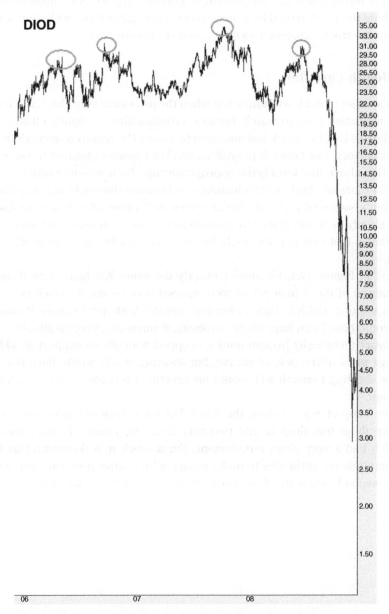

FIGURE 17.3 The lower high following the trio of higher highs marked a change in direction.

First Top Date: 9/18/2006   Top Price: $28.96   Percentage Loss: −90%
Last Top Date: 8/11/2008   Posttop Price: $2.95

though the difference between those highs wasn't significant. The fourth high, however, was the first instance of a lower high, and this—coupled with the fact that the support level at $22 was an area of high risk—suggested that a top might be in place.

It is unimportant that these four tops aren't identical in price. What is important is that the stock's ability to create a higher high was signaled by the fourth circle. In addition, the recent dip beneath $22, threatening important support, also signaled increased risk. Those long the stock would have been wise to recognize this subtle shift and make an exit before the stock expressed its directional shift more fully.

Coventry Health Care, Inc.

Of course, it's easier to trade a multiple top when the prices are very close. For bulls, this provides an important level to watch, because crossing above a tightly clustered range of prices indicates that the stock has managed to garner the required strength to resume its upward trajectory. For bears, it provides a level to consider shorting the stock, since any price action above that level is the appropriate zone for a stop-loss order.

The safest place to short in such instances is beneath the confirmation point, since a stock hitting a series of highs at similar prices isn't proof of a downturn itself. The stock might simply be working its way through a consolidation zone, and once it pushes above resistance, that rise in price might be very fast, clobbering anyone who is short the position.

Coventry, in Figure 17.4, hit almost exactly the same $62 high price three times, and the instances of those high prices were spaced very far apart, which is reassuring for a person seeking multiple highs. Shorting this stock simply because it was at this high price would have been imprudent (although, it turns out, very profitable), because the stock wasn't technically broken until it dropped beneath its support at $44. There is a very large price difference, of course, but shorting at $62 would have been guessing, whereas shorting beneath $44 would be executing a trade based on a legitimate technical event.

Once this support was broken, the stock fell for a very extended period. An interesting fact about this drop is that two very large gaps down in price took place, each of which had a very clean retracement. For a stock in a downturn this lengthy, there were multiple opportunities to make money with a short position: first, when $44 was broken; second, when the first gap was closed; and third, when the second gap was closed.

FIGURE 17.4 Coventry's triple top preceded a severe drop in value.

First Top Date: 2/9/2006   Top Price: $63.89   Percentage Loss: −88%
Last Top Date: 1/8/2008   Posttop Price: $7.97

Lindsay Corporation

Double tops are easier to trade and track than the prior examples, and Figure 17.5 shows a double top whose highs were mere pennies apart. Importantly, these highs were also

FIGURE 17.5 The double top, the simplest possible formation, at almost identical price levels.

First Top Date: 4/22/2008   Top Price: $122.29   Percentage Loss: −81%
Last Top Date: 6/17/2008   Posttop Price: $23.19

spaced far enough apart—the first, April 22, and the second, June 17—to be a legitimate formation. This example also illustrates a clean retracement. After the stock broke support at $95, it fell beneath $80, but then by August 4 it recovered to precisely beneath the former support line. As with so many other chart examples in this book, this provides a great opportunity for bulls and bears alike. For bulls, it offers a welcome second chance to get out as a decent price, because it is unlikely a stock in this formation is going to be able to overcome its former support level, and for bears, it creates a fantastic shorting opportunity with relatively little risk.

Boeing Corporation

Some retracements are only partial, which proves that it can be difficult waiting for a full retracement to take place, since such an opportunity may never come.

The double top in Boeing, Figure 17.6, is similar in form and spacing to Figure 17.5. The tops were on July 25 and October 2, 2007, and these prices were only pennies apart. When you are examining a heavily traded stock that makes an extremely clean double top like this, it merits watching, because that price symmetry is no coincidence.

Support was at about $85, and BA fell as low at $66 before turning around. It managed to claw its way back as high as $81, but it didn't get to its former support level, four dollars higher, before resuming its downturn and eventually getting beneath $28. Those waiting for an $85 price would have been sorely disappointed.

If you are waiting for a retracement, you might want to scale in to a position slowly as retracement is approached, instead of waiting for the perfect price. You could, for example, enter a third of the position at 50 percent of retracement, another third at 75 percent of retracement, and a final third upon full retracement, should it ever take place. If the stock is strong enough to take it all the way, then your average price will be pretty good. On the other hand, if the price only gets, for instance, 60 percent back up the retracement zone, you will at least have a partial position in place to extract some profits out of the trade.

FIGURE 17.6   Here is another nearly perfect double top.

First Top Date: 7/25/2007   Top Price: $99.97   Percentage Loss: −72%
Last Top Date: 10/2/2007   Posttop Price: $27.56

SUMMARY

There's an old saying in trading that trees do not grow to the sky. In other words, even the healthiest stock isn't going to rise forever, and monitoring for instances where the price ascent seems to be exhausting itself is the best way to take your profits while they are still safe. In the course of your charting, when you see instances of similar tops taking place over a long span of time, circle those tops to monitor them, and draw a line where you see a base of support beneath those tops. You're going to want to watch for:

- Similar highs.
- Plenty of space between those highs.
- An easy-to-identify base of support.
- And, should it occur, a violation of that support, which is your confirmation point.

The double top is the easiest of these to identify, but over a longer-term chart, multiple highs can help you keep track of subtle shifts in a stock's momentum that foretell of a change that bulls will not want to see, but that bears will welcome.

CHAPTER 18

Pennants

The pennant pattern is extremely similar in most respects to the flag pattern (see Chapter 12), except that its lines are convergent rather than parallel. The two lines containing the price bars point toward a common end, and this consolidation pattern typically suggests a continuation of the trend.

Some of the patterns in this book can be quite long-term, spanning years or even decades. The pennant pattern is nothing of the sort. It is, instead, a rather short-term pattern typically lasting just a few weeks, and it is a continuation pattern, allowing a security to take a breath before moving in its dominant direction.

DEFINITION OF THE PATTERN

The first requirement for a pennant pattern is that it be preceded by a strong move in the first place. That move can be up or down, but it must be strong and sharp, since the entire basis for a pennant pattern is that it represents a brief pause in the action of an overall powerful move. Even though prices may form pennant patterns in the midst of markets that are meandering, the fact that they aren't in the context of a strong move negates their import.

Next, the pennant should be countertrend to the general trend. Because of its countertrend nature, the pennant should be downward sloping for a bullish move and upward sloping for a bearish move. It is acceptable for the pattern to be flat, in the form of a symmetric triangle, irrespective of direction. Buying or selling action is supposed to abate during the formation of the pennant—often on dwindling volume—and it makes sense that the dominant direction would be opposed while the pennant is being formed.

The pennant itself is defined as a group of prices that are cleanly bounded by a pair of converging trendlines. If the lines are parallel, the pattern is a flag, which is covered in a different section. The pennant itself shouldn't be terribly lengthy; a length of three months is probably the longest acceptable timeframe, and a more typical age will be a month or less.

Finally, when the price breaks out of the pennant pattern, that breakout should be accompanied with an increase in volume. The trend is eager to resume itself, and after weeks of waiting, buyers (or sellers, as the case may be) should push the equity back into its longer-term trend with an abundance of activity.

Even though pennants aren't particularly big patterns, the moves they portend can be substantial. The distance from the beginning of the broad trend (whether up or down) to the beginning of the pennant is sometimes known as the *flagpole* (a bit of a misnomer), and its height is the figure you want to use to compute the measured move. That move is calculated by adding (or, in a downtrend, subtracting) the price value to the end of the pennant pattern.

For instance, if a stock was trading at between $20 and $22 for a long time, and then it suddenly made a rapid ascent from $12 to $20 before starting its pennant pattern, the flagpole would be $8 in height (that is, $30 minus $22, since $22 is the value when the stock changed from trading in a tight range to soaring higher sharply). Let us assume the pennant was formed by a gentle down sloping pattern lasting three weeks that took the price back down, but then the bulls stepped in again on big volume and broke out of the pennant at $28. The measured target would therefore be $36, since $28 (the breakout level) plus $8 (the flagpole's height) equals $36.

PSYCHOLOGY BEHIND THE PATTERN

Let's look at a real-life example of a pennant pattern to understand the thinking behind the crowd trading it. Figure 18.1 shows the big-box retailer Costco Wholesale (symbol COST). The stock moves from about $54 to $65, and this pole is $11 high, implying that, upon pattern completion, the move will be $11 higher.

The pennant lasts basically for the entire month of October 2010, as bounded by the lines in Figure 18.1. This consolidation lets the weaker hands take their profits on the bullish side. The price launches above the pattern on November 4, and with a price of $63 at the breakout, a target price of $74 is created. It nails this price almost to the penny by January 3, 2011, which is the first time COST encounters any meaningful weakness in its current uptrend.

Thus, the poles on both sides of the pennant—from 54 to 65 and from 63 to 74—are equal, and this pennant has illustrated its predictive power and has served as a consolidation point exactly midway in the up-move.

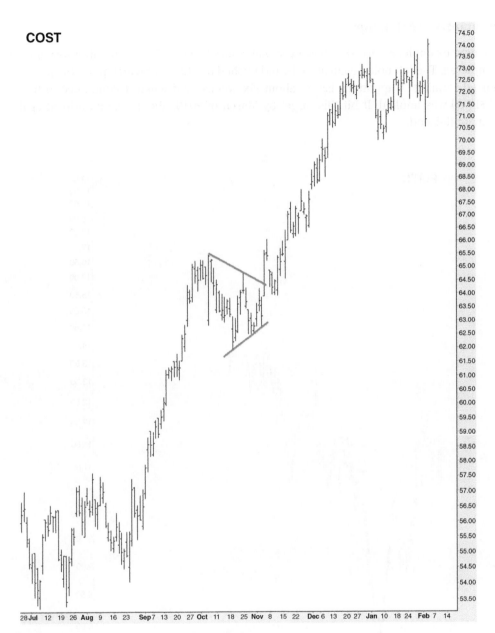

FIGURE 18.1 The stock of retailer Costco formed a pennant formation at precisely the midway point of its rally.

The following examples show you the pattern's start date, end date, breakout price, and percentage change after the pattern's completion.

Parametric Technology

The next example, Figure 18.2, has a very substantial gain of 74 percent after its pennant completed. The left pole began at $7.18 and pushed to $12.87, at which point the pennant started forming. The pattern lasted about six weeks, and when it completed, a target of $17.69 was implied. It hit this target by March of 2010, about nine months after the pennant finished.

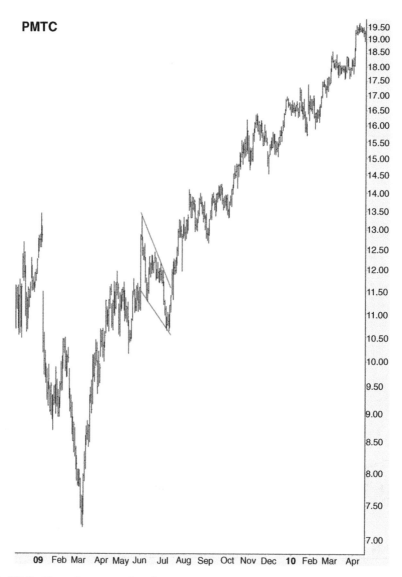

FIGURE 18.2 The price move after this pennant, 74 percent, was substantial.

Pattern Start: 6/1/2009   Breakout Price: $11.50   Percentage Change: 74%
Pattern End: 7/15/2009   Postbreakout Price: $20

Although the right pole took much longer to complete than the left pole, the target was still met, and there was no meaningful interruption in the series of higher highs and higher lows that transpired upon the pennant's completion.

Hanesbrands, Inc.

Because pennants are countertrend formations, they can suggest to some chartists that something is going wrong with the stock. This is obviously not the case with completed pennants, however, since successful ones break to the upside (in the case of a bullish continuation). Figure 18.3 provides an illustration of this.

FIGURE 18.3 The pace of the increase slowed after this pattern, but the target was achieved nonetheless.

Pattern Start: 6/10/2009   Breakout Price: $14.20   Percentage Change: 120%
Pattern End: 7/14//2009   Postbreakout Price: $31.45

Hanesbrands enjoyed a price raise from about $5 to $18, and then its price weakened. Some would have mistakenly assumed that the stock's rally was through, as it lost over 25 percent of its value. The stock broke out at $14, though, implying a target price of $27, which it nailed almost to perfection by November 9, 2009 (it was a few pennies short of the goal). Interestingly, the stock encountered a bout of weakness almost immediately after its target was reached, and dropped almost 30 percent. This illustrates the value of having a solid target in mind when you base a trade on a pattern.

Kimberly-Clark Corporation

The value of patterns, besides providing insight to direction and price, is that they can help you attain a good price on a trade in a timely manner before the stock moves too quickly above or below a reasonable entry price. Kimberly-Clark, shown in Figure 18.4, moved from about $40 to $51 over a few months in early 2009, and then it began to consolidate in a pennant formation during all of June and the first half of July.

It moved a little above this pattern on July 15 and pushed demonstrably above it the next day, July 16, which would have been a clear buy signal. The price paid would have been about $51 per share. Just a few days later, on July 23, the price gapped up strongly, climbing about 8 percent for the day. A person already in position with KMB would have been pleased to see such a strong confirmation of the expected bullish move. A person unaware of the technical event that had just taken place might rush in to buy the security too late, increasing their risk by doing so.

Of course, it would have worked out for this latecomer in any case, as we can see from the chart. However, if the stock had weakened, the person who entered at $54 has to tolerate more risk than the person who entered at $51. In any case, the breakout at $50, added to the prior pole height of $11, yielded a target price of $61. This target was matched by November of that year, and it was even exceeded by a few percent. At this point, the stock sold off and lost about 15 percent of its value, proving to the person who closed the position profitable at the $61 target that they had made the right choice.

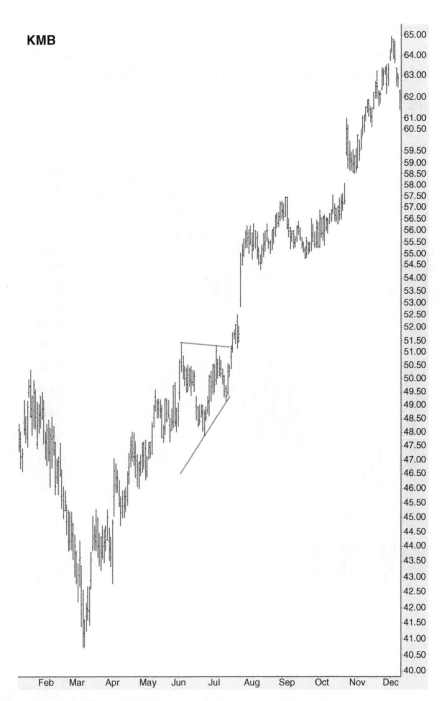

KMB

FIGURE 18.4 Identifying this pennant would have permitted a trader to get into the stock before it made its huge gap higher several days later.

Pattern Start: 6/2/2009   Breakout Price: $50   Percentage Change: 30%
Pattern End: 7/16/2009   Postbreakout Price: $65

Ralph Lauren

Clothes manufacturer Ralph Lauren, whose chart is in Figure 18.5, exhibited a pennant during precisely the same time frame as the prior example. The pattern range matches

FIGURE 18.5 The breakout from this pennant was particularly sharp.

Pattern Start: 6/2/2009   Breakout Price: $53   Percentage Change: 79%
Pattern End: 7/15/2009   Postbreakout Price: $95

almost to the day, although the percentage gain, 79 percent, was much more significant than the 30 percent gain of the last illustration. The reason for this is because the left pole had a large percentage gain, implying an equally large target price.

The left pole spanned from $31 to $59, a difference of $28. The breakout at $53 suggested a target of $81, achieved by November 10. There is some nice time symmetry here as well, since the left pole took a little more than three months to complete, and the right pole also took a little more than three months. The stock continued to be strong until it reached $95.27, well above the target, at which time it lost more than a quarter of its value during some overall market weakness.

Medtronic, Inc.

Our final example of a pennant, Figure 18.6, is in the shape of a symmetrical triangle. The price action preceding this pattern lifted the stock from $23 to $34, an $11 difference, and the pattern was broken to the upside at $34, implying a $45 target price. This target was hit on January 11, 2010.

One interesting footnote to this pattern is that it didn't exceed this target very much before it began a sustained sell-off, losing over a third of its value. By the time the selling abated, the price had retracted the entire gain that Medtronic had enjoyed after its pennant. A person taking a buy-and-hold approach would have seen the entirety of their 37 percent profit wiped out and would instead be looking at a small loss. We see yet again how valuable it is to have a target in mind, and even if you don't exit the position completely at the target, at least keep your stop-loss orders tight after the target is achieved.

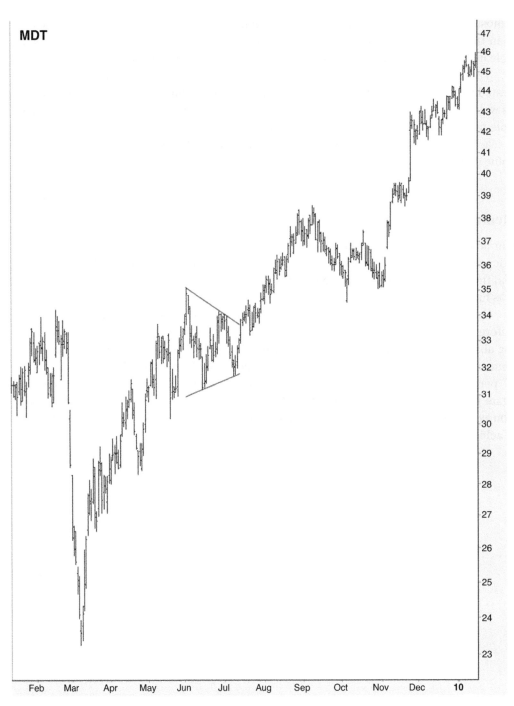

FIGURE 18.6 Medtronic had a 37 percent price gain after this pennant completed.

Pattern Start: 6/2/2009   Breakout Price: $33.38   Percentage Change: 37%
Pattern End: 7/15/2009   Postbreakout Price: $45.58

SUMMARY

The pennant isn't an easy pattern to spot during the course of real-time trading, and you may find it helpful to use a pattern recognition system (such as Prophet Patterns, which is built into ProphetCharts) to identify these as they are taking shape. The pattern does not form terribly often, but when it does, you can find it a valuable ally in pinpointing a target price and know when—if ever—the pattern has signaled that the trend in progress is about to continue with its second half.

CHAPTER 19

Rounded Bottoms

Probably the simplest, cleanest, and easiest-to-identify pattern in technical analysis is the rounded bottom (also called the saucer bottom). As the name suggests, this pattern indicates the price action has a curve at the bottom of a price decline, setting up for a reversal to the upside. Some of the most powerful and long-lasting price movements take place after a rounded bottom, and they usually represent relatively safe trades since the market has spent so much time hammering out a bottom and clearing bears and nervous holders out of the security.

DEFINITION OF THE PATTERN

At the risk of oversimplifying, the definition of a rounded bottom is a price pattern that gradually decreases in price, stabilizes for a while, gradually increases in price, and then finally breaks above resistance on strong volume. Figure 19.1 provides an example with the security RAX (Rackspace Hosting, Inc.). The price slowly moved from about $22 to $16 over a period of half a year, then reversed and started slowly moving higher. In September, the stock overcame resistance at the $22 level on strong volume and went on to a 50 percent price gain over the coming several months.

This example shows the two core elements of this kind of pattern—a clean, well-defined base that resembles a relatively smooth saucer, and a "punching through" of the price on hearty volume. This volume surge affirms renewed interest in the stock, since all recent buyers are now enjoying a profitable position.

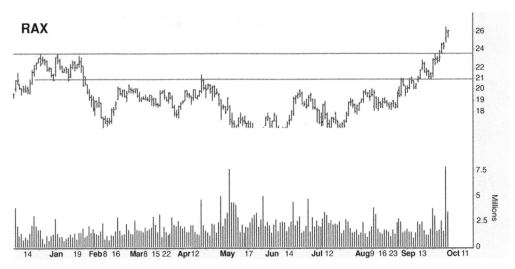

FIGURE 19.1 Strong volume on the breakout isn't required, but it greatly increases the chance of good profits later.

PSYCHOLOGY BEHIND THE PATTERN

The psychology behind a mass of buyers holding a security at a particular price is important, and in a way it is the very basis of technical analysis. Generally speaking, traders prefer profits to losses. Owners of a security whose price moves higher will feel increasingly positive about that stock and will be compelled to buy more, because their profits are increasing. If there is a large mass of such buyers, this kind of buying can feed on itself.

A stock that has been trapped within a small price range for a long term will have two important ingredients for a potential upside move: (1) a large quantity of buyers within that price range, eager to add to their position if the stock breaks out of the range, and (2) a strong support level at that price range, which will create a firm floor for prices if an initial breakout weakens. If a stock breaks above its price range and then starts sinking, that same mass of owners of the stock is going to be reluctant to sell their holdings as the price softens, which will cause the price to firm up as sellers dry up. This group of security owners within that price range is a potent force for both pushing the stock higher as well as protecting the stock from falling through the well-established price range.

One nice feature of breakouts is that they often give traders a second chance to get in after the breakout. This temporary softening in prices after the breakout is known as a pullback, and it is caused by a portion of the owners of the stock anxious to bank their modest profits on their stock's newfound price activity.

Imagine a hypothetical group of 1,000 people, each of whom owned shares in a company that had been trading between $10 and $12 for years. If the stock finally breaks out and hits $15, you can understand the excitement of these owners, since they have been holding a do-nothing stock for years that is finally showing signs of life.

Although most of these owners may be patient enough to let their profits build, there is going to be a subset of this group that will want to get out of the stock immediately and take their gains. The psychology behind this group is understandable, too—after all, their stock has done absolutely nothing, and now it is giving them an opportunity to get out with some extra cash. So some people—let's say 100 out of the group of 1,000—immediately place orders to sell the stock at the current market price.

This influx of selling is going to cause the price to soften, at least temporarily. It usually will head back to the upper end of its former trading range, at which point selling will dry up since any newfound profits the group enjoyed have now vanished, eliminating the compulsion to sell the stock for a quick profit. It is important that the price remain above the breakout level, since doing otherwise invalidates the pattern's integrity.

This temporary softening of prices is the pullback, and those people watching the stock chart closely can take advantage of this by acquiring the stock at the "prebreakout" price. It is an especially attractive opportunity since the stock has, in a manner of speaking, tipped its hand about its price direction since it has finally broken out of its price range.

EXAMPLES

Some incredible gains can be enjoyed with the completion of a rounded bottom, as you will see with the following example charts.

Cal-Maine Foods

The examples in this chapter sometimes represent patterns that span years. By no means does this suggest that rounded bottoms need to be in place over very long stretches of time. The visual aspects of the pattern should be roughly the same whether you are looking at price action over a 10-year or a 10-minute span of time.

The first example, Cal-Maine Foods, belongs to the "multiyear" category. The saucer spans over six years (the chart in Figure 19.2 shows only the rightmost half of it). The stock meandered for year after year, but when it finally broke above $2.65, volume picked up appreciably. By way of example, a typical day for this stock was June 25, 2003, when it traded 7,600 shares. By December of the same year, there were days when nearly 5 million shares were being traded.

The price itself had a fantastic run-up before easing back, climbing 646 percent by February 2004, which was only eight months after the breakout.

CALM

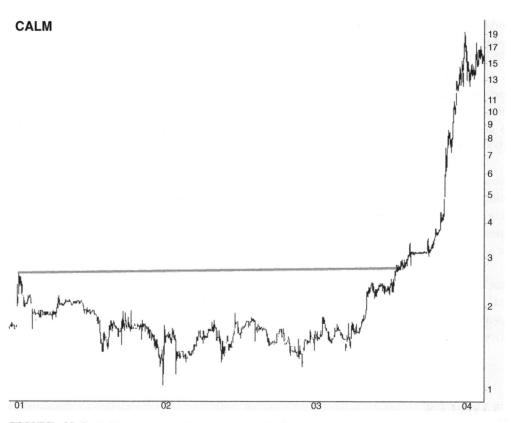

FIGURE 19.2 Cal-Maine enjoyed a gigantic, triple-digit percentage run-up in just eight months after breaking out from a six-year-long saucer pattern.

Pattern Start: March 1997   Breakout Price: $2.65   Increase in Value: 646%
Pattern Breakout: July 2003   Postbreakout High: $19.96

Mechel Oao

The next chart, Figure 19.3, is a good lesson in considering how tolerant to be of pull-backs. The saucer pattern spanned more than a couple of years, and finally, on April 4, 2007, the price broke above the horizontal line representing resistance. The problem, though, is that the price kept moving above and below this line repeatedly until June 13, at which time it broke higher again, this time to a new high by July 12, and then it started softening again. By August 16, it was yet again below the breakout line, having lost about 30 percent of its peak value.

Those who had bought the stock on the initial breakout and used a conservative stop-loss level would have been stopped out of the position promptly. Those who kept trying to get into the security, only to be stopped out repeatedly, would be generating little more than commissions for their broker and losses for themselves while the stock oscillated around the important $11.36 price level.

Looking back, we now know that the August 16 low was the bottom price for the stock as it began its true ascent, quintupling in price by May 2008. The vital lesson to take away from this is that nowhere is it written that, once a pattern is complete, its price will absolutely not be going beneath that breakout level again, only to ultimately fulfill its potential. There's no question that the saucer pattern of MTL was well defined and, with hindsight, we know it was terribly profitable. What must have been maddening for those trying to trade this, however, was that the stock spent April through August noodling around its breakout price and confounding bulls and bears alike.

The solution to this problem, which is to use much wider stops, carries with it a cost, since there is also no guarantee that having liberal stop-loss levels will ultimately reward you with a good price. After all, MTL's drop beneath its breakout level could have been a signal that the price was heading down to $7 again. The prudent thing to do is respect the price line, but there's no harm in continuing to monitor a chart like this on a regular basis to see if, as in MTL's case, it eventually shakes off the selling and begins steadily moving in the intended direction.

FIGURE 19.3 Mechel Oao provides a confusing period for traders as it kept violating its breakout level for months before finally pushing higher.

Pattern Start: October 2005   Breakout Price: $11.36   Increase in Value: 402%
Pattern Breakout: March 2007   Postbreakout High: $57

Sina Corporation

In sharp contrast to the prior example, Sina Corporation (symbol SINA; shown in Figure 19.4) broke above its saucer on October 28, 2002, and never came close to violating its breakout level. A convincing argument in favor of owning this stock was the volume increase on that day. The prior trading day, October 25, there were 56,000 shares traded. On October 28, the breakout day, 1,111,000 shares traded.

The cleanness of the pattern and the surge in the volume after the breakout were very positive signs for the bulls, and this is one of the more extraordinary examples in the book of how much a stock can move based on these advantages. Between October 2002 and January 2004, SINA moved up an incredible 1,736 percent before it began to retrace any meaningful portion of its gains. This is the kind of eye-popping return that can make technical analysis so exciting.

FIGURE 19.4 This is an exceptionally clean saucer bottom.

Pattern Start: February 2001   Breakout Price: $2.56   Increase in Value: 1,736%
Pattern Breakout: October 2002   Postbreakout High: $47

Agrium

Agrium, shown in Figure 19.5, is a bit unusual in that its breakout line is tilted. An upward-tilting line is not only not a problem for a saucer; it's actually a positive, because it suggests subtle strength underneath the stock that is easing prices higher even while the pattern is being formed.

As with Figure 19.3, however, AGU generated the same challenge for traders, since between April 29, 2004, and May 19, 2004, it dipped below its breakout level. Had a person been stopped out of their position, they would have had a small loss, but once the stock regained its footing later in 2004, it would have been acceptable to reenter based on the renewed breakout.

AGU

FIGURE 19.5 The slightly upward-tilting breakout line is bullish for the stock.

Pattern Start: February 1996   Breakout Price: $13.25   Increase in Value: 692%
Pattern Breakout: October 2003   Postbreakout High: $105

Gold

The exchange-traded fund for gold, symbol GLD, was introduced to the market in November 2004, and since that time is has become one of the most consistently and widely traded financial instruments in the United States. Funds such as this provide a highly liquid mechanism for participating in commodities markets without actually dealing with the peculiarities and leverage of the futures markets.

The saucer itself began forming almost immediately after the initial public offering, and as shown in Figure 19.6, the breakout occurred on September 15 with a healthy increase in volume. GLD pushed a little higher, then it eased gently back down to its breakout level again on November 4. This represents an ideal opportunity to buy, because the stock has already demonstrated its ability to move higher (in this case, to lifetime highs) on stronger volume, and it is affirming its support level, thus giving you a safe stop-loss price. Even though the initial gain of 27 percent for GLD isn't as eye-popping as some of the other examples in this chapter, it only took a few weeks to get to that level, and gold itself went on to much, much higher prices in the years that followed.

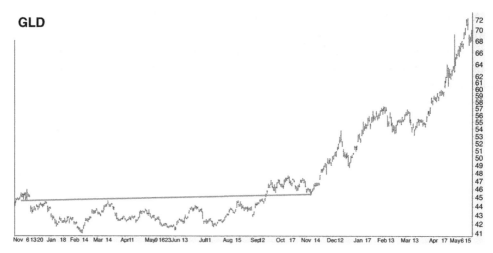

FIGURE 19.6 This is a very clean retracement back to the breakout line.

Pattern Start: December 2004   Breakout Price: $45   Increase in Value: 27%
Pattern Breakout: September 2005   Postbreakout High: $57

Illinois Tool Works, Inc.

Illinois Tool Works (symbol ITW), shown in a multidecade chart in Figure 19.7, sports a 479 percent rise in price after its saucer breakout. What is especially interesting about this instance is how much farther the stock went in the years to come. The gains from the initial rise are measured only until 1987, since a significant drop in the market represented the first meaningful downturn in price for ITW (even though the position was

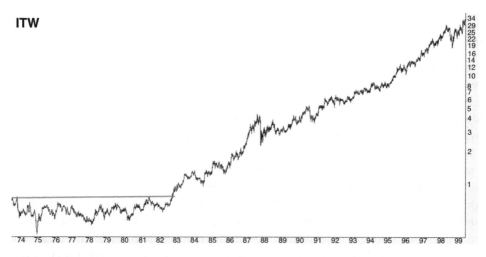

FIGURE 19.7 This very long-term pattern illustrates that even a decade-old saucer can have tremendous power.

Pattern Start: March 1973   Breakout Price: $0.75   Increase in Value: 479%
Pattern Breakout: October 1982   Postbreakout High: $4.34

still very profitable). As impressive as the quintupling in price was, the stock went on to repeat that performance several times more through the 1990s, as its percentage change entered the quadruple digits.

The main point in this example is that rounded bottoms are not only valuable for the short- and medium-term gains they provide, but they are often harbingers of the kinds of generation-long uptrends that can turn a portfolio from simply profitable to life-changing.

Merck

It took several attempts for Merck to exceed its $1 (split-adjusted) resistance level—the summers of 1981, 1983, and then, at last, 1985 (see Figure 19.8). It may seem hard to believe, but this breakout presaged an era for this security that saw its price rise over sixtyfold by its peak in 2000. On a much shorter timeline, it made a 343 percent move by September 1987, which was the first time it experienced anything that might have been considered a pause in its ascent.

FIGURE 19.8 Although the 343 percent rise of this stock was amazing, the price actually went on to much higher levels later in its history.

Pattern Start: February 1973   Breakout Price: $1.00   Increase in Value: 343%
Pattern Breakout: March 1985   Postbreakout High: $4.43

Murphy Oil Corporation

The other examples in this chapter exhibit fairly good symmetry between the left and right halves of the saucer. This is not a requirement, however, as Figure 19.9 illustrates. In this instance, the climb higher for prices was a slow, arduous affair. What's more important than the length of time it took is the fact that the $5.64 price level was respected as a resistance level. Although this saucer could have broken up much earlier, such as

1990, and still have been a perfectly good saucer pattern, it took an additional six years to hammer out a meaningful base.

It should also be mentioned that, even after the breakout, the stock experienced a substantial drop in 1998, but this drop never sent prices beneath the breakout price. The price levels you use as your stop-loss prices are on a chart-by-chart basis, so it is unknown whether your own position would have "survived" such a serious dip in prices. But a person willing to stay in the position, so long as prices were above the initial breakout level, would have held onto this security for the long haul.

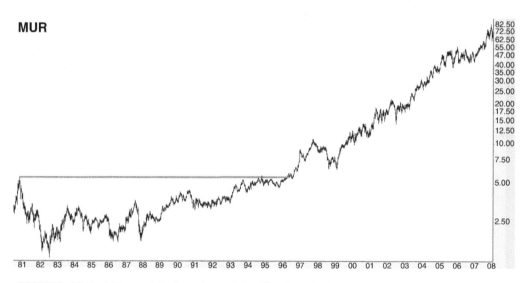

FIGURE 19.9 This stock had a substantial pullback in the late 1990s, but the price still did not dip below the initial breakout level.

Pattern Start: November 1980   Breakout Price: $5.64   Increase in Value: 1,451%
Pattern Breakout: April 1996   Postbreakout High: $87.5

Whole Foods Market, Inc.

The organics-oriented grocery chain Whole Foods Market came public in 1992, and from 1998 to 2001 it formed a well-defined saucer pattern that took more time moving up (1999–2001) than it took going down in the first place (1998). The interesting thing about this breakout was the length of time that the retracement took.

The initial breakout gave the stock about a 44 percent increase in price within eight months, but then it started succumbing to overall stock market weakness and hit a bottom on July 24, 2002, having lost all of its postbreakout gains. What's amazing is that it retraced to its breakout point perfectly, even though it did so many months after the fact. This provided a superb opportunity for newcomers to the stock to enter a long position and—for those fortunate enough to have made money on the initial 44 percent climb—to take the proverbial second bite at the Apple. By retracing, but not violating, this line, the stock affirmed the importance of that price level as support. See Figure 19.10.

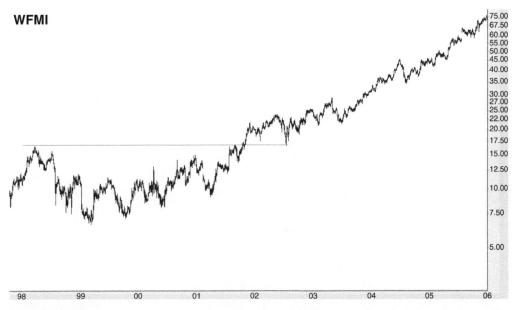

FIGURE 19.10 Here is another example of an almost perfect touchpoint on the breakout line.

Pattern Start: March 1998   Breakout Price: $16.70   Increase in Value: 343%
Pattern Breakout: October 2001   Postbreakout High: $74.00

SUMMARY

Of the many patterns described in this book, the rounded bottom is one that deserves more attention than most of the others. It is easy to identify, provides a clean stop-loss level, and can precede some dazzling price performance. Keep in mind also that this pattern doesn't necessarily have to appear at the bottom of a long bear market. It can serve as a continuation pattern as well (that is, an ascending stock can pause for a while as it shapes a saucer before continuing higher). Lastly, pay close attention to volume; nothing affirms a breakout better than a large number of traders piling on board.

CHAPTER 20

Rounded Tops

The chart formation called the rounded top is precisely what it sounds like—a topping pattern, implying a significant move lower, that is made up of a series of higher highs and then higher lows, which taken altogether create a rounded effect.

DEFINITION OF THE PATTERN

The first prerequisite for the pattern is that it has to be preceded by a sharp rise in price. The point of finding the pattern in the first place is to sell the stock short, close a long position, or buy put options on it—whatever your trading objective might be—in anticipation of a drop in price. Unless the stock has already risen substantially, there will be too much support beneath the price level to create the opportunity for a substantial drop.

Capital One Financial, shown in Figure 20.1, had risen significantly when it started forming its rounded top in early 2003. In 2004, 2005, and the first half of 2006, it made a series of higher highs, but the rate of ascent of those highs diminished each time, forming the beginning of the rounded top you can see drawn here after the fact.

Starting in mid-2006, the stock subtly changed direction and began making a series of lower highs at increasingly sharp angles. This gentle progression of higher highs and then lower highs is the next requirement, because that is the geometric requirement for drawing out the upper portion of the oval shown.

During the creation of the rounded top, a horizontal line similar to the head and shoulders' neckline is established. If and when this support line is broken, a sell signal is in place, assuming that the rounded top is mature enough to constitute a valid pattern.

THE PATTERNS

COF

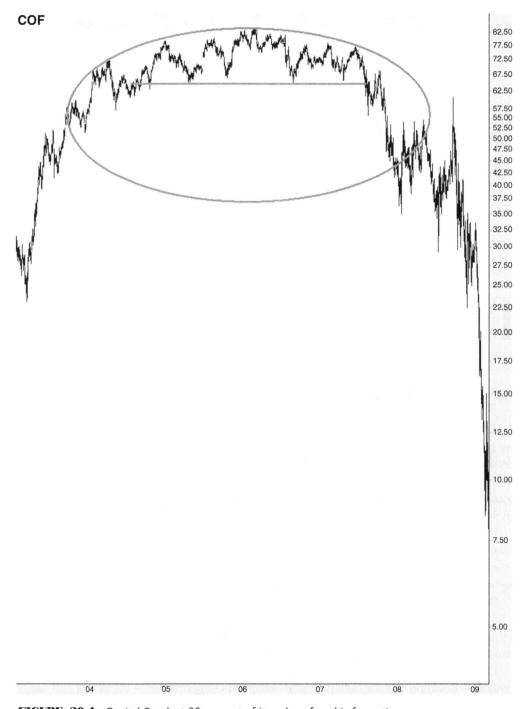

FIGURE 20.1   Capital One lost 88 percent of its value after this formation.

Sometimes, but not always, the price will retrace back to the former support line, which represents the lowest-risk opportunity for a person to sell the stock short. There are occasions when the price will exceed this former support level, as it did with the example in Figure 20.1. So long as the price does not violate the progression of lower highs, the pattern is still intact.

PSYCHOLOGY BEHIND THE PATTERN

Imagine a stock that has been moving steadily higher for a period of two years, starting from $10 and soaring to $50. Its owners are elated at their gains, and they have grown accustomed to a stock that does little but ascend in value.

The stock reaches a new lifetime high, and some of the holders decide for various reasons to take their profits and exit. Some might think the fundamentals are too rich; others might believe the market in general is headed for a turning point; others might simply want to cash their profits and put them to other uses. The stock sells off some, as it is inclined to do from time to time, and not many take notice of it.

Over the coming months, the stock continues this series of buyers taking control and then sellers taking control, and although the majority of owners continue holding their position, they are getting increasingly nervous each time the stock dips, because the stock seems to be running out of the proverbial gas, failing to move as robustly as it once did.

At some point, unknown to anyone at the time, the stock makes its final high price. The stock moves lower, and then higher again, but this time, it does something it hasn't done in years—it fails to get past its former high. It's not like a panic is taking place—far from it, because the stock is still near the highest price it has ever achieved—but it has stopped short of pushing any higher, establishing its first lower high. A trend change has taken place.

Now as the stock resumes its oscillations downward and upward, the dips get deeper, the lifts don't get quite as high, and the pace of the decline starts to pick up. By this point, a chartist could see that the top is taking on a rounded shape. If she can determine a price that seems to represent support, then she might take note of it, because that is going to be the break point that marks when the stock is in danger of falling hard. In this case, let us suppose the support level is at $40.

One evening, the company makes its regular quarterly earnings announcement, and it's a little short of expectations. When the regular trading opens the next morning, the stock opens at $39.50 and spends the day falling, closing finally at $38.73. Owners are increasingly worried that a sea-change has taken place with their former high-flier, and selling intensifies, along with volume.

A few weeks later, the stock hits $34 and begins attracting buying interest. It takes several weeks, but the stock makes its way past $35, $36, $37, and finally reaches $39.50, thanks to a series of analysts reissuing their "Buy!" recommendations on the security.

Unfortunately for those long the position, this is as far as the price will get, because the mass of owners who bought above $39.50 just want to get out of this stock, so the overhead supply overwhelms any further attempts to push the stock higher.

Selling begins anew, and as people realize their losses on the stock are probably only going to get worse, more and more of them sell out of their position. Now the stock begins a swan dive, plunging quickly past the recent low of $34 and not finding any real support until $25. The slow and subtle shift that took place with the rounded top has finally expressed itself in a plunge, and the event is over.

EXAMPLES

The following are some examples of this very important topping pattern.

Marinemax, Inc.

Beginning in 2004, Marinemax experienced a substantial and sustained rally that lifted it to a price that would approximate its lifetime high (see Figure 20.2). It sold off and, after a V-shaped bottom, rallied again to a price just a little higher than the prior high. It sold off again—harder, this time—and enjoyed another rally that took a little longer than before but also carried the price a little higher. So in this case, the stock experienced three slightly higher highs, each of which would be nicely enveloped by the oval that has been drawn on the chart.

When the selling began, it was strong enough to take the stock to a lower low compared to its prior low, and even on the recovery the stock was not able to get back up to the boundary of the displayed oval. The deterioration in price after this point was steady and, although not violent, it was unrelenting. After years of consolidating in this range of high prices, it broke support at $18 and pierced the boundary of the oval. There was a modest recovery at this point that, as we would expect, pushed the price just to the underside of the violated pattern (that is, the oval), and then the price commenced a waterfall decline that erased 93 percent of its value when the break took place.

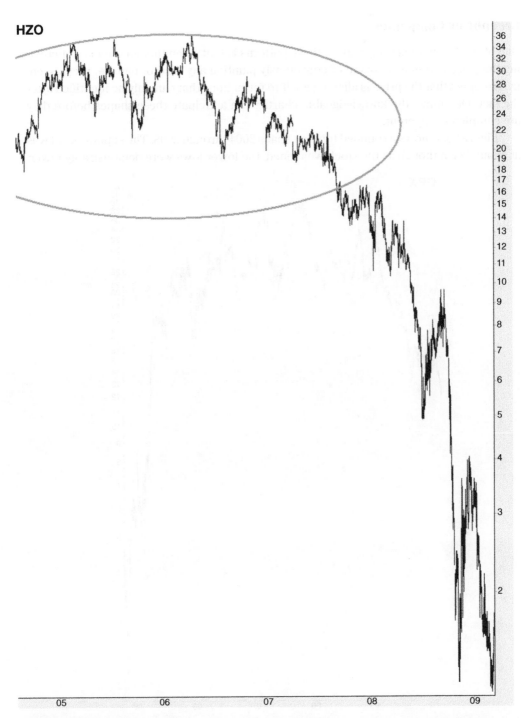

FIGURE 20.2 The lower highs on this security were much lower than the defining oval since the selling was so strong in late 2006 and early 2007.

Pattern Start: 11/2004   Price at Break: $18   Percentage Change: −93%

Pattern Break: 8/2007   Postbreak Price: $1.19

Greenbrier Companies

One of the fascinating things about these patterns is that, even though the market creating the price action is unaware of consciously painting any kind of pattern, it can seem in retrospect that the price is aligning itself to formations that can only be identified after the fact. Of course, the knowledgeable chartist can anticipate these shapes before they are completely apparent.

Figure 20.3 shows a rounded top that spans 2004 through 2008. The support level was at about $24, although as the stock weakened, the lower lows were demonstrably lower.

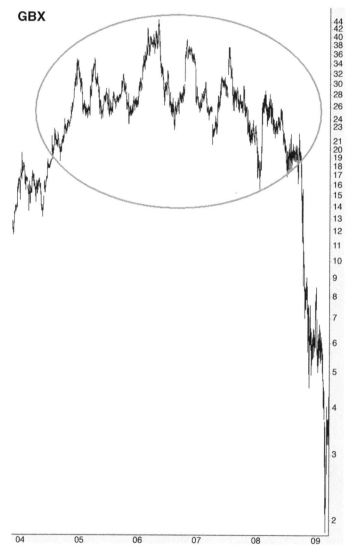

FIGURE 20.3 One interesting thing about this rounded top is that the oval that defines it also nicely captures its first drop and the resistance before its final plunge commenced.

Pattern Start: 10/2004   Price at Break: $23   Percentage Change: −92%
Pattern Break: 6/2008   Postbreakout Price: $1.86

The last lower low, at about $16, touched the inside of the oval perfectly, and something very interesting happened next: The stock rallied to nearly $30 (but did not break the trend of lower highs) and then, when it sold off again, it stalled at the inside of the oval again (which was, by definition, higher in price).

To someone simply looking at the price chart, it would seem that the stock had changed course, since it had stopped falling at a point reasonably higher than the prior low. To a person tracking this formation by means of an oval (which is the most convenient tool for tracking a rounded top), they would recognize that the price was simply hanging onto support within this oval, and a price fissure beneath this level would crack the price like the egg that seemed to be containing it.

And that is precisely what happened. The stock snapped beneath the boundary and began plunging with ferocious speed. Although it briefly consolidated between $5 and $8, forming a flag (a different pattern covered elsewhere in this book), it resumed its plunge to beneath $2. It should be noted that this drop was also interesting for those learning about the flag pattern, since the left flagpole and the right flagpole were well matched.

Abercrombie & Fitch Company

The clothes retailer Abercrombie & Fitch (symbol ANF) illustrates an almost perfect rounded top with a very clean support level at $64 (see Figure 20.4). On the left side of the oval, you can see three higher highs, and on the right half, three similar points resembling a mirror image. Indeed, you could fold this chart in half at about September 2007 and see the astonishing symmetry between the rise and the fall.

The comparison ends there, however, because stocks often fall much faster than they rise. Although it is not drawn here, take note of the firm support at about the $64 level. There were four different times that the chart challenged this level, but when it finally broke, it broke hard and lost over $14 within just a few sessions. The buyers mounted a counterattack and, just as swiftly, pushed the stock back to almost precisely the same level that had formerly served as support.

The huge mass of buyers who had accumulated the stock between $64 and $80 were by this point eager to get out, and the sudden recovery from its initial plunge was welcomed by a barrage of sell orders, sending the stock into an almost vertical fall. By the time the stock had bottomed, it was worth one-fifth of its price at the break-point.

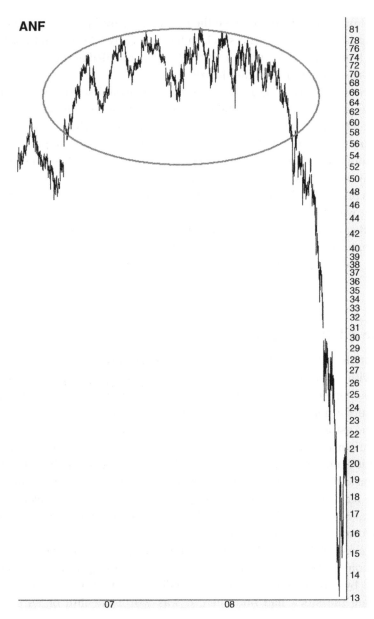

FIGURE 20.4 The support level illustrated here was at about $62.

Pattern Start: 9/2006   Price at Break: $64   Percentage Change: −80%
Pattern Break: 6/2008   Postbreakout Price: $13

Atlas Pipeline Partners

Let us look at an example where the supporting line has been drawn. Figure 20.5 shows that the $30 price level was the support level for Atlas Pipeline Partners (symbol APL)

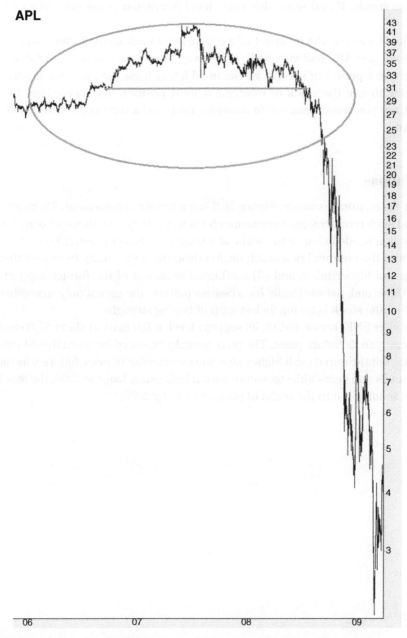

FIGURE 20.5 Not all rounded tops have a retracement, as is evident here.

Pattern Start: 10/2006   Price at Break: $30   Percentage Change: −93%
Pattern Break: 7/2008   Postbreakout Price: $2.15

for nearly two years. The shape of this chart doesn't adhere to any other specific topping pattern, such as a head and shoulders, but it does conform nicely to the oval drawn. For a person watching this chart, there are only two things to note: (1) that the pattern of higher highs and then lower highs remains intact, and (2) that the supporting price level is steady. If and when that price level is violated is the time when action is required.

As with any pattern, the prospect of a retracement back to the former support level is not assured, and APL had very little in the way of a retracement once $30 was broken. There was a period of several weeks in which at least the price fell gradually, so those seeking to exit the stock or establish a short position had ample time to do so, but the pattern you sometimes see of a sudden drop and a dramatic retracement didn't happen here.

Sonic Solutions

In contrast to the prior example, Figure 20.6 has a terrific retracement. There are three reasons that such retracements have so much value: (1) they give those who are long the position a much-needed chance to escape at a somewhat better price, (2) they give bears who recognize the potential of a much farther drop the opportunity to reduce their risk by shorting at a higher price, and (3) it affirms the import of the former support (now resistance) level and, paradoxically for a bearish pattern, the ascent only strengthens the argument that the stock is taking its last gasp of buying strength.

We see after SNIC broke $12.18, its support level, it fell hard to about $7.50 and then rallied precisely to its failure point. The price actually bounced between this $4 range for many weeks, but the initial push higher after the *shock event* of price failure was the best chance for bulls and bears alike to secure such a high price. Later in 2008, the stock sold off terribly, sending it into the realm of penny stocks by 2009.

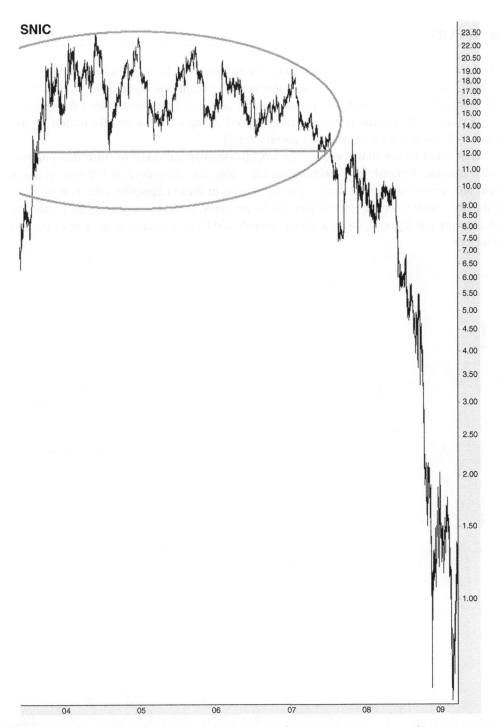

FIGURE 20.6 This stock retraced very nicely after its first drop, creating a marvelous opportunity for short sellers or those who didn't get out in the first place.

Pattern Start: 8/2003   Price at Break: $12.18   Percentage Change: −95%
Pattern Break: 7/2007   Postbreakout Price: $0.57

SUMMARY

All of the examples in this chapter were drawn from the bear market from late 2007 through early 2009. The reason is that the market conditions leading up to 2007 were so strong (although wavering in the summer of 2007) and the conditions following the peak gradually deteriorated into an unmitigated collapse. Thus, the formation of the domes—the rounded tops—was just about perfect.

This is not to say that it requires a worldwide financial crisis to form this pattern. Under normal circumstances, formations this clean are infrequent, but if you do see a chart shape resembling the domes you have seen in these examples, take careful note of the horizontal price support so you can be prepared to exploit a potentially profitable trading opportunity; and, if you are long, you should be prepared to make a graceful and rapid exit.

CHAPTER 21

Support Failure

The topic of support failure covers not so much a specific pattern as an event that can take various forms. The general idea is that a stock has, for a certain amount of time, respected a given price level as support. That is, the stock has remained above this level (which may be a specific price or a drawn object on the chart) until, for whatever reason, it breaks beneath this level.

Support failure is a signal to the bulls to get out of their position and a signal to the bears to short the stock or, alternately, buy puts on it.

DEFINITION OF THE PATTERN

There are a couple of general categories of support failure that will be covered in this chapter, and they are different in their appearance but similar in their behavior.

The first is price failure, an example of which is shown in Figure 21.1. Price failure is an instance in which a certain absolute dollar price or a fairly narrow price range has been respected for some length of time as a level under which the stock will not fall. It represents, by definition, a state of equilibrium between buyers and sellers—a stalemate, if you will—at which buyers eventually have regained control.

With the Dow Jones Utility Index example, there was strong support between 330 and 350 on the index. It spent five years above this level, getting as high as about 575, and each time the index sold off, it respected this price range as support. Early in 2008, there was a lot of trading within the price range, and the rally after this point was more subdued than those of the past.

Finally, in the middle of 2008, the index fell under 330 and lost over one-third of its value before the year was over. What's more interesting is that, even after this big fall, the index climbed all the way back up to just beneath its former support range. Sometimes

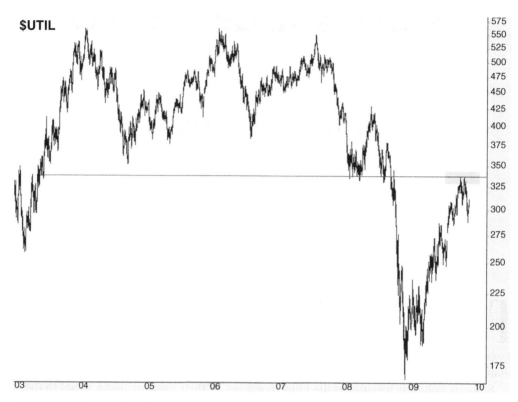

FIGURE 21.1   The highlighted portion shows where the utility index hit resistance.

a price failure will result in a rapid retracement soon after the initial drop; other times, like this one, it will complete its fall before performing the retrace; and at other times, no retracement will be seen at all.

The other style of price failure is a trendline break. Unlike the failure of a specific dollar price, this event occurs when the price has used an ascending trendline for support, bouncing off and above it at least twice before, but then breaks the line. As with price failure, a trendline failure might yield a rapid retracement, a deep fall followed by a retracement, or no retracement whatever. We will examine some trendline breaks further on in this chapter.

PSYCHOLOGY BEHIND THE PATTERN

In the case of a price failure, the psychology is fairly easy to understand. The mass of buyers and sellers will have, over time, silently established an agreed-upon price in which they reach a stalemate. The sellers are no longer able to create sufficient downward pressure on the stock, because that price level—for whatever reason—offers enough value to prospective buyers that they are willing to acquire shares at that level. The more instances in which this support level is reached, the more buyers accumulate at that level.

You could think of this in terms of the average price at which the entire population of buyers purchased a stock. Suppose a stock keeps falling to $30 and stays there for about a week while many trades are executed at that level. The more times trades are executed at $30, the closer the average price gets to $30, and the greater the number of individual holders who have bought the stock at $30. Psychologically, that level is going to represent the difference between a profit and a loss for these buyers.

Since the price keeps bouncing higher, most of these buyers become accustomed to enjoying a profitable position on the stock, and they will find the idea of seeing a profit turn into a loss increasingly distasteful. Some portion of them will set stop-loss orders at levels just beneath $30 to minimize their chances of suffering a meaningful loss.

Therefore, if support at $30 is violated, those stop-loss orders are going to get executed, creating more selling pressure. Others, of their own free will, will decide to execute sell orders at the market price. Even if the price dips to $29 and then starts fighting its way higher, there is going to be a wall of owners at $30 that wants to get out with as small a loss as possible. Greed has already swapped places with fear, and the overhead supply is going to be large.

A trendline break is harder to explain, because it isn't as straightforward as a specific price or price range. Only a portion of the traders is going to be following the trendline. By definition, though, a trendline shows a certain momentum, direction, and strength to a stock's price movement, and when any of those properties are weakened by more selling than has taken place in recent history, then the stock is likely to change to a downtrend. A trendline break is a relatively early indicator of this change.

EXAMPLES

The successful identification of support failure can create some excellent shorting opportunities. Here are some examples to help light the way.

Diodes, Inc.

Figure 21.2 shows a security with solid support at $22. It held this level for years, although it was violated in very tiny ways on four different occasions. When you encounter a stock that has pierced its support by a few pennies and then jumps back above support, you can either adjust the support level slightly lower to accommodate this violation or simply accept these exceptions as brief but meaningless events.

The fourth of these rapid price explorations beneath support brought the stock to $19.50, but as in the past, this dip was reversed the same day. The important thing about this brief dip is that violating that low, $19.50, signaled that a much larger price drop was

DIOD

FIGURE 21.2 Even long after the stock had bottomed, the former support level was attained. After this much time, the trading opportunity had probably passed.

Pattern Start: 12/2005   Price at Break: $22   Percentage Change: −86%
Pattern Break: 9/2008   Postbreakout Price: $3

finally ready to take place. During this final break, the stock lost a staggering 86 percent from the $22 support level and, many months later, climbed back to the exact same $22 level that had been its support before. It is doubtless there were buyers at $22 who were relieved (and perhaps more than a bit surprised) to have another opportunity to get out at such a small loss after they had seen their stock get so brutally crushed.

Allied Capital Corporation

For those who like to short stocks, the chart in Figure 21.3 is a thing of beauty. This is the kind of event that is as close to free money as bears will ever encounter, since the stock has very solid support, falls beneath it, and then quickly retraces to the exact same level.

The way to benefit from a chart in real time is clear. If you are monitoring such a stock, and you want to keep your risk to a minimum, you can simply wait for a solid retracement. This retracement may or may not happen. If it doesn't, you simply don't take the trade, and if it keeps falling, it is just another missed opportunity that is inevitable in one's trading career.

If it does retrace, then you short as much as you comfortably can, placing the stop-loss a small amount above the entry price (perhaps 1 percent above, for example). The amount of overhead supply and fear that is going to exist in such a formation is going to be on the side of the short-sellers, and it would take an extraordinary amount of buying strength, or some bullish exogenous event, to put the bulls back in power. No such fate awaited the bears, however, as they prospered from a 95 percent drop in price after the retracement finished.

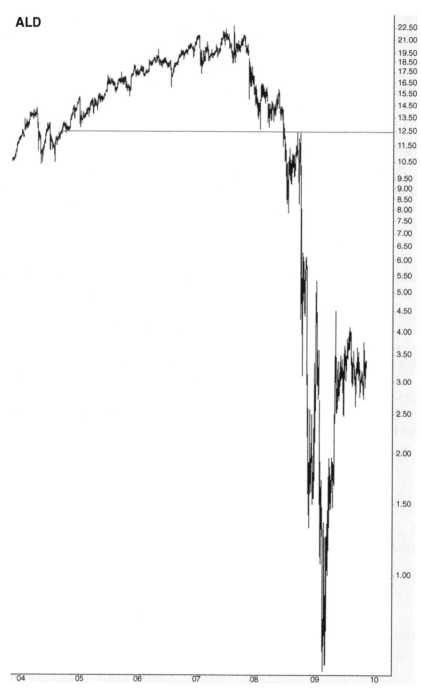

FIGURE 21.3 This is about as perfect a retracement opportunity as you will ever see.

Pattern Start: 10/2004   Price at Break: $12   Percentage Change: −95%
Pattern Break: 6/2008   Postbreakout Price: $0.58

American International Group, Inc.

The support price of $684 of this next example, Figure 21.4, might seem surprisingly high, but it is only because the stock fell so much that it went through a reverse split. If you ever need proof that a stock has no obligation to retrace, then AIG should do the trick. The stock gapped down on May 9, 2008. Virtually every trading day between then and July 15, the closing price was lower than the opening price, and by then it had already lost about half its value.

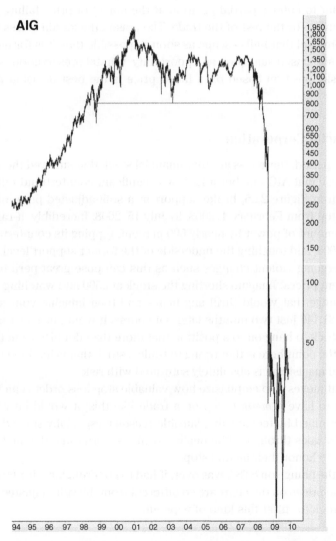

FIGURE 21.4 Once support was violated, there was absolutely no pause in AIG's plunge.

Pattern Start: 11/1998   Price at Break: $684   Percentage Change: −99%
Pattern Break: 5/2008   Postbreakout Price: $5.53

This is an uncommon example, of course, because AIG was at the epicenter of a financial earthquake unlike any the world had ever seen. However, there are certainly ample examples of a stock whose selling pressure is so intense that it never has a chance to retrace.

There is a lesson here for bulls and bears alike. For bulls, it emphasizes that broken support should be the one and only signal you need to get out of a position. There's no sense waiting and hoping that the stock will retrace, because the price just beneath support is in all likelihood the best price you're going to get for many years to come.

For bears the lesson is similar, but not quite as important. Those looking to short a security may want to enter a partial position at the outset of price failure and await a possible retracement for the rest of the trade. The reason the lesson is less important is because it is more vital that bulls escape as soon as possible than it is for bears to maximize their trade size based simply on an opportunity. Capital preservation is paramount, and exiting a risky position based on a failed price is the best decision in almost all such cases.

Sterling Financial Corporation

During the same period, there was another financial stock that suffered the same 99 percent price collapse that AIG did, but it had two significant countertrend rallies. Sterling Financial, shown in Figure 21.5, broke support at a split-adjusted price of $1,271 and fell almost nonstop from February 4, 2008, to July 15, 2008. Incredibly, it rallied with almost the same amount of power by nearly 500 percent, topping its countertrend rally on September 19, 2008, and touching the underside of the former support level.

Stocks undergoing violent changes such as this can pose great peril to those who enter at imprudent prices. Imagine shorting the stock at $500 and watching it go to $150 per share—a plunge that would thrill any bear—and then imagine your shock as the stock soared to $1,146 just two months later. Of course, it would be sheer insanity for a person short a stock to hang on to a position that more than doubles from their original entry price, but the point here is that trying to trade a stock that is lurching up and down during a financial maelstrom is absolutely saturated with risk.

These violent moves also emphasize how valuable stop-loss orders can be. A person would not want to have a *mental stop* on a trade like this; it would be wiser to set a stop that is determined by technically plausible reasons, especially since the emotional gyrations a trader goes through while dealing with a security like this might overcome his or her ability to honor their mental stop.

By the time the plunge on STSA was over, it had to go through a 1-for-66 reverse split (which is why the prices on the chart are so different from the split-adjusted prices). It is very rare for a stock to suffer this kind of wipeout.

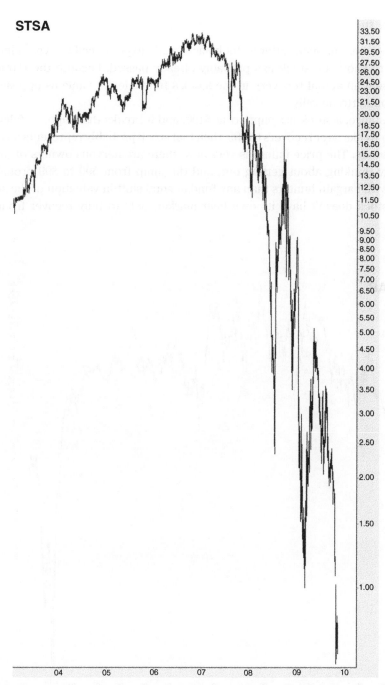

FIGURE 21.5 The extreme nature of this retracement is nothing short of startling.

Pattern Start: 5/2004   Price at Break: $1,271   Percentage Change: −99%

Pattern Break: 10/2007   Postbreakout Price: $15

Photronics, Inc.

When a retracement happens after a stock has already experienced a severe plunge, the opportunity to short the stock has probably already passed, because the retracement might represent an actual recovery in the stock's fundamental value as opposed to an emotional countertrend rally.

If, for instance, a stock has support at $100, and it breaks that support, falls to $90, and then two weeks later recovers to $99, then that stock probably represents an exciting short opportunity. The price failure is very new, there are nervous owners of the stock still seriously thinking about getting out, and the jump from $90 to $99 probably has more to do with bargain hunters than any fundamental shift in valuation of the security. After all, a stock doesn't have its own bear market, only to fully recover from it two weeks later.

FIGURE 21.6 The overhead resistance of this stock guaranteed that it would be years, or even decades, before the stock would be able to reach its former glory.

Pattern Start: 10/1994   Price at Break: $7.19   Percentage Change: −95%
Pattern Break: 6/2008   Postbreakout Price: $0.33

Take the illustration of Figure 21.6, for instance. The stock lost 95 percent of its value almost without interruption, and it retraced most of that fall, but it took it over a year to do so. A year is far much time to consider something a shortable retracement. The public has had a huge amount of time to digest the news surrounding the stock, and although the former support level surely represents an important threshold of resistance for years to come, the stock is unlikely to suddenly lurch downward when it gets near resistance.

Indeed, this stock went on to meander even higher, completely retracing the drop by December 2010. A person shorting this stock at about $5 based merely on the fact that the stock had retraced from a very bad fall would have found themselves terribly frustrated, since the stock continued an awkward climb to prices 40 percent above the entry level.

The lesson here is that it is imprudent to try to take advantage of a retracement that is more than a few months older than the initial breakdown. You want to be taking advantage of the market's emotional bounce-back—which takes only weeks or a few months—and not take the risk of a stock actually mending itself on a sustained basis, which it can do with a lengthy price recovery.

Dynegy, Inc.

If you are watching a stock's support level, and it drops beneath support, should you short it at once? And what happens if it simply goes back above resistance? Do you cover the short immediately?

These are trading decisions only you can make, but one thing is certain—just because a stock drops beneath support doesn't guarantee it won't rise above it. A stock price can tease bears repeatedly by dropping below, and then rising above, support. If it does this too much, you might want to lower the support line you are using since the noise happening around your current support line suggests that perhaps true support is a little lower.

Figure 21.7 provides an example of a stock that fell below support and, within just two sessions, was back above it. It would be a big mistake to hold on to the short, thinking that the violation of support doomed the security to a rapid fall. Indeed, DYN rallied about 45 percent after the support failure of September 27, 2001.

The wiser action is to set a stop-loss order at a price above which you believe the short no longer makes sense. Whether that is 3 percent, 5 percent, or some other figure is up to you (although it probably is well less than 10 percent, since you don't want to expose yourself to too much risk). With a stop-loss, a trader would not have been in the DYN position for more than a day or two before getting stopped out, and they could have watched the 45 percent price climb without being harmed any more by it.

The interesting follow-up to this is that on November 30 of the same year, DYN fell below the $160 level again (the y-axis of this example is different due to a large reverse split later on). This time, it was not a fake-out. About four months later, the stock had fallen and retraced to the same horizontal line, and then it was time for a collapse in price.

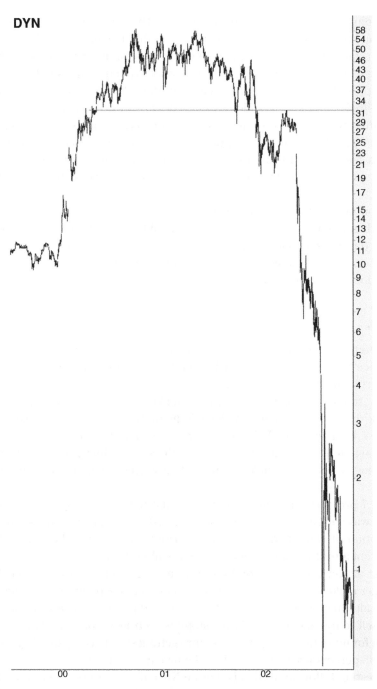

FIGURE 21.7 There was an extremely short-lived false break well before the true break, but a trader with a prudent stop-loss would not have been in that trade for more than a few days.

Pattern Start: 5/2000   Price at Break: $160   Percentage Change: −97%
Pattern Break: 11/2001   Postbreakout Price: $5

Honeywell International, Inc.

Stocks, like people, have personalities, and the price action helps articulate a stock's personality over the long haul. Sometimes this personality can express itself in fascinating ways, such as a stock that falls and rises in similar ways. Stock can sometimes offer mirror images of their price action during times when they are either bullish or bearish.

The next two examples, Figures 21.8 and 21.9, are excellent examples of this unusual phenomenon. The defining parameters behind most stock patterns—support and resistance—is the reason for this, because the tug-of-war between bulls and bears can cause a top to form in much the same way as a bottom forms.

Honeywell, which is in Figure 21.8, had support at about $50. When it violated this level, it didn't plunge but instead grasped tightly to the $50 level, like iron fillings to a magnet. The stock did not seem to want to fall from that price, and over a period of nearly three months, it confined itself almost exclusively to a price range of $46 to $50. It is rather unusual to see an otherwise dynamic stock lock itself into such a tight range for such a long period of time.

At last the price drop came, and it fell from $50 to $22, a loss of 56 percent. What's interesting here is that the stock had experienced a multiple top pattern, defined by four major high prices of about $60, followed much later by a double-bottom pattern. And, just as $50 had represented support before, now $35.50 offered a resistance area.

Just as the stock did not suddenly collapse when it pushed below $50, it didn't soar higher when it pushed above $35.50. Instead it clung to the vicinity of the resistance line, and when it finally did break free after February 2010, it moved on to much, much higher prices.

The takeaway from this example is that Honeywell's behavior had similarities in both directions. While anthropomorphizing a stock can be hazardous, the fact is that there are human beings behind a stock's price, and the way the collective consciousness of those humans acts with a certain stock can express itself in similar ways whether it is moving up or down. Trading a small number of stocks actively can educate you about the personalities of these securities, providing insight as to which securities you get along with and which of them are at odds with your own trading personality.

HON

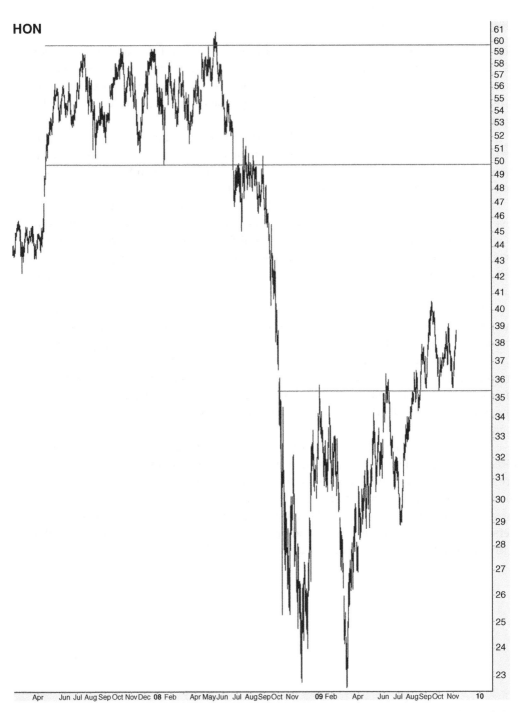

FIGURE 21.8 Here we see a stock with both a bearish pattern—support failure—and a bullish pattern—overcoming resistance.

Pattern Start: 4/2007   Price at Break: $50   Percentage Change: −56%
Pattern Break: 6/2008   Postbreakout Price: $22

Atlas Pipeline Partners

An experience similar to Honeywell's is shown in Figure 21.9, the 90 percent loss for Atlas Pipeline and its subsequent recovery. The stock's support at $31 was violated, and then the stock fell very hard, pausing late in 2008 but completing its plunge in early 2009. It then formed an inverted head and shoulders pattern, the majority of which is shown in this chart, and proceeded to climb almost all the way back to its failure level.

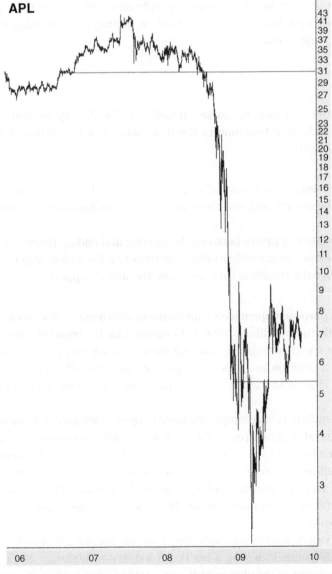

FIGURE 21.9 This is another example of a stock whose price was completely brushed that managed to form a bullish pattern afterward.

Pattern Start: 10/2006   Price at Break: $31   Percentage Change: −90%
Pattern Break: 7/2008   Postbreakout Price: $3

One reason this kind of thing can happen is that the free fall that took place offers very little in the way of resistance on the way back up. In other words, there are virtually no owners of the stock at the prices bounded by the free fall. In the case of APL, the fall from $31 to $3 was very rapid, and there were very few clusters of trading activity to create zones of resistance when the stock was trying to trade higher.

In addition, for an event this dramatic, the reasons behind the fall have much more to do with panic than reality. The final stages of the plunge in late 2008 and early 2009 represented a lot of panic selling, and once people had time to assess the plausible values for these securities, they were comfortable acquiring them at what they correctly recognized were bargain prices.

Aflac, Inc.

We direct our attention now to broken trendlines. To identify broken trendlines, of course, one has to have a trendline in the first place. The properties of a well-drawn trendline are as follows:

- It connects at least two points of a graph (because this is a supporting trendline, these would be low prices), and the more points it touches, the more valid and useful the line is.
- It is never violated by prices between the starting and ending points. In other words, all of the stock prices are either below the trendline (in which case the line is resistance) or above the trendline (in which case the line is support).

A trendline's purpose depends on your position with a particular stock. If you have a position in a stock, the trendline's value is to ensure that the trend of the stock is intact, so that when the trend is violated, you exit your position as profitably as possible. If you do not have a position in a stock, the purpose of a trendline is to show you when a possible trend change has taken place so that you can consider taking a position in the stock.

Drawing a trendline is very simple for most people, since laying down a straight line to bound the uptrend or downtrend of a stock makes intuitive sense. The art, however, is discerning when to redraw a trendline. As a stock moves, it may become appropriate to redraw a trendline to take into account the more complete price data. The danger, of course, is that you can wind up fooling yourself. If your trendlines become so elastic that they bend and move no matter what direction prices are heading, then you have eliminated their value.

When prices violate a trendline, however, it should normally be heeded. To illustrate this point, imagine yourself driving a car down a deserted highway. Since you want to understand the concept of trendlines well, you decide to not look at the road ahead but simply open your door and keep your eye on the median line. You have no idea how the road will twist or turn—or whether it will continue to be straight.

For a while, the yellow line whizzes by more or less in the same place. It sometimes moves a little away from the car, but it soon returns to be just outside the driver's door. Suddenly, the median line moves underneath your car, disappearing from sight. You'd better look up quick to see what's happening, because the road must be turning!

That's sort of what trendlines are like (although not nearly as dangerous—at least in the physical sense). They provide a line that prices should stay above (if the line is support) or below (if resistance), and if prices should stray across the trendline, something has changed. As with your car, it doesn't necessarily mean a crash is ahead, but you'd better start paying better attention.

The insurance company Aflac, Figure 21.10, enjoyed the benefit of a supporting trendline for over eight years. Because this trendline was so well established, it was also terribly important. Because the trendline was broken, the stock soared one last time, nearly making a new lifetime high before cutting through the trendline on October 3, 2008. The longevity of the trendline made this violation a serious one, and the stock dropped 80 percent in the midst of a broad sell-off for all financial securities.

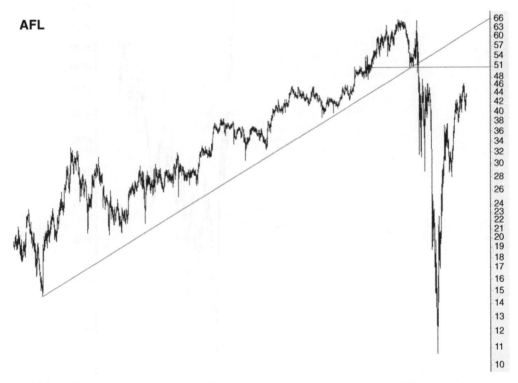

FIGURE 21.10 The trendline break here followed a final attempt at a new lifetime high.

Pattern Start: 3/2000   Price at Break: $49   Percentage Change: −80%
Pattern Break: 10/2008   Postbreakout Price: $10

Abercrombie & Fitch Company

As with other patterns, a trendline break can sometimes produce a retracement. One of the cleanest of these in modern stock market history was offered by the fashion retailer Abercrombie & Fitch (see Figure 21.11). The stock broke its trendline on June 26, 2008,

FIGURE 21.11   The retracement to the broken trendline shown here is superb.

Pattern Start: 9/2006   Price at Break: $62   Percentage Change: −79%
Pattern Break: 6/2008   Postbreakout Price: $13

lost 23 percent of its value, then rebounded absolutely perfectly and to the penny to the underside of its trendline. This area is circled in the figure for emphasis.

It is extremely unusual to see a break-and-retrace that is this clean, but if you do, you should consider yourself the recipient of a potentially thrilling trading opportunity. A retracement at this level has a mountain of overhead supply that is going to collar the price at that level, and the broken trendline is a stock signal that the stock is heading lower. And lower it did head, cutting 79 percent off its price after the break-point.

Broker Dealer Index

Trendlines are every bit as useful and valid on indexes as they are on any other financial instrument. Indexes also have much longer histories than most stocks, providing the opportunity to lay down much longer-term, and thus more potent, trendlines.

The broker-dealer index, symbol $XBD, is shown in Figure 21.12 with a thirteen-year-long trendline. This trendline survived the bear market of late 1999, the even larger bear market of 2001–2002, and all the ups-and-downs in between. What it didn't survive, however, is the financial crisis, and it broke the $200 level in January 2008, eight months before the extreme selling of the crisis took hold. This would have served as a superb warning signal for the market in general, and for financial stocks in particular.

FIGURE 21.12 The longer the trendline, the more potent the failure.

Pattern Start: 12/1994   Price at Break: $200   Percentage Change: −75%
Pattern Break: 1/2008   Postbreakout Price: $50

Morgan Stanley High Tech Index

Our next example of a trendline violation is via another index, the Morgan Stanley High Tech Index (symbol $MSH), captured in Figure 21.13. The trendline here is over five years long, and it was ruptured in January 2008.

The most important thing to note about this chart is that the price retraced to the underside of its trendline, and unlike price failure, a retracement on a trendline can acquire a price *higher than the original break-point*. The trendline, by definition, is going higher. Therefore, if a stock cuts beneath that trendline and then, over a period of months, climbs its way back up to the underside of that same trendline, the price can absolutely be higher than it was when it first broke down.

In this case, the price failed on January 4, 2008, at about $587. It fell through March 17, and then it climbed through May 19, reaching a high of $622, a level about 6 percent higher than when the trendline failed. Keep this in mind when selling short based on a broken trendline, because you may still be in a perfectly valid trade and suffer a loss. The price can creep along the underside of the trendline for as long as it likes, and your losses can continue to grow, even though there is still nothing technically wrong with your trade.

Of course, you wouldn't want to hold on to such a trade forever, particularly if a new lifetime high was reached. Those trading $MSH—perhaps by way of put options—didn't have to face that difficult circumstance, since the index resumed its fall after May 19, stopping only after the price was less than half its level from the trendline break.

FIGURE 21.13 In this case, the price pushed back to the underside of the failed trendline.

Pattern Start: 10/2002   Price at Break: $588   Percentage Change: −52%
Pattern Break: 1/2008   Postbreakout Price: $283

SUMMARY

Placing trades based on support failure can be a great way to make money when markets are turning soft. Those who only profit from the market during uptrends are foreclosing themselves from profiting from the bear markets, which inevitably are going to happen every few years.

Between the two styles covered in this chapter, price failures are probably easier to track and trade, especially since the risk of holding on to a losing short is less when you have a specific price level to watch. However, both trendline breaks and price failures are potent allies for bearish trades, as long as the trendlines and horizontal price levels (respectively) are carefully rendered by the chartist.

CHAPTER 22

Automatic Patterns

T he basis of a large portion of technical analysis is pattern recognition—that is, the ability to spot one of the classic technical patterns (such as a wedge, a head-and-shoulders, a triple bottom, etc.) and estimate in what direction and by what amount the price is likely to move.

This book is all about recognizing patterns and applying them to your own trading, but getting some assistance in finding candidates based on a set of electronic eyes is a great time-saver. Pattern recognition is hard enough for humans, so it is especially hard for computers, since the subtleties of some patterns can produce a lot of false positives. However, an automatic way of seeking patterns can at least gather up good candidates for your own analysis. A few of the larger products on the Internet for this task are:

- **Recognia** (www.recognia.com): This Canadian-based outfit covers a huge universe of financial instruments—65,000 as of this writing—from all over the world. The product has been around for years, and its feature set and robustness are excellent. Recognia focuses on providing their services through brokerages, but individual subscriptions are available as well.
- **AutoChartist** (www.autochartist.com): This is a service that scans for patterns in real-time, including Fibonacci patterns. They have enhanced this to be an excellent tool for foreign exchange traders as well.
- **Thinkorswim** (https://www.thinkorswim.com/tos/client/index.jsp): The thinkorswim brokerage is the only one that provides ProphetCharts, and they charge nothing for access to the product. ProphetCharts includes Prophet Patterns, which is the built-in system for finding any of the most popular technical patterns on U.S. or Canadian stocks over the past five years.

Because it is my own creation, and I know it deeply, I'm going to discuss ProphetCharts. If you are using a brokerage other than thinkorswim but still want access to ProphetCharts, you can also get it from Investools (www.investools.com) by way of their Investor Toolbox product. Even if you have no plans to use ProphetCharts, scanning the contents of this chapter will give you an idea what an automated pattern recognition system is capable of doing to save you time in your own prospecting for opportunities.

PATTERNS IN PROPHETCHARTS

The Prophet historical price database automatically keeps track of patterns as they emerge. Getting to this information is simply a matter of establishing the parameters of your search so the qualifying symbols can be delivered to your copy of ProphetCharts.

The first thing you do is choose Find Patterns from the Patterns menu, as shown in Figure 22.1.

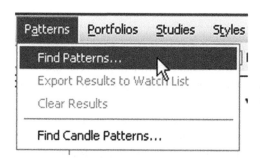

FIGURE 22.1 You can access up-to-date patterns results by clicking Find Patterns.

The Find Patterns dialog box comes up, and within that box there are five different tabs: General, Patterns, Ratings, Watch Lists, and Filters. You can choose any of these five tabs to fine-tune the nature of your pattern search. We will go through each of these tabs individually.

The first tab, General, is the one that shows up when you first bring up the Find Patterns dialog box (Figure 22.2). It has a variety of checkboxes, drop-down menus, and radio buttons. As with the vast majority of the choices available in Find Patterns, you don't have to make selections in every single one of these parameters. They are mostly there to give you the ability to customize your search.

The General tab has the following parameters:

- **Find Symbols with Patterns:** You need to check this box in order to activate the search function. As the description indicates, the resulting symbols will show up in the Patterns module.
- **Order Results By:** There is a dropdown menu here with eight different choices for you to establish the basis of sorting the results. The default, sorting by Symbol, is usually best.

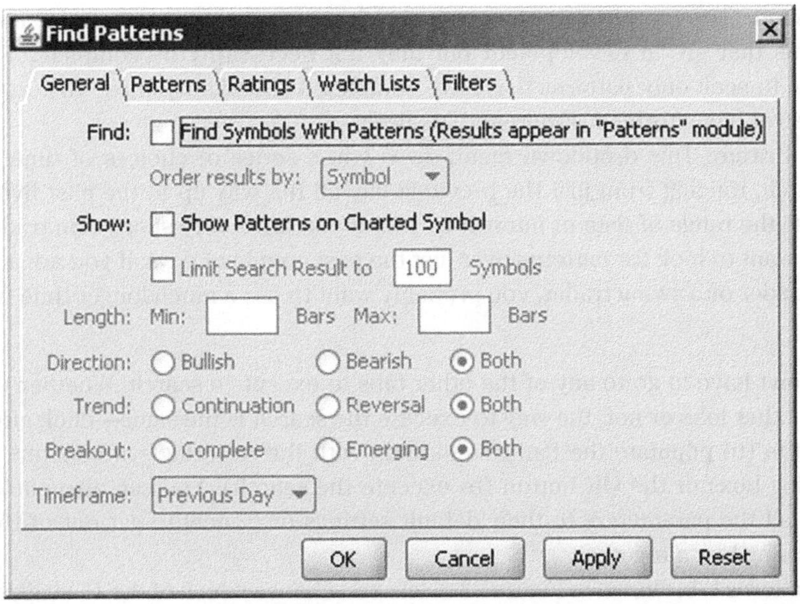

FIGURE 22.2 Of the five tabs, General has the most important parameters.

- **Show Patterns on Charted Symbol:** If you check this box, ProphetCharts will automatically draw the lines that constitute the basis for the symbols found. It is very likely you'll want to check this box, since the whole point of the pattern recognition engine is to see the patterns.
- **Limit Search Results:** You can restrict the quantity of symbols that are displayed here. If you enter a number that is smaller than the resulting list, the excess symbols will not be displayed.
- **Length:** There are two fields here—Min and Max—which let you state the number of price bars that will make up your search. For instance, if you were searching daily charts for patterns, and you wanted to see only patterns between 50 and 200 days in length, you would enter 50 in the Min box and 200 in the Max box. It is a pretty good idea to set a Min value, because the longer the price pattern, the stronger and more reliable it tends to be.
- **Direction:** Here are three radio buttons—Bullish, Bearish, and Both. You must choose one of these to state whether you want to seek bullish patterns, bearish patterns, or both.
- **Trend:** There are also three radio buttons here—Continuation, Reversal, and Both. Trend is an important distinction when seeking patterns. If you want to seek patterns that are echoing their general trend (for instance, if you want to seek bullish patterns that are in stocks that are already behaving bullishly), choose Continuation; if you are looking for changes in direction (such as bearish patterns in bullish stocks), choose Reversal; if it doesn't matter, choose Both.

- **Breakout:** The pattern recognition engine is always monitoring prices, including patterns that are in development but may not necessarily be complete. You can choose to seek only patterns that have completed (Breakout), those that are in the process of being formed (Emerging), or Both.
- **Time Frame:** This dropdown menu gives you a series of choices of time frames to search, ranging from just the previous day all the way up to the past five years. Choose the range of data of interest to you; if you are a very short-term trader, you might want to look for patterns over just the past couple of days; if you are a longer-term trader or a swing trader, you probably want to use a much longer time frame.

You don't have to go to any of the other tabs to execute a search. Whether you use any of the other tabs or not, the way to execute the search is the same—click either the Apply button (to populate the Patterns module with the resulting symbols but remain in the dialog box) or the OK button (to execute the search). You can also click Reset to change all the parameters to their default settings or Cancel to get out of the Find Patterns dialog box altogether.

The Patterns tab, shown in Figure 22.3, lets you choose which of the 16 available patterns you'd like to seek. You can choose anywhere from one to all 16 of the checkboxes; the Select All and Clear All buttons will save you time by checking all (or unchecking all) the boxes. If you are looking only for interesting patterns, you might as well leave all of them checked, but if you are honing in on a favorite (such as the inverse head-and-shoulders pattern), check only the specific patterns you want.

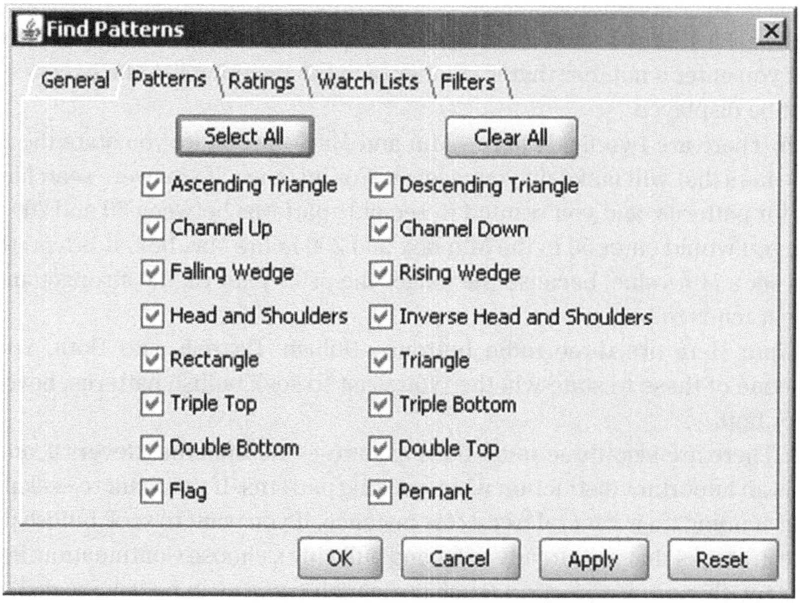

FIGURE 22.3 There are 16 patterns available in the recognition engine.

The third tab, Ratings (Figure 23.4), lets you establish a minimum and maximum value for the quality of patterns you are seeking. These figures range from 0 (lowest quality) to 5 (highest quality), and the default is 0 for minimum and 5 for maximum for all six parameters (which means nothing is filtered out).

The six parameters dictate how clean the patterns are in several respects—Overall is the general quality of the pattern; Initial Trend is how clean the price action was leading up to the pattern; Breakout Strength is how much power the price has when moving out of the pattern; Volume Increase is how strong the volume increase was during the breakout; Uniformity is how well-shaped the pattern is compared to the ideal; and Clarity indicates the confidence level that the price will move to the target.

Generally speaking, you should just leave these settings as they are, but if you'd like to tighten up the search to look for higher-quality patterns, you can change the Min value in the Overall parameter to 4 (or even 5), which will greatly limit the results.

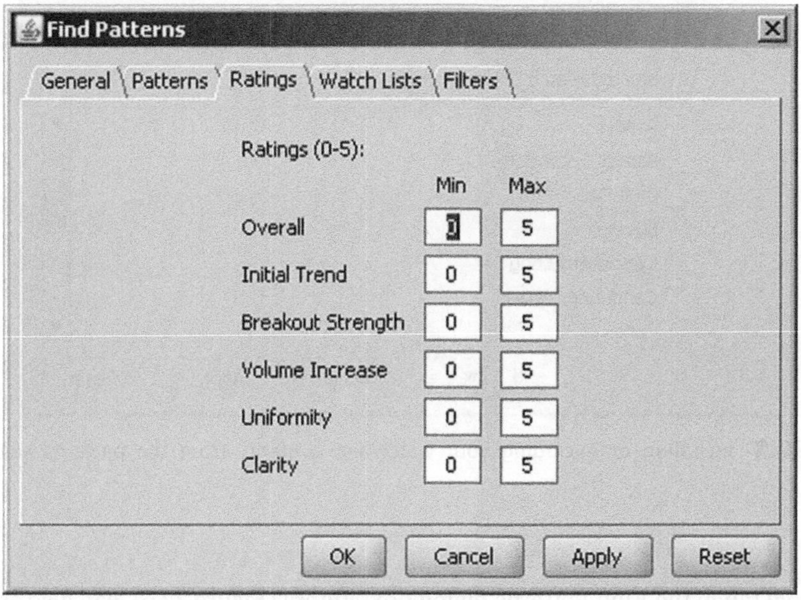

FIGURE 22.4 Most of the time, you probably will want to just leave the default settings.

The fourth tab, Watch Lists (Figure 22.5) is extremely helpful, because it lets you constrict a search to only the symbols found within or without your watch lists. For instance, if you want to seek only the patterns for symbols that you were already following, you would choose the radio button "In any of my Watch Lists" (you would also check the checkbox titled Limit Patterns). This way, *only* symbols that you already follow will be displayed in the resulting Patterns module.

You may instead want to seek symbols that aren't in any of your watch lists. After all, you are looking of new opportunities, so you might want to exclude those items you are already following. In this case, you would click the "Not in any of my Watch Lists" radio button.

You might even choose something not quite as stark as total inclusion or exclusion: Instead, you might want to include (or exclude) specific watch lists. In this case, you would click the third radio button, which also includes a dropdown menu, to seek symbols that are already in (or already not in) the watch lists that you specify by clicking the checkboxes beneath.

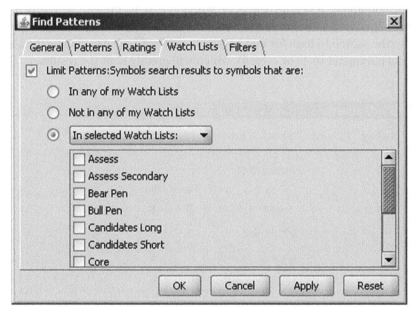

FIGURE 22.5 Including or excluding your watch list contents from the patterns search will save time.

The final tab in the Find Patterns dialog box, Filters (Figure 22.6), can also save you time by not bothering to show you symbols that you don't find interesting in the first place. It offers a number of parameters to refine the search:

- **Options Available:** If this box is checked, only stocks for which options are available will be presented. This is particularly valuable if you are an options trader, but even if you are not, it will at least focus the search on stocks that are widely traded enough to have options in the first place.
- **Average Volume:** You can set a Min and Max level for the average volume. The main benefit of this is to set a Min amount so that you are not looking at thinly traded stocks.

- **Start Price:** You can set a Min and Max for the price at the beginning of the pattern; this is probably not that important, since it is the ending price that is more crucial.
- **End Price:** If you want to avoid stocks that are out of a certain price range (for instance, stocks less than $5), you can set a Min and Max level for the ending price of a stock.
- **Exchange:** By default, this setting is All, but if for some reason you only want to find stocks that trade on the NYSE, American, or NASDAQ stock exchanges, you can choose the appropriate checkboxes here.

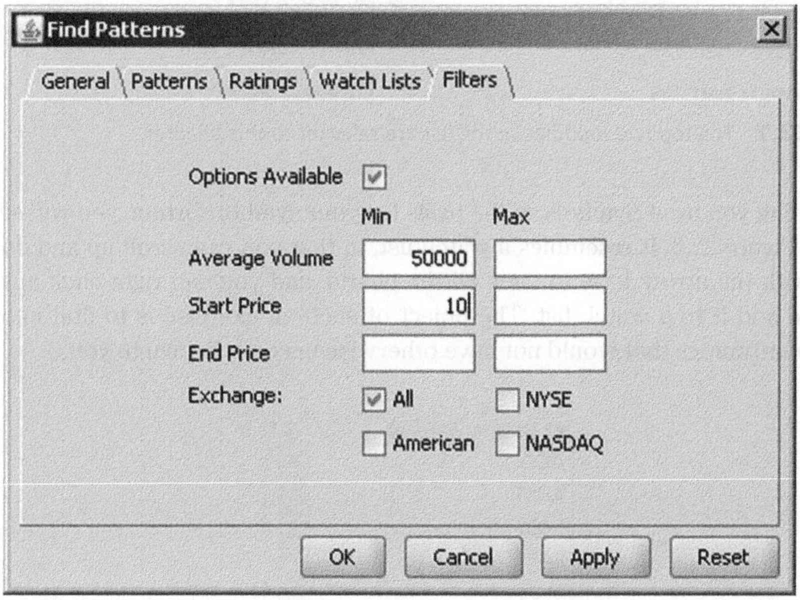

FIGURE 22.6 You should restrict your search to seek only the stocks that you would consider trading.

Doing a Pattern search is quick, easy, and intuitive. Most of the time, you'll probably only need to use a few of the parameters to construct the search you want. Once you're ready, just click OK.

WORKING WITH THE RESULTS

In order to see the symbols resulting from your search, you need to make sure the Patterns: Symbols module is turned on. Figure 22.7 shows the two relevant modules to this chapter, both at the top of the list. If there is a checkmark next to a module name, then that module is available to you.

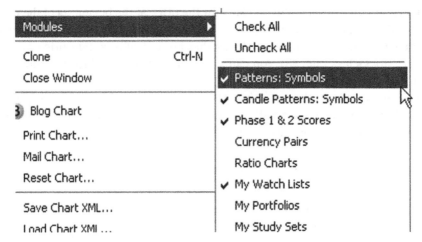

FIGURE 22.7   The top two modules in the list are relevant to this chapter.

Assuming you used Symbols as the basis for your symbol sorting, you will see a list similar to Figure 22.8. It resembles a watch list, in that you can scroll up and down the symbols with the arrow keys to view all the charts, and you can right-click any of the symbols to add it to a watch list. The object of such an exercise is to find interesting trading opportunities that would not have otherwise become known to you.

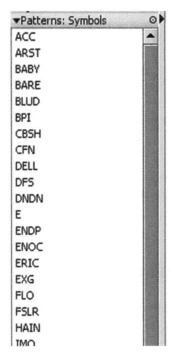

FIGURE 22.8   The symbols resulting from your patterns search are shown in this module.

When you begin looking at the symbols, you will see automatically-generated lines drawn on the charts (in addition to any drawn objects of your own). These lines represent all the patterns found for the time period you have specified. In many cases, you will see multiple patterns on the same stock, such as in Figure 22.9. If you mouse over any particular line, it will display an information box telling you the pattern that is found, its start and end date, and its anticipated target.

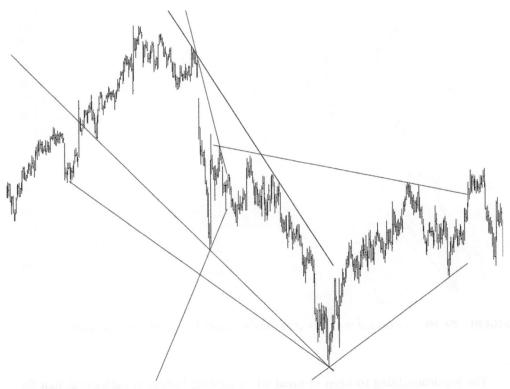

FIGURE 22.9 If you decide to use Show Patterns on Chart Symbol in the dialog box, you will see lines automatically drawn on your charts, showing any discovered patterns.

Something else interesting and useful happens when you mouse over a pattern line: A rectangle appears showing the target zone. If the target is bullish, the rectangle is tinted green; if the target is bearish, the rectangle is tinted red. The rectangle is placed on the chart appropriate for the target time range (which is the width of the rectangle) and the target price (which is the height). Figure 22.10 provides a bearish example.

FIGURE 22.10 The shaded rectangle shows the anticipated range of the price move.

The important thing to keep in mind when viewing historical patterns is that the completion of a pattern typically happens when the price crosses beneath the supporting trendline (for bearish patterns) or above the resisting trendline (for bullish patterns). Looking at Figure 22.11, for instance, the pattern was completed at a price of about $14.50 when the stock gapped down and pierced its lower trendline. At that time, the prediction system called for the stock to fall somewhere between $12.1188 and $13.3853 between the dates of 11/20/2009 and 2/7/2010. As you can see, the price did indeed fall within that date and price range, indicating that a successful prediction was made.

We've seen a couple of bearish examples—let's look at some bullish ones. Figure 22.12 shows a bullish projection (the rectangle), calling for a stock that was about $34 at the time of the signal to climb to above $40. Mousing over the pattern shows us the name of the pattern (Triangle), its direction (Bullish), its predicted price range, and its prediction period. Because some time has passed since the pattern was predicted,

Triangle. Bearish Pattern
Predicted Price Range: 12.1188...13.3853
Prediction Period:
From: 11/20/2009
To: 2/7/2010

FIGURE 22.11 This is an example of a successful bearish prediction.

we can see the result, which was that the prediction succeeded (just to be clear, some predictions succeed, and some do not; there is no such thing as a 100 percent reliable system).

Of course, even when a price moves into its prediction rectangle, there is no reason it will not keep going in the same direction. Figure 22.13 illustrates that the price kept moving up after the time range of the rectangle. If you were making use of this prediction in a real trade, you would probably want to seriously consider closing the position once the price entered the rectangle. After all, anything inside the rectangle is considered a success, and there is no guarantee that the price will move into the upper boundary of the projected price movement (indeed, there is no guarantee that the rectangle will be penetrated by the prices at all).

The pattern search engine isn't meant to be a substitute for your own thoughtful analysis; it is intended primarily as a source of ideas that you might not have had without access to this tool.

Triangle. Bullish Pattern
Predicted Price Range: 40.3016...47.4579
Prediction Period:
From: 7/22/2009
To: 5/12/2010

FIGURE 22.12   Here is an example of a successful bullish prediction.

Triangle. Bullish Pattern
Predicted Price Range: 21.7373...34.2709
Prediction Period:
From: 2/5/2009
To: 7/16/2009

FIGURE 22.13 There is no reason prices cannot move above their bullish projections or below their bearish ones.

PATTERN FAILURES

It's important to understand that plenty of patterns are not realized. Stocks that are pro-jected to have bullish moves might plunge in value, and bearish projections might instead be faced with a soaring stock price. So, again, the results from a patterns search should be viewed as nothing more than a list of symbols to chart and consider on your own.

Figure 22.14 illustrates a failed bullish prediction. The entire time span has been traversed, but the price didn't even come close to getting inside the rectangle.

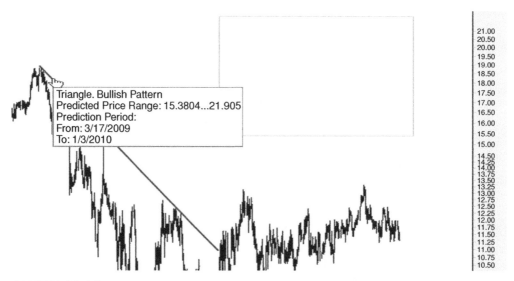

FIGURE 22.14 A failed bullish price projection.

Figure 22.15 provides an even more interesting example, because not only did the price not get into the rectangle, but it subsequently fell away sharply once the projected time range had passed. This is a good illustration of why one should not simply hold on to a position based on a hoped-for outcome. If you were to enter a position based on a projection, and the time span passes entirely without the anticipated price being realized, it's probably time to move on (all other aspects of the chart being equal).

Double Bottom. Bullish Pattern
Predicted Price Range: 44.6753...49.0508
Prediction Period:
From: 3/3/2008
To: 7/9/2008

FIGURE 22.15 The price fell away sharply after the predicted price movement was not realized.

PUTTING THE PATTERNS TO WORK

No matter what system you use, it is imperative you put these symbols to the test with your own eyes and mind. As fond as I am of computers, I do not trust them to make good trading decisions. The symbols derived from an automatic pattern recognition tool are prospects—nothing more—that you should load into a watch list and examine, one by one, with your own charting program. If you find only 10 terrific opportunities out of a list of 200 prospects, that is at least 10 charts you didn't know about in the first place. Smoking out those formerly unknown opportunities is what using a system like Prophet Patterns is all about.

Trading and You

CHAPTER 23

Setting Stops

Having a stop-loss order on each position in your portfolio is, in my opinion, vital to responsible trading. Some traders dismiss stops as being unnecessary. Perhaps they think that a *mental stop* will be sufficient (a mental stop is a pledge to yourself to get out of a position if you think it's going wrong). Other more conspiracy-minded individuals believe that market makers gun for stops, taking small traders out of positions with some magical knowledge of their stop-loss levels.

Both of these notions are silly. Having a mental stop in place of a real stop is a way of cheating yourself out of trading with integrity, and in a market as big as ours, the idea that market makers have nothing better to do than omnipotently push prices up and down in order to zap small retail traders out of their positions is absurd.

GENERAL GUIDELINES

In case you are not acquainted with a stop-loss order, it simply is a standing order to execute a trade based on a certain condition. Typically this condition is one in which a price is violated to the upside (for short positions) or downside (for long positions). A stop-loss order may sit in your account for days or weeks without ever executing, but that's the entire idea: It is there just in case something happens, and it may never be executed.

When a stop-loss order is entered, it can be input as a market order or a limit order; the latter requires an execution to be at a certain price. Again, I offer no nuances here: Using limit orders on a stop-loss order is silly. The entire basis for a stop-loss order is to get out of a position as quickly as possible, and basing this aforementioned exit on the hoped-for existence of a bid price of a certain level is folly. I use market orders, and I suggest you do the same.

The price you choose for your stop-loss should be based on this one question: *At which price is my basis for holding on to this position violated?* In other words, what price tells you that your logic for being in the position is no longer valid? This price, of course, depends on the chart and whether it is a long or a short position. The following categories will provide some guidance as to what kinds of stops are appropriate for various kinds of positions.

BELOW SUPPORT

A long position that is based on a breakout to the upside should have a stop based on support failure. In other words, if the position violates support, the position should be exited. Some of the patterns covered in this book in which this kind of stop would be relevant include:

- Ascending Triangle
- Cup with Handle
- Flag
- Inverted Head and Shoulders (IH&S)
- Pennants
- Rounded Bottoms

For example, if a stock was in a rounded bottom pattern, and its resistance line was at $30, and it broke above resistance, then its stop-loss level would be its newfound support at $30. Note that in all of these classifications that resistance becomes support and support becomes resistance. This is the nature of breakouts: There is a role reversal, so be careful to not let the semantics confuse you.

Therefore, when we think of a stop being set below support, we are referring to the line that used to be regarded as resistance but now, since the pattern has broken out, is defined as support. Of course, if the price (hopefully) progresses higher and higher, you will not keep the stop-loss at this level. In other words, the aforementioned example of a stock breaking above resistance at $30 would not be applicable once the stock had moved, for instance, to $50. You would instead update the stop as described next.

ABOVE RESISTANCE

Setting a stop just above resistance would be appropriate for a short position that is based on support failure. Setup types that fall under this definition are:

- Descending Triangle
- Head and Shoulders

- Rounded Tops
- Support Failure

The caveats mentioned in the preceding section, Below Support, apply here as well. So, as an example, if a stock had support at $40 and broke beneath it, your stop price would be at $40.01 (or a little higher, if you wanted to provide a small amount of wiggle room for your security). If the price continued to move lower, you would update the stop to a more conservative level, increasing the likelihood of guaranteeing a profit on the trade.

ABOVE TRENDLINE

The *above trendline* method is a little more complicated: The stop price is in a constant change of state because it is based on a nonflat line. Setups in which this category apply are:

- Ascending Wedge
- Channel (top of range)
- Diamond Top

The point here is that the price should not go *above* the trendline (which represents resistance). One day this stop might be $32.55, the next it might be $32.75, and the next $32.95. One of the peculiarities of stop prices based on an ascending trendline is that you can remain in position (which is probably a short one) even as the position moves more and more against you. You can't do this forever, of course, so you might seek other criteria as a basis for exiting the position in case the price keeps drifting higher.

BELOW TRENDLINE

Here we set the stop just *below* the trendline above which the price has broken. The setups belonging to this style are:

- Channel (bottom of range)
- Descending Wedge
- Diamond Bottom

Let's take the example of a diamond bottom: if the price broke above the trendline at $25, then the stop-loss would be somewhere beneath $25. As you move right on the time axis, the price level of the diamond's trendline will get lower and lower. As with the "Above Trendline" section, you probably will want a secondary basis to decide when the position should be closed out due to unacceptable losses, since you don't want to hang on a position indefinitely merely because it is above a trendline with an infinitely downward slope.

MOST RECENT LOW

In a way, this is the stop-loss basis that you most want to have, because it is predicated on having a long position that is moving progressively higher in price. The two categories where you use this are:

- General Price Ascent
- Multiple Bottoms

The perfect kind of long position is one that *scallops* higher in price. As a hypothetical situation, imagine a stock that you bought at $20 and which subsequently moves to $25. Imagine the price forming a tiny saucer between $24 and $26 and then moving higher to $30. It then forms a small saucer between $29 and $31 before moving higher to $35, and so forth.

With each lurch higher, you would update your stop-loss level to the most recent low. With this simplified example, your stop-loss levels might be $19.99, $23.99, $28.99, and finally $33.99. This is an extremely simplified example, of course, but the point is that you can have the best of both worlds: (1) you are virtually guaranteed a profit, even if it's not the maximum profit, once the stock makes a reasonable move away from your initial entry point; (2) at the same time, you are keeping your risk sensible and responsible by keeping your stop-loss level fresh and up to date.

If the stock eventually moves to $500, that's terrific, but you don't want your stop loss at $19.99 sitting there forever with that kind of price gain. The order is there to help protect as much of your profit as possible while at the same time keeping you prudent as a trader.

MOST RECENT HIGH

This type is for short positions and is relevant with these setups:

- General Price Descent
- Multiple Tops

Everything stated in the "Most Recent Low" section applies here, except in reverse. With a short position, you are hoping the price keeps slipping lower. You want to spot the most recent high price in a cluster of prices as the basis for your stop-loss order. If the price moves above that local high, then the pattern you want to see—an ongoing series of lower lows and lower highs—has been violated, and you'll want that position closed at once.

SPECIAL CASES

There are a couple of setup categories whose rules for stop-loss merit special mention.

Gaps are one such case. You'll want to initially set your stop at the price at which the gap would be more than closed. For instance, let's say the low price on a Monday was $45.40 and the stock opened on Tuesday at $42. The stock moves higher through the day, and you short it at $44.75. You would set your stop at $45.41, since that would not only close the gap but exceed it.

Simply stated, you want to avoid a situation in which the gap is completely closed. A second example could be an upside gap: Suppose a stock closed on a Monday at $70.50 and opened Tuesday at $74.25. It drifted somewhat lower on Tuesday, and you bought it at $72.75. Your initial stop would be at $70.49, just beneath the lowest range of the gap.

The other family of setups that is a special case is the one related to Fibonacci patterns, because the lines that comprise these patterns define the stop-loss levels, and setting the stop depends on where the price is in relation to those levels. For instance, Fibonacci retracements consist of a series of horizontal lines and are drawn on the basis of two criteria: (1) whether you are long or short and (2) where the price is relative to those lines, which determines what the stop should be. It would be similar to the methods described in the "Above Resistance" or "Below Support" sections.

No matter what the situation, the most important thing about stops is to keep them fresh. If you have the time to do so, going through your positions once each trading day and updating your stops is a very good idea, since the markets are always moving. Keeping your stops fresh strikes the perfect balance between maximizing profit and minimizing risk.

CHAPTER 24

On Being a Bear

For this chapter, I switch to the first-person voice, because being a bear is a somewhat personal topic. In my trading, I have made a specialty of being a short (that is, betting that a security will go down), and I've learned a few things about short-selling over many years of doing so. I'd like to share some of that knowledge here.

THE PHILOSOPHY OF SHORTING

As mentioned earlier in this book, selling a stock short simply involves selling a security which you do not own, pledging that you will buy back the same stock at a later date (and hopefully at a lower price). There are many financial instruments you can short (and many ways you can short the market by going long, such as purchasing put options), but I will use stocks as the focus in this chapter, since that is the simplest and most popular method.

Over the many years I've been trading and writing my blog, people have often asked me why I tend to be a bear in the first place. Let me first state that I am quite aware of a couple of reasons why a person *shouldn't* be a bear:

1. **The whole world is against you.** From the Federal Reserve, to the investment banks, to CNBC, to Jim Cramer, to the brokerage houses, everyone on the planet seems to want the market to go up forever. There is a huge vested interest in the markets going skyward for eternity. So by being a bear, you are definitely going against the crowd.

2. **No one gets rich being a bear.** Fortunes like Warren Buffett's are made by investing in stocks that reap multithousand percent gains or more. In the many chapters you've seen in this book, the gigantic, life-changing gains come from long positions.

325

The most successful shorts go down 99 percent, and something like that almost never happens. There is virtually no one on the Forbes 400 that got there by being a bear, although there are plenty of big hedge fund managers that have done so.

Having said that, allow me to explain myself and hopefully shed some light on my position. I have four primary reasons, some of which are quite rational, and others that are not:

1. **Impatience:** I'm not the most patient soul in the world. And the fact is that markets fall much faster than they rise. For instance, on February 27, the market plummeted over 500 points in just a few hours. It usually takes weeks to go up that much. The financial turmoil in late 2007 and throughout 2008 is a fine example: it took only 15 *months* to wipe out gains that had required a *decade* to form. So I'm drawn to fast-moving markets.

2. **Worrywart:** I'm a worrier by nature. I wouldn't go so far as saying I'm a pessimist, but usually I tend to see the things that will go wrong more easily than I see the things that will go right. (I should add that this is a skill that is quite handy when one is raising young children.)

3. **Unconventional:** Somehow I'm wired to want to be different. I like to stand apart from the crowd. To be a bear is by its very nature to be weird and different. If you happened to be this way during the 1980s and 1990s, it was also terribly unprofitable!

4. **Social Observation:** One of the few verbs I remember from four years of Latin in high school is *speculare*, from which we derive the term *speculate*. This verb doesn't mean "to gamble," as some might guess, but instead "to observe." I am a speculator, and as such I am an observer. And what I am noticing in the present environment, and based on my long-term analysis of markets, points to a multiyear downturn followed by remarkable, long-term growth.

PRACTICAL GUIDE TO SHORT SELLING

In simplest terms, short-selling is no different from the normal buying and selling of a stock, except that you are doing it backward. Bulls want to buy low and sell high; bears want to sell high and buy low.

There are obstacles, however, that exist for bears that bulls need not contend with. You should be aware of these pitfalls:

- **Locating the Stock:** If you want to buy a stock, your broker will always be happy to oblige. But if you want to sell a stock, they have to find it first. Typically, the larger the brokerage, the easier it is for them to locate the stock for you. Some brokerages have lists that you can consult of stocks that are easy for them to borrow. Generally speaking, the more widely traded a stock is, the easier it will be to find. If you find yourself often frustrated with your broker's lack of inventory, and you are serious about short-selling, you might consider changing brokers.

- **The Uptick Rule:** As of this writing, this rule is no longer being used, but there is talk of bringing it back in some form very soon. The uptick rule, in its prior form, deemed that a person could not sell a stock short unless there was an uptick in its price; that is, unless the stock traded at a price higher than it did before, indicating there was at least some level of buying. This is, sadly, an example of how the market is constructed to be against the bears—notice there is no *downtick* rule on the books—but the logic was that the markets should not permit a stock to fall mercilessly, dragged down by the incessant selling pressure of bears.
- **Buy-Ins:** Once you are in a short position, your brokerage can force you out of that position, even at a price that you'd prefer not to take. This is known as a buy-in. Recall that, in order to sell a stock that you do not own, you need to borrow it from someone else. Well, that someone else might want it back; more particularly, if the broker's inventory of that given stock shrinks to the point that they need to recover shares that are sold short, they may need to take you out of that position.
- **Dividends:** If you own a dividend-paying stock, you enjoy being paid a (usually small) dividend periodically from the company. If you are short a stock, the reverse is true: You actually have to pay the dividend yourself, in behalf of the company, since the rightful owner of the stock is still due their dividend. So this creates a true cash cost to being short a particular security (which means you might want to focus on stocks that don't pay a dividend in the first place).
- **Squeezes:** You have probably heard the term *short squeeze* before, but perhaps you're not sure what it meant. When a large number of individuals have short positions in a given stock, they all are obliged to buy back that stock at some point. But let's assume that a stock has been performing well, and it keeps pushing to new highs (or at least technical levels that are damaging to bears). Those who are short the stock will be compelled to close their positions in order to stop the pain, and that creates more buying pressure on the stock. This buying pressure, in turn, compels other shorts to cover their positions, and this cascade of buying feeds on itself. This is what is known as a short squeeze, because eventually all the bears on that stock are falling all over themselves to get out, which, ironically, is terrific for the bulls. So it is best to avoid stocks that are already heavily short (there are entire web sites devoted to tracking the short interest on stocks, showing, relatively speaking, how many shares are short for a given company's stock float).
- **Emergency Rules:** There are times when extraordinary circumstances in the market lead to extraordinary measures being taken. Since those who regulate markets tend to be in favor of upward markets, and opposed to down markets, these measures are almost without exception designed against bears. During the historic week of September 15, 2008, the SEC put rules in place banning short-selling on an entire class of widely traded financial stocks. This caused havoc in the markets, particularly on securities that were based on bearish financial positions. So during

tumultuous times, be warned that the laws and regulations might be changed right under your feet.

There is one other risk often mentioned when the topic of short-selling arises, and that is how potential losses are infinite. In other words, if a person pays $10 a share for a stock, the most he is risking is $10 per share, because a stock can never be worth less than zero. However, if a person is short a stock and pledges to buy it back, there is no limit to how high the stock can go, and thus a person's theoretical risk is unlimited.

I think this argument has a point, but in general it's pretty silly. I remember when I was learning to scuba dive that some people would get completely unhinged at the vastness of the ocean. The ocean is gigantic, it can be miles deep in places, and even in a normal dive spot, there may be a hundred feet of uninterrupted water beneath you. Yes, that's all true, but you're *buoyant*, and it's a bit preposterous to equate being a hundred feet above the sea floor with being a hundred feet in the air.

By the same token, although one's potential risk of loss is indeed unlimited, there are three basic risk management tools that can render this point virtually moot:

1. **Position Size:** There's no reason any particular position has to constitute a large percentage of your portfolio. I personally tend to have a very large number of positions, so even if I get a nasty surprise in one stock, it has a very minor effect on my overall portfolio.

2. **Stop-Losses:** If a person has no stop-loss order and is content to let a stock that he has sold short rise forever, then, yes, he can lose much more than the sum of his original investment. But that would be foolish: you should always have a stop-loss order on all your positions, if you want to remain prudent.

3. **Price Ranges:** The simple fact of the matter is that, even with an earnings blowout or a corporate takeover, it is very rare that a stock (unless it is a penny stock) pushes up hundreds of percent in value overnight. Even if a short position moves against you, the percentage loss is usually going to be quite modest. I try to keep my risk to less than 10 percent for any one position, which is far enough away from "unlimited" to make me comfortable.

EXCHANGE-TRADED FUNDS

Prior to 1993, there was no such thing as an exchange-traded fund (ETF), but as of this writing, there are over 1,500 of them. These are financial instruments that trade very much like stocks but can represent a wide variety of slices of the financial world, including sectors, countries, and inverse funds (which is of interest to us in this chapter).

The function of ETFs was largely covered in the world of mutual funds prior to their creation, but mutual funds have some pretty big disadvantages for active traders, not the least of which is that they can only be bought or sold at the end of the trading day. ETFs, on the other hand, trade through the day (and, for the most popular issues, after hours as well), and some ETFs are among the most popular investment vehicles in the world.

For those looking to take on bearish positions, there is an added benefit: because of the existence of inverse funds, one can take on a long position while actually being short the market. This was useful to me, for instance, in 2008, because I had money in a 401k that I wanted to use on the short side, but the custodian forbid anything except long positions. I took advantage of the existence of inverse funds to produce an extremely substantial gain that year (regrettably, in extending its mission of apparently protecting investors from themselves, the same custodian went so far as to ban trading of ETFs altogether in 2009).

There are a number of firms that offer inverse funds, a couple of which are Rydex and ProShares. With a regular brokerage account, you should be able to buy and sell pretty much any ETF in existence, and even if you are required to have only long positions, you can still be short the market.

There are new ETFs being created all the time, but here are a few examples of how to take on bearish positions using ETFs:

- **Index ETFs:** These were the first ETFs ever created, with SPY being the original back in 1993. SPY, for example, follows the movement of the S&P 500; QQQQ follows the NASDAQ 100, and IWM follows the Russell 2000. Most index ETFs are extremely heavily traded and thus very liquid, and these represent the most direct way to short an entire market. You could sell short the SPY, for instance, to be short the S&P 500 index.
- **Sector ETFs:** These cover entire sectors, such as semiconductors, consumer staples, and so forth. These represent a good way (for bulls and bears alike) to take a position on an entire industry as opposed to a single stock or a whole index.
- **Commodity ETFs:** Most stock traders aren't interested in getting directly involved in the commodities market by opening a futures account; these ETFs allow you to take advantage of price swings in gold, silver, agricultural commodities, or a variety of other baskets. If you wanted to take a bearish position on gold, for instance, the symbols GLD and GDX are both very heavily traded gold ETFs.
- **Inverse ETFs:** These are similar to other ETFs, except that they go up when the underlying instruments go down. For example, the symbol DOG is the inverse of the Dow 30 index, so if on a given day the Dow 30 goes down by 2 percent, then DOG would climb about 4 percent.
- **Leveraged ETFs:** Finally, leveraged ETFs are supercharged versions of regular ETFs, since they move more than 100 percent of the direction of the underlying instrument. Various coefficients are available, such as 1.5, 2, 3, and even 4. For instance, the symbol TWM is a double inverse fund on the Russell 2000, so if on a given day the Russell went down 1.5 percent, meaning its ETF (the IWM) would also be down 1.5 percent, then the TWM would be up about 3 percent, since the movement is doubled. Likewise, if the Russell went up 1.5 percent, the TWM would go down 3 percent.

Now let's take a moment to review a very important point about leveraged ETFs. There is a very insidious reality about leveraged ETFs that it seems a lot of people do not understand, which is that unless a given index or sector (on which the ETF is based) moves very consistently in the direction you desire, the value of your ETF will probably suffer even if, over the long haul, the direction you want it to move is realized.

Let's take an oversimplified example: let's suppose you had a double-inverse ETF on a given index, and let's give it the value of $100. On a Monday, the index goes up 5 percent, meaning your ETF goes down to $90. On Tuesday, to your relief, the index goes down 5 percent. Are you back to where you started, since the index has moved in your direction by precisely the same amount it moved against you the prior day? No, because your $90 ETF goes up 10 percent in value, which is $99. So you are down 1 percent, even though, over the course of those two days, the index hasn't budged.

Now imagine this process repeated over and over, and you will soon realize that the value of the ETF can wither away, even if the market is generally moving in your direction. If the index kept wiggling up and down, day after day, the ETF would be down 40 percent in 100 trading days (and this isn't even taking into account fund expenses and other slippage, which would damage the fund even more).

A surprising number of supposedly sophisticated investors didn't realize this when they bought into ultra-ETFs, because both bullish- and bearish-oriented leveraged funds tended to suffer unless their movement was relatively consistent in the intended direction. Late in 2008, two new instruments based on financial stocks were introduced: their symbols were FAS (triple-bullish) and FAZ (triple-bearish). The extraordinary thing is that *both funds lost most of their value* even though they are opposites. Amateur observers would have assumed that one would prosper while the other suffered, but both of them did poorly (and very savvy traders shorted as much of both of them as they could when they were initially brought to market).

PUTS FOR LEVERAGED PROFITS

If you are not well acquainted with options, here is a simple explanation: Options give you the right (but not the obligation) to buy (in the case of a call option) or sell (in the case of a put option) a particular financial instrument at a particular price within a certain amount of time. Options are derivative instruments, meaning they are based upon something else (which might be an index, a stock, a commodity, or the like).

An option's price is crudely composed of two components: its intrinsic value and its time premium. Let's take the example of a call option on Apple Computer that expires in June of a certain year—let's say that it is currently April—and gives you the right to buy 100 shares of Apple at $200 per share. Let's assume that Apple is currently trading at $210 and the option in question has a value of $15. In this instance, the intrinsic value of the call is $10 (because it is worth $10 to pay $200 for a stock that has a market price of $210) and its time premium is $5 (because there is uncertainty about what the price will do between April and June, and people are willing to pay a premium for that uncertainty). The option itself, by the way, would cost $1,500, since it controls 100 shares, not just one.

A put option is similar, except insofar as it gives you the right to sell something at a given price (which is known as the strike price). Let's use the Apple example again, only this time we're dealing with a put instead of a call, and let's suppose the price of the option is $5. In this case, there is no intrinsic value, since having the right to sell Apple at $200 when the market price is $210 isn't of interest to any economically rational person. In fact, there is *negative* intrinsic value of $10, which means the time premium is $15.

As you might guess, one of the appealing things about options is the leverage they provide. And, generally speaking, the calmer a market is, the greater the leverage. The reason for this is that time premiums will be much higher in volatile markets, because people are scared and are willing to pay a high premium, as opposed to calm, sedate markets. It's little different from the cost of hurricane insurance in Florida versus the same insurance in Iowa—the premiums are going to be vastly different.

So let's return to Apple again and assume that we thought the stock was going to fall. Let's further suppose that the market has been extremely benign, and faith in Apple's upward price trajectory is deeply embedded among investors, so a June put option with a strike at $200 is selling for just 10 cents (the stock price, as with the earlier incarnation of this example, is still $210). An option priced at 10 cents means each contract (which controls 100 shares) is $10, so let's say you took on an aggressively bearish position and bought 1,000 of these contracts for a total cost of $10,000.

The next morning, Apple announces something very bad for its stock price, and it plunges $20 to $190 per share. You have put options with a $20 strike, and these now have an intrinsic value of $10 each. In addition, because people are suddenly very nervous about Apple, there is a $5 time premium, making the price $15. You are now the (ecstatic) owner of $1.5 million in Apple puts, which you promptly sell for a breathtaking profit. Later that day, you buy everyone in your town the latest iPod.

Now, this is a bit of a silly example, but it shows you the power of leverage. Because if you took the same $10,000 and shorted 48 shares of Apple (which is what you could do in a cash account at $210 per share), even with the $20 plunge, you would have netted $960—a far cry from one and a half million dollars. Of course, the reality is that your $10,000 in options will in all likelihood expire worth $0, netting a $10,000 loss if you hold on to them until the very end, but sometimes options holders can experience astronomical gains.

If you do decide to give options a try, here are some words of advice:

- **Don't get stars in your eyes:** Stories like the one about Apple are compelling, but so is reading about lottery winners. The vast majority of the time, those purchasing high-risk options wind up losing the entire investment. It's better to start small and aim low.
- **Avoid out-of-the-money options:** Try to get options with some intrinsic value. Buying cheap out-of-the-money options makes for hypothetically higher percentage returns, but the odds are stacked much more heavily against you, and the time

premium you will be paying will be much greater. Buying in-the-money options is safer, more conservative, and (at least at the time of purchase) gives you the assurance that you are at least purchasing something that has worth.

- **Avoid nearby expiration dates:** As with out-of-the-money options, options that expire relatively soon are going to be very cheap and tempting to beginning traders. There is a phenomenon in options pricing known as theta burn, which essentially is the rate at which a time premium decays as the expiration date nears. The decay looks like a plunging roller coaster as the final weeks of an option's lifespan take place, so it is best to get an option that is at least a couple of months out to give your position a reasonable chance of working out.

Buying in-the-money, far-out options is more conservative than getting out-of-the-money options that expire in a week, but it's radically safer. You might miss a hit-it-out-of-the-ballpark trade now and then, but you will likely avoid a lot of losses, too. The bottom line is that leverage is a two-edged sword, and the same power that makes breathtaking returns possible is also able to provide you with 100 percent losses.

THE PHILOSOPHY OF SHORTING

The nature, definition, and manifestation of good and evil are subjects I have often pondered. All cultures, philosophies, and religions have their own views on these subjects. Some of them dismiss the idea that evil even exists. This is something with which I disagree.

The definition of evil that strikes me as the most accurate is "That which destroys life and liveliness."

But how does one comprehend goodness? Do we simply invert the aforementioned definition, yielding "That which *creates* life and liveliness"?

I think that is a step in the right direction. But to my mind, the concept of goodness conjures up a variety of other properties, as well. In no particular order, I can think of attributes such as:

- Balance
- Harmony
- Order
- Love
- Faith
- Compassion
- Generosity
- Kindness
- Honesty
- Bravery
- Moderation

These qualities are not likely to be challenged. But there are some subtleties in human nature and behavior that make the topic of goodness more complex.

Self-Perception

Most people don't adhere to a standard yardstick of principles and behaviors when placing themselves on a continuum of good and evil. People are, in my view, self-interested creatures, and it is tempting to consider another person evil, when in fact he or she may be simply dissimilar or have a different worldview.

I seriously doubt that when Osama bin Laden was alive, he would gaze at his reflection in the mirror hanging on the cave wall, cackles mischievously, and declare, "How wonderfully evil I am!" Nor do I imagine that Hitler or Stalin thought of themselves as evil. They were obsessed by their own worldviews and motives, and those who stood in opposition to their plans must either get out of the way or be destroyed.

Yet a great majority of people would agree that Hitler and Stalin were, in fact, evil. What's required to make this sort of assertion is a sense of proportion and a broad perspective.

Is Heroism Chosen?

What constitutes a hero?

On a regular basis, newspapers and television shows relate tales of individuals who, in the face of danger to themselves or loved ones, decide to act with remarkable courage and strength in order to create a positive outcome. A man runs into a burning building to save the life of a stranger; a woman dives into a frozen lake to rescue a teenager; a wounded soldier drags another injured soldier off a battlefield to prevent him from being killed.

These are all heartwarming tales, and as sentimental as I am, I'm probably even more affected and moved by these stories than many other people. But do heroes *choose* to be good, or are they simply wired that way? And if they are wired that way, are they any more deserving of our praise than are people who are blessed by other genetic dispositions, such as having blond hair or a nice singing voice?

In the long run, I don't think anyone really cares if it was a person's conscious choice or not to behave heroically. The fact is that they did, and the action itself gives that person heroic attributes. It is all the more alluring and praiseworthy to the public that these decisions are usually made in a split second. Perhaps deep inside we're all wondering whether we would have acted the same way; we question if we have that much goodness within ourselves.

What Does This Have to Do with Shorting Stocks?

The reason I bring this subject up is that I believe there is a misunderstanding about the actions of traders and what those actions represent. Specifically, the public seems to have the notion that buying stocks (and being bullish) is good, whereas selling or shorting stocks (and being bearish) is bad.

Let's start with a few basic facts:

- Unless one's trading size is so gigantic compared to a given security's volume that you are going to push the market substantially up or down, your actions are immaterial to the market as a whole.
- Unless you are actively and effectively spreading malicious untruths about a given organization or security, you are trading morally.
- Your participation in an aftermarket does nothing to help or hinder a public company.

Let's focus on that last point. If you buy 5,000 shares of AAPL, the company Apple doesn't care. You're not helping them, or their employees, or their sales, or their customers, or their management of expenses. If you short 5,000 shares of AAPL, likewise, the company doesn't care.

Now, if it were 1976, and Steve Jobs and Steve Wozniak came to you for startup funding, and you gave it to them, Apple would care very much. Because you are providing them what they need to create a business. And if, in 1980, you as an investment bank agree to underwrite their public offering, Apple again cares, because you are providing them with a source of financing that will help them grow as a business.

But once a company's stocks are publicly traded, your actions as a trader really have nothing to do with them. Sure, a company (and more particularly, its shareholding employees) *likes* to have its stock bid up to higher prices. But your actions as a trader aren't creating any good (or evil) for that organization. You are operating in a realm outside the bounds of that enterprise.

Creation and Destruction

Some people get the idea that bears are malicious, nasty, grubby creatures that relish the thought of destruction and collapse. I can't speak for all bears, but I would say for myself—and I would think most sane people—that this notion is absolute junk.

An objective technical trader:

- Examines a chart.
- Reaches a conclusion.
- Acts upon that conclusion.

There is nothing malevolent in the above. *Nothing.* If I believe the stock BIDU is going to fall and I choose to short it, then I am taking actions that I hope will be profitable for me. I am taking a risk. Yes, I am *hoping* the stock will fall, because that benefits me and aligns with my analysis. It feels good to be right, and it feels good to take a profit.

But this hope has nothing to do with wishing ill on others; it is simply a supposition made based on analysis.

Others might say that bears want America to fail, or that they hate America. Again: This is nonsense. I love this country. I built a business here, creating employment, products, and profits—and I sold it to a much bigger firm. I raise my family here. There is, on the whole, no other place I'd rather live.

But my perception that this country is going very bad places doesn't make me un-American. If anything, my willingness to perceive and talk about these concerns makes me that much *more* of an American. I would like to see this country come out on the other side of this mess in one piece. I would say blind optimists who figure things will get better just because they *ought* to get better are unpatriotic because they are apathetic.

As for corporations: if you really want to destroy a company, then create a stronger competing company!

Who do you think had a more destructive effect on Yahoo!: (a) short sellers, or (b) the founders of Google? I think that even a *million* short sellers couldn't even approach the damage that the two cofounders of Google created. So Joseph Schumpeter's notion of "creative destruction" wins the day.

The Amorality of Trading

For 99.9 percent of traders out there, trading is an *amoral* act. You're not *good* by virtue of buying; you're not *evil* by virtue of selling; you're not behaving in a *virtuous* manner by being bullish; you're not being *malevolent* by being bearish.

What about the circumstance in which you actually make a profit as a direct result of the suffering of others?

Let's suppose that, on September 10, 2001, you were strongly of the opinion that airlines were going to go down in price, so you put all of your trading capital into puts on American Airlines, United Airlines, and the like. September 11 happens and—when the market finally reopens on the 17th—your puts soar in value by hundreds of percentage points (I do not know what the options actually did during that month, but I am guessing this is close to the truth).

Was there evil intent in your trade? Did you contribute to an evil cause? Did you assist the terrorists? No, of course not.

Did you (unwittingly) profit because of a terrorist act? Yes. Does this make you evil? Based on the hypothetical circumstances I have described, I would say the answer is no.

Now, it certainly might *feel* unseemly if you were in this position (and we won't even go into a potential visit from federal authorities, curious about your prescient timing). Your profits might feel like blood money to you—perhaps you might even donate all the profits to the Red Cross, since it would seem like the right thing to do.

I propose that you have no sin which you need to atone for, although I do agree it might be fitting, and erase a perceived stain on your soul, to surrender the profits, since the circumstance would be profoundly unusual.

But, let's face it, 9,999 times out of 10,000, a profitable short sale or put position doesn't do well because of an event that causes human suffering. But I think the wise bear keeps his mouth shut about profiting from a company's troubles: No matter how morally neutral a trade might be, there is still room in this world for decorum and common sense.

The bottom line, for me, can be expressed as simply as this . . .

You simply *are*, and your trading *is*, and the markets *are*. These things are neutral, and it is your *relationship* to the market that will dictate your profits and losses. Outside of those boundaries, nothing matters, and no one need care.

CHAPTER 25

A Guide to Real-Life Trading

T he goal of this book has been to study a variety of common chart patterns, using real-life examples, in order to understand their behavior and applicability to your own trading. To augment this knowledge, there are some basic guidelines about any kind of trading that will be helpful to most people who decide to trade, be it professionally or casually, and we review those in this chapter.

TRADING RULES

It is often tempting for people to keep a list of their own trading rules, particularly as they generate losses that they regret and wish to avoid in the future. Keeping a diary of trading experiences is a valuable exercise, but what often happens with a list of rules is that the list grows so long and arcane as to be almost useless. The old saying about how you can never step into the same stream twice holds true for trading, and over the months and years that you are trading, you will be faced with a never-ending set of changing circumstances.

I've got my own list, but it is short and sweet—only seven rules. I ignore some of these rules from time to time, and virtually every time I do, I regret it. If one day I can follow these rules consistently, I'll be a much better trader for it. An acronym for the rules listed below is SOB FEES, which is appropriate considering how many tears were shed while learning them.

1. **Stops:** A stop price must be in place at all times for all positions.
2. **Opening Bell:** No new positions should be initiated in the first 30 minutes of any trading session. In addition, after-hours trading is to be avoided altogether, since the volume is terribly thin and thus prone to easy manipulation.

3. **Balance:** This rule is the hardest of all to define, but because it is impossible to know with certainty the future direction of the market, a balance between bullish and bearish positions is the most prudent. In addition, if you are heavily weighted either bullish or bearish, and if the market moves strongly in your favor intraday, you should consider taking on a large opposite day-trade position for insurance, in case that intraday move reverses.

4. **Freshness:** Positions should be regularly refreshed for the sake of updated stops. This is especially important when the market has moved in your direction by a meaningful amount so that you can lock in some profits with tighter stops.

5. **Emotional Awareness:** Use emotional awareness to your advantage, understanding that fear often accompanies reversals in your favor and hubris often accompanies reversals against your positions.

6. **Exits:** The only acceptable exit is either being stopped out of a position or reaching a target price that has a clear technical rationale, and even in cases of the latter, partial exits are preferable to outright closes.

7. **Sizing:** Initial position sizing must be consistent among instrument types irrespective of anticipated opportunity.

Following these rules consistently isn't easy. But every year I get a little better at it, and every year I do better in my trading. I urge you to consider making these rules an important part of your trading life.

Let us now examine some of these rules from a different perspective with three simple components: how to open a position, how to hold a position, and how to close a position.

HOW TO OPEN A POSITION

When a person opens up a position, they are at their most optimistic. There are many different profit possibilities available to a person: the classic *buy low/sell high*, the oft-ignored *buy high/sell higher* (such as is the case with strong performers that seem too expensive for much of the investing public), and, for short-sellers, *sell high/buy low*.

No matter what your disposition is on a stock, there are five easy-to-follow rules that will probably save you a lot of trouble and money. They are as follows.

Don't Enter a Trade in the First 30 Minutes of the Trading Day

Although you may be eager to jump into a trade the very moment the market opens, it is wise not to do so. The fact is that there is a tremendous amount of noise in the first 30 minutes of the trading day. Amazingly, a significant percentage of stock orders are placed even before the opening bell. This creates a rather distorted picture of the market at the first part of the day.

It is, of course, all right to let a stop order close out a position for you (more on this later) in the first 30 minutes. After all, it is the job of a stop order to get you out of a trade if it needs to do so. But letting the smoke clear out of the market is essential before you enter any new positions. Even if you pay a little more for a stock by waiting out the first half hour, it will be immaterial if the position turns out to be a good one.

Pay a Good Price

"Pay a good price" may sound like absurd advice, akin to "never lose money." But the point is simply this: When you examine a chart, you have an opportunity to see what constitutes an attractive price for a security. This will depend strictly upon the chart, so there is no predetermined rule for all securities. If, for example, a stock explodes out of a basing pattern and quickly rises from its former resistance level of $15 to $25, you may decide to wait until the stock is $17 or less before purchasing it. It may never reach that level again, and you may find yourself denied the opportunity of profiting from future growth. But rushing into a stock just after it has had a major price ascent may put you in a position of unnecessary risk.

The key is to make a decision for yourself (preferably not during market hours, so that you can calmly and rationally decide what a fair price would be) as to what price you are willing to pay for the security. You want to seek a good risk/reward ratio. The risk is measured by calculating the price you would pay for a security versus the price at which you would be stopped out of the position, while the reward is based on the difference between the target price for the security and the price you would pay for it.

For example, assume you were willing to pay $16 for a stock with a target price of $36 and a stop price of $14. The risk is $2 and the potential reward is $20, which is a risk/reward ratio of 10. In other words, you are risking $1 for every $10 in reward you are seeking. That's a very attractive ratio. On the other hand, it is unlikely you would want to buy into a stock at $34 with a stop price of $15 and a target price of $40. Even though there's still a potential profit to be had, the risk/reward profile doesn't make it worthwhile.

You cannot control how high the stock will go, but you can certainly control what you pay for it. Therefore, you have much more say in the risk you are willing to undertake as opposed to the reward you may or may not make. Therefore, determine your price in advance and don't pay anything higher, as tempting as it might be. It often pays to wait for the stock to return to the level you seek.

Trade Active Securities Only

Although there are tens of thousands of stocks and options that trade in the U.S. equity markets, only a few thousand of them trade in volumes that are significant enough to be worthwhile. Although you may find a chart with a very alluring pattern, be sure to check its average daily volume to ensure that you don't get stuck with a security that has too thin a market.

The problem with a thin market is twofold: First, there is typically a substantial bid/ask ratio. In other words, for a heavily traded security, you will enjoy a very tight bid/ask ratio. The QQQQ, for example, might trade with a bid of $36.02 and an ask of $36.03, because there are so many people making a market in this security that a penny spread is sufficient. On the other hand, a security that trades just a few thousand shares a day might have a bid of $43.20 and an ask of $45.00. This means that the moment you enter the position, you have a $1.80 per share loss on your hands.

The other problem is that you are far more vulnerable to someone who is gunning for your stop price. As you will read next, having a stop price is crucial for responsible trading. But if a market is extremely thin, it becomes very little trouble for others in the market to push the market either up or down and execute orders based on existing stop prices. You will not experience this kind of problem in actively traded shares.

As for what defines *actively traded*—it is best to trade securities that trade at least a million shares a day, but at a minimum, you should avoid anything that trades less than 250,000 shares per day unless the chart is so spectacular that it is worth the extra risk.

Have a Stop and Target Determined in Advance

Just as you should have a price you are willing to pay determined in advance, you should likewise figure out a stop price and a target price.

As a reminder, a stop price is a price below which (or, if you are short, above which) a market order will be instantly executed. For instance, let's say you bought 5,000 shares of AAPL at $350, and you set a stop price of $347.99. As long as AAPL trades at $348 or above, your order will not be executed. But if any trade at $347.99 or lower goes through, there will be an instant order submitted to the market to sell your position at the best available price.

The reason stops are so crucial is that they allow you to dispassionately get out of bad trades. You should never, ever have a position without a stop price. In fact, the moment you get your order filled, you should place the stop order. It is far too tempting to talk yourself out of selling a stock if it falls and you don't have a stop order in place. By automating the process, you remove the emotional element from getting out of a bad trade.

The target price is less important, because it is much harder to judge how far a stock will go, and it is likely that if a stock moves in the direction you anticipate, you will update your target. But a target is important to judge the risk/reward ratio of a potential position.

If you are trading options, there is a special point. It isn't wise to place a stop order based on the option price itself. Options are typically far too thinly traded to make this a reasonable approach. What makes more sense is to go with a broker that offers Contingent Orders. This means that if the underlying security falls above or below a certain price, then the order to close the option position is placed. Stocks are far, far more heavily traded than their options, so this is absolutely the best way to go to protect your option positions.

Trade on Completed Patterns Only

Patterns do not form overnight. They take weeks, months, or even years to form. And when they are about 70 percent to 80 percent complete, it becomes easy to see what pattern might ultimately take shape.

In a situation like this, it is very tempting to enter a trade based on the supposition that a pattern will complete. For example, perhaps you are looking at a head-and-shoulders chart that has the left shoulder, the head, and about half of the right shoulder. You can clearly see what the pattern would look like if it were to complete as expected. You can also see that you will make more money getting into the position now, since the area between the neckline and the current price of the stock represents that much more profit to you. In other words, you want to beat the crowd before they realize the pattern has broken.

As tempting as this is, you should wait for the pattern to complete before taking action. An incomplete pattern isn't a pattern at all—it's simply something that may become a pattern. You will find that jumping the gun like this will backfire so many times that it simply doesn't become worth the extra profit you might make. So wait for the trendline to be crossed, the neckline to be violated, and the resistance level to be overcome. Don't rush in before the chart is ready for you.

HOW TO HOLD A POSITION

Once you're in a position, having steadfastly followed the previous five rules, now what do you do? The easiest thing to do is sit back and let your positions take care of themselves. If your stock reaches your target, terrific, you can cash in your profits. If your stock gets stopped out, that's okay, because you've managed your loss and kept it reasonable. But too often people meddle in their portfolios and cause themselves harm they never intended. Let's review three rules to help avoid this.

Let the Winners Run

This is one of the most basic rules offered to traders: Cut your losses and let your winners run. It would seem obvious that traders should let their profits grow. The reason this often doesn't happen is based on a human impulse articulated by another old saying: "You'll never go broke taking a profit."

People love to take profits, and often they take them far too soon. For every person who enjoyed a 1,000 percent return on a stock, there are hundreds of other people who bought the exact same stock at the exact same time and took a 10 percent profit and felt they were financial geniuses—until the stock kept moving higher. It feels good to take a profit, because it means you not only get to pocket the extra cash, but you also eliminate the risk of holding the position in the first place.

Unfortunately, instead of letting winners run and cutting losses short, it is human nature to let losers run and cut winners short. A person holding a losing stock will always find many reasons to hold onto that position, hoping that it will turn around. And a person with a profit has the urge to bank that profit as swiftly as possible. But small profits can never pay for large losses, and in the end, taking this approach will create a shrinking portfolio.

So what you should do instead is simply hang onto the position as long as it doesn't violate your stop price (or until such time as it reaches your target). This is how multi-hundred percent returns are created.

Let Your Stops Manage Your Losers

Stop orders are your friend. Placing a stop order the moment you are in a position does a couple of very good things for you. First, it relieves you from the duty of staring at a computer screen, monitoring your positions. If the stop price is hit, you'll be taken out at once. Second, it injects a healthy dose of responsibility into your trading. Determining and setting a stop price with a calm, rational, objective mind set will save you a fortune in the long run.

For years there has been a late-night TV ad for a kitchen appliance in which the host says to the audience, "Set it, and forget it!" This is, for the most part, also true of stop orders for your positions.

Keep Your Stops Updated

When you initially establish a stop price, you are doing so at a price below the current value of the stock (or above the current value, if it is a short position). But if the stock moves in the direction you anticipate, the stop price is going to become less and less relevant. As a position matures, a stop price's function should change from minimizing your loss to instead preserving your profit.

For example, if you bought 1,000 shares of a $20 stock and set a stop price of $18, you have $2,000 at risk. If the stock moves up over time to $100, it would be silly to continue to have an $18 stop in place. There is no reason to risk the entirety of your profits after a stock has moved that much.

Instead, it pays to check your charts on a regular basis and update the stop prices based on the most recent chart activity. For example, let's say the same stock just mentioned traded at about $25 for several weeks before moving higher. You may decide to update your stop price to $24.99 since there seems to be a strong new level of support at $25. You could therefore lock in $5 of profit and still allow the stock to go higher.

Some brokers offer *trailing stops*, which base the stop price on a percentage of the stock's current value. This is much like laying down a moving average on top of a chart and stating to sell the stock if it crosses below that moving average. If you don't have time to update your stops regularly, this is a nice compromise, since it automates the act and ensures that you can lock in some profits. The only trouble is that trailing stops aren't really based on the pattern per se, since they are little more than a raw moving average based on recent price activity. But they are certainly better than leaving your initial fixed stop price in place forever.

HOW TO CLOSE A POSITION

St. Teresa of Avila wrote, "More tears are shed over answered prayers than unanswered ones." A trader might paraphrase this as, "More tears are shed over profits than losses." The reason is that a closed profitable position often goes on to become a *wildly* profitable position, and you missed most of the ride.

I've offered five rules for opening a position and three rules for holding a position, but there's really only one rule for closing a position: Close it when your target has been reached or your stop has been violated. It's as simple as that.

Never do an ad hoc close. In other words, don't decide in the moment to rush out of a position for any reason—that reason might be the thrill of a sudden profit, or the shock of a sudden loss, or anything in between. As long as your stop is in place, let the position run, and if your target is met, terrific—close it out. Until then, allow the seeds you've planted to grow, undisturbed.

When you do close a position, you may want to jot down some notes about what you learned from that particular trade. If you lost money, can you figure out if your analysis was wrong? If you made money, are there things you did correctly that you want to remember for future trades? There is always something to be learned from a properly closed position, whether you made money or lost it. Over the course of time, these trading lessons will form a helpful mosaic for your ongoing career.

TIME AND MONEY

One aspect of being a trader that is simultaneously appealing and nerve-wracking is that the results a trader generates are just about the purest reflection of whatever talent they might have. In other words, the talent is almost perfectly correlated with the result.

This is not the case with most other endeavors. Let's say you are a fifth-grade schoolteacher. You have certain talents that are germane to the job—patience, discipline, knowledge, a rapport with young people, a rapport with their parents, the ability to wake up and get to school on time, and so forth. There are dozens of attributes that factor into your potential success in that occupation.

How does one measure the result? That's a tough question—it could be measured by the change in test scores from the start of the year to the end, or by the relative performance of that class versus similarly aged classes in the same school, or by the results of a satisfaction survey that the students fill out, or the results of a similar survey of parents. As you can see, defining *success* in this occupation is very hard.

Similar challenges would be faced in determining the success of a lawyer, a dentist, or a bricklayer.

In addition, what happens between input (skills) and output (results) is subject to the interaction of the person with the environment. In the case of the teacher, the environment is mainly the students and the school's culture; for a lawyer, it would be clients and coworkers; for a bricklayer, it would be the job site, the tools, and interactions with other subcontractors.

But the perception of the success in any given occupation can by fudged quite a bit. You can be a lousy Senator but still appear to be competent and get elected repeatedly. You can be a crummy teacher but thrive simply because your students like and admire you.

A trader, though, has just one asset: his or her ability to apply their edge, whatever it might be, in the never-ending turmoil that represents a given market. The edge might be in the form of skillful charting, insightful fundamental analysis, or a deep understanding of a certain industry.

But since a trader's measurement of success is simple—their profit/loss statement—there's no fudge factor involved. All you've got is talent, and all you've got to show for it is a numeric result.

So let's say you were hired to sit on a manhole cover in order to prevent zombies from coming out of it. You are being paid 100 percent for your time. You are applying no talent at all to this occupation—the only asset you are bringing is your body's mass (it could be argued that some folks are more talented than others even in this respect, but let's keep it simple).

If you are a sales clerk at a high-end clothing store, you are being paid partly for your time (someone needs to be there to open the store for business and to make sure the merchandise isn't stolen) but also partly for your talent (your knowledge of clothes, of what looks good on a particular person, etc.).

No one is going to pay for a trader's time. You can sit there all year long, working your tail off, and if the talent isn't there, you're not going to get a stipend. In fact, you are going to work very hard for the privilege of losing money.

Of course, the market's behavior has a direct relationship on the results your talent brings, but that is the biggest task of all: to hone your skills so that the market's behavior ultimately becomes irrelevant to your ability to generate profits.

THERE IS NO HOLY GRAIL

My philosophy on trading has this important premise: it's all about your relationship between yourself and the market. However, no one can control the market; you can control only yourself, to a degree. And it is the complexity of yourself *vis-à-vis* an ever-changing market that makes the entire enterprise of being a trader simultaneously fascinating, exasperating, and thought-provoking.

Instead of latching onto one particular trading method, I have, over the years, adopted a handful of methods, and I've put them into my own unique trading stew. I am refining it all the time—monitoring vectors and weighting some more and some less. But this concoction is best suited for me and who I am. It may not work as well for most other people.

It's important to embrace one's ignorance. I seek mastery by considering myself a dunce who is in search of knowledge. By no means am I suggesting piling on rule after rule, method after method. I view the act of trading as not much different from making an ongoing series of bread loaves. I'm changing the recipe a little each time, and I'm kneading and kneading the dough (that is, my positions, their weighting, and their stops) in order to try to get the result I'm after. This results in a delicious loaf of bread—or in a nice, outsized profit.

The fact that learning to be a great trader is a very personal journey is why I stopped buying business books many years ago. When I was in my late teens and early twenties, I bought business books all the time. I figured they would help me become a more successful businessperson. They didn't.

I've got shelves full of these books, and I don't think I learned a thing from any one of them. It's not because I didn't read them carefully. But the fact is that most how-to books might as well be titled *If You Do What This Person Did, You Will Be Like This Person*. But you know what? That person is that person; he or she isn't you. And the circumstances in which that person thrived (whether we are speaking of Jack Welch, Tom Peters, Steve Jobs, or Mark Zuckerberg) are unique to that person. If you want to read a biography, great—read a biography. But if you want to be like that person—well, that spot's already been taken.

This isn't to say there's nothing to learn from books. But I think books related to business or trading are best applied to either (1) the actual mechanics of trading techniques and their application; and (2) learning from the successes and failures of others in order to pick up templates to compare to your personal experiences. I don't have any illusions that I'm going to be a Paul Tudor Jones. But I do draw inspiration from his resilience in the face of defeat and his successful use of past markets to present ones.

CLOSING THOUGHTS

Making money in the market isn't easy. So much of human nature is geared to poor trading habits that it is difficult to overcome the challenges to being a good trader.

You have some advantages on your side now, however. You are, by virtue of the fact you are reading this book, interested in improving yourself as a knowledgeable trader. You have seen hundreds of examples of technical analysis in real-life charts to understand how to observe and apply these lessons. And you know some critically important rules of the road that lead to sound trading.

Good luck in your endeavors, and make a point of revisiting this book whenever you need a refresher. I hope it will be a powerful guide as you chart your way to more profitable and consistent trading.

And stay in touch! You can learn more by visiting my blog (www.slopeofhope.com), and if you want to write to me, my e-mail address is trader.tim.knight@gmail.com. Thank you, and good trading to you.

Index

A. *See* Agilent Technologies, Inc. (A)
AAPL. *See* Apple, Inc. (AAPL)
Abercrombie & Fitch Company (ANF):
   rounded tops pattern, 273–274
   support failure and, 294–295
ABFS. *See* Arkansas Best Corporation (ABFS)
Acadia Realty Trust (AKR), 233–234
AEP. *See* American Electric Power Company,
   Inc. (AEP)
Affymetrix, Inc. (AFFX), 170–171
Aflac, Inc. (AFL), 294–295
Agilent Technologies, Inc. (A):
   gaps and, 165–166
   multiple tops pattern, 232
Agrium (AGU), 260–261
AIG. *See* American International Group, Inc.
   (AIG)
AINV. *See* Apollo Investment Corporation
   (AINV)
Alcatel-Lucent (ALU), 199–201
ALD. *See* Allied Capital Corporation (ALD)
Alexandria Real Estate Equities, Inc. (ARE),
   125–126
Allegheny Energy, Inc. (AYE), 190–191
Allied Capital Corporation (ALD), 283–284
Alpha Natural Resources, Inc. (ANR), 107
ALU. *See* Alcatel-Lucent (ALU)
ALVR, 8–9
Amazon.com, Inc. (AMZM), 57–59
American Electric Power Company, Inc.
   (AEP), 115
American Express Company (AXP), 135
American International Group, Inc. (AIG),
   285–286
AMZN. *See* Amazon.com, Inc. (AMZM)
ANF. *See* Abercrombie & Fitch Company
   (ANF)
ANR. *See* Alpha Natural Resources, Inc. (ANR)
APL. *See* Atlas Pipeline Partners (APL)

Apollo Investment Corporation (AINV),
   99–100
Apple, Inc. (AAPL), 124–125
ARE. *See* Alexandria Real Estate Equities, Inc.
   (ARE)
Arkansas Best Corporation (ABFS), 47–48
Ascending triangles:
   definition, 33–35
   examples, 35–43
   generally, 33, 43
   psychology, 35
Ascending wedges:
   definition, 45–46
   examples, 47–53
   generally, 45, 53
   psychology, 47
ASGN. *See* On Assignment, Inc. (ASGN)
Atheros Communications, Inc. (ATHR),
   159–160
Atlas Pipeline Partners (APL), 275–276,
   293–294
AutoChartist, 301
Automatic patterns:
   Internet products for, 301
   pattern failures, 314–315
   ProphetCharts pattern finder, 302–313
   putting patterns to work, 315
Avon Products, Inc. (AVP), 220–221
AXP. *See* American Express Company (AXP)
AYE. *See* Allegheny Energy, Inc. (AYE)

BAM. *See* Brookfield Asset Management
   (BAM)
Banco Santander (STD), 45–46
BDX. *See* Becton, Dickinson and Company
   (BDX)
Be Aerospace, Inc. (BEAV), 168–169
Bear market, 278
Bear Stearns crisis, 192

Bears vs. bulls, 4
BEAV. *See* Be Aerospace, Inc. (BEAV)
Becton, Dickinson and Company (BDX), 77
Bemis Company (BMS), 167–168
BEN. *See* Franklin Resources, Inc. (BEN)
BEXP. *See* Brigham Exploration Company
    (BEXP)
Bezos, Jeff, 57
Black Monday crash, 16
Boeing Corporation (BA), 239–240
BRCM. *See* Broadcom Corporation (BRCM)
Brigham Exploration Company (BEXP):
    diamond pattern, 110
    inverted head and shoulders (IH&S)
        pattern, 206–207
Broadcom Corporation (BRCM), 184–186
Broker Dealer Index ($XBD), 297
Brookfield Asset Management (BAM), 38–39
BTU. *See* Peabody Energy Corporation (BTU)
Bulls vs. bears, 4

Cal-Maine Foods (CALM), 257–258
Capital One Financial (COF), 267, 268
Carnival PLC (CUK), 146–147
Caterpillar, Inc. (CAT), 119–120
CBS Corporation (CBS), 158–159
Channels:
    defined, 55–56
    examples, 57–68
    generally, 55, 68
    psychology, 57
Chart setups:
    bulls vs. bears, 4
    generally, 3–4
    history repeats itself, 11–13
    patterns working together, 13–14
    prediction, value of, 4–6
    prices pushing through, 8–11
    shorting/being short, 6–7
    support and resistance, 7–8
    using this book, 14
Chesapeake Energy (CHK), 9–11
Chevron Corporation (CVX), 77–78
China index ($CZH), 112
China Yuchai, 42–43
CHK. *See* Chesapeake Energy (CHK)
Citi Trends (CTRN), 60–61
Closing positions, 343
COF. *See* Capital One Financial (COF)
Costco Wholesale (COST), 244–245

Coventry Health Care, Inc. (CVH), 236–237
Crash of 1987, 16–17
CTRN. *See* Citi Trends (CTRN)
Cubic Corporation (CUB), 121
CUK. *See* Carnival PLC (CUK)
Cup with handle:
    definition, 69–70
    examples, 72–74
    examples, longer-term, 75–79
    generally, 69, 79
    psychology, 70–71
CurrencyShares Euro Trust (FXE), 36
CVH. *See* Coventry Health Care, Inc. (CVH)
CVX. *See* Chevron Corporation (CVX)
Cycle trades, 56
Cytori Therapeutics (CYTX), 93–94

Darden Restaurants, Inc. (DRI):
    gaps and, 161–162
    head-and-shoulders (H&S) pattern, 189
Dell, Inc. (DELL), 117
Descending triangles:
    definition, 81–83
    examples, 83–89
    generally, 81, 89
    psychology, 83
Descending wedges:
    definition, 91–92
    examples, 93–102
    generally, 91, 102
    psychology, 92–93
Diamonds:
    definition, 103–105
    examples, 105–110
    generally, 103, 110
    psychology, 105
Diodes, Inc. (DIOD):
    multiple tops pattern, 235–236
    support failure and, 281
Dish Network Corporation (DISH), 164–165
Double bottoms. *See* Multiple Bottoms
Dow Jones Industrial Average, 5
Dow Jones Industrials ($INDU), 136–137
Dow Jones Transportation Index ($TRAN),
    221–222
Dow Jones Utility Index ($UTIL), 279–280
DreamWorks Animation SKG, Inc. (DWA),
    148–149
DRI. *See* Darden Restaurants, Inc. (DRI)
DST Systems (DST), 218

DTE Energy Company (DTE):
  flag pattern, 150–151
  multiple bottoms, 227–228
Duke Energy Corporation (DUK), 50
DWA. *See* DreamWorks Animation SKG, Inc.
  (DWA)
Dynegy, Inc. (DYN), 289–290

eBay, Inc. (EBAY), 173–174
Echelon Corporation (ELON), 37–38
EFA. *See* iShares MSCI Index Fund (EFA)
EFX. *See* Equifax (EFX)
Elliott Wave, 22
ELON. *See* Echelon Corporation (ELON)
ELX. *See* Emulex Corporation (ELX)
EMC Corporation (EMC), 78–79
Emerson Electric Company (EMR),
  118–119
Emulex Corporation (ELX), 51–52
Encore Wire Corporation (WIRE), 98–99
Equifax (EFX), 156
Essex Property Trust, Inc. (ESS), 122
Eurodollar (EUR/USD), 114–115
EWZ. *See* iShares MSCI Brazil Index (EWZ)
Excel cells, 28–29
Exchange-traded funds (ETFs):
  generally, 337–338
  shorting and, 328–330
Exide Technologies (XIDE), 36–37

Failures, pattern, 314–315
False breakout, 102
Federal Realty Investment Trust (FRT),
  122–123
FEI Company (FEIC), 91, 92
Fibonacci fans:
  definition, 111–112
  examples, 114–126
  generally, 111, 126–127
  psychology, 113
Fibonacci patterns, stop prices and, 323
Fibonacci retracements:
  definition, 130–131
  examples, 132–138
  generally, 129–130, 139
Find Patterns function, 302–313
First Marblehead (FMD), 171–172
Flags:
  definition, 141–142
  examples, 143–152

  generally, 141, 153
  psychology, 142–143
FMD. *See* First Marblehead (FMD)
Franklin Resources, Inc. (BEN), 74
FRT. *See* Federal Realty Investment Trust
  (FRT)
FXE. *See* CurrencyShares Euro Trust (FXE)

Gaps:
  definition, 155–157
  examples, 158–174
  generally, 155
  psychology, 157–158
  stop prices, setting, 323
GBX. *See* Greenbrier Companies (GBX)
GD. *See* General Dynamics Corporation (GD)
GE. *See* General Electric Company (GE)
General Dynamics Corporation (GD), 101–102
General Electric Company (GE), 135–136
Genworth Financial, Inc. (GNW), 86–87
GeoMet, Inc. (GMET), 83–84
GLD. *See* Gold (GLD)
GMET. *See* GeoMet, Inc. (GMET)
GNW. *See* Genworth Financial, Inc. (GNW)
Gold (GLD), 261–262
Gold bugs index ($HUI), 116
Goodrich Corporation (GR), 123–124
Google (GOOG), 170
Google Finance, 26
GR. *See* Goodrich Corporation (GR)
Greenbrier Companies (GBX), 272–273

H&S. *See* Head and shoulders (H&S)
Hammering out a bottom, 218
Hanesbrands, Inc. (HBI), 247–248
Harris Corporation (HRS), 59–60
Harte-Hanks, Inc. (HHS), 222–223
HBI. *See* Hanesbrands, Inc. (HBI)
HD. *See* Home Depot (HD)
Head and shoulders (H&S):
  definition, 175–176
  examples, 178–196
  generally, 175, 197
  neckline, importance of, 177–178
  psychology, 176–177
HHS. *See* Harte-Hanks, Inc. (HHS)
Holding positions:
  keep stops updated, 342–343
  let the winners run, 341–342
  let your stops manage your losers, 342

Holly Corporation (HOP), 162–163
Home Depot (HD), 227–228
Honeywell International, Inc. (HON), 291–292
HOP. *See* Holly Corporation (HOP)
Hovnanian Enterprises, Inc., 195–196
HRS. *See* Harris Corporation (HRS)
Hutchinson Technology, Inc. (HTCH), 178–179
HZO. *See* Marinemax, Inc. (HZO)

IH&S. *See* Inverted head and shoulders (IH&S)
IIN. *See* Intricon Corporation (IIN)
Illinois Tool Works, Inc. (ITW), 262–263
Incyte Corporation (INCY), 62–63
Industrial Sector ETF (XLI), 214–215
Ingersoll-Rand (IR), 87–88
Intricon Corporation (IIN), 95–96
Inverted head and shoulders (IH&S):
    definition, 199–201
    examples, 202–215
    neckline, importance of, 202
    psychology, 201
IR. *See* Ingersoll-Rand (IR)
iShares MSCI Brazil Index (EWZ), 61–62
iShares MSCI Index Fund (EFA), 188
Isle of Capri Casinos, Inc. (ISLE), 191–192
ITW. *See* Illinois Tool Works, Inc. (ITW)

JPC. *See* Nuveen Multi-Strategy Income and
    Growth Fund (JPC)
JWN. *See* Nordstrom, Inc. (JWN)

Kimberly-Clark Corporation (KMB), 248–249
KKD. *See* Krispy Kreme Doughnuts, Inc.
    (KKD)
KMB. *See* Kimberly-Clark Corporation (KMB)
Krispy Kreme Doughnuts, Inc. (KKD), 163

Lam Research Corporation (LRCX), 137–138
Las Vegas Sands, 81, 82
Lindsay Corporation (LNN), 238–239
Louisiana-Pacific Corporation (LPX):
    ascending triangle pattern, 41–42
    channel pattern, 64–65
LPX. *See* Louisiana-Pacific Corporation (LPX)
LRCX. *See* Lam Research Corporation (LRCX)

Major Market Index ($XMI), 132–133
Manitowoc Company, Inc. (MTW), 75–76
Marinemax, Inc. (HZO), 270–271
Masco Corporation (MAS), 208–209

Mattson Technology (MTSN), 205–206
MDT. *See* Medtronic, Inc. (MDT)
Mechel Oao (MTL), 258–259
Medtronic, Inc. (MDT), 251–252
Mela Sciences, Inc. (MELA), 187
Merck, 263
MIPS Technologies, Inc., 108–109
MMM. *See* 3M Company (MMM)
Morgan Stanley (MS), 192–193
Morgan Stanley Technology Index ($MSH),
    104–105, 298
MS. *See* Morgan Stanley (MS)
MTL. *See* Mechel Oao (MTL)
MTSN. *See* Mattson Technology (MTSN)
MTW. *See* Manitowoc Company, Inc. (MTW)
Multiple bottoms:
    definition, 217–219
    examples, 220–230
    generally, 217, 230
    psychology, 219
Multiple tops:
    definition, 231–232
    examples, 233–241
    generally, 231, 241
    psychology, 233
MUR. *See* Murphy Oil Corporation (MUR)
Murphy Oil Corporation (MUR), 263–264
Mylan, Inc. (MYL), 204–205

Newport Corporation (NEWP), 202–204
Nordstrom, Inc. (JWN), 133–134
Novellus Systems, Inc. (NVLS), 84–85
Nuveen Multi-Strategy Income and Growth
    Fund (JPC), 65–66
NVLS. *See* Novellus Systems, Inc. (NVLS)
NZD/USD cross-rate, 130–131

Oil Services ETF (OIH), 105–106
On Assignment, Inc. (ASGN), 49–50
Opening positions:
    active securities only, 339–340
    complicated patterns and, 341
    not in first 30 minutes, 338–339
    pay a good price, 339
    stop and target determined, 340–341

Panic selling, 294
Parametric Technology (PMTC), 246–247
Pattern failures, 314–315
Pattern recognition. *See* Automatic patterns

Peabody Energy Corporation (BTU), 73–74
Pennants:
  definition, 243–244
  examples, 245–252
  generally, 243, 253
  psychology, 244–245
Personal trading journey:
  Alex and JavaCharts, 19–21
  Black Monday crash and, 16–17
  earliest interest in markets, 15–16
  Internet/World Wide Web and, 18–19
  Kandinsky project, 21
  lessons learned, 22–23
  ProphetCharts lives, 23–24
  Prophet.net web site themes, 24–30
  prophet's beginning, 18
  slope of hope, 22
  technical tools, 17–18
PetSmart, Inc. (PETM), 224–225
Photronics, Inc. (PLAB), 288–289
PLD. *See* ProLogis (PLD)
Plug Power, Inc. (PLUG), 67–68
PMTC. *See* Parametric Technology (PMTC)
PNM Resources (PNM), 142–143
PolyOne Corporation (POL), 211–212
ProLogis (PLD), 181–182
ProphetCharts pattern finder:
  patterns and, 302–307
  results, working with, 307–313
Prophet Financial Systems, 18–21
Prophet.net web site themes:
  Analyze, 27–28
  Explore, 24–27
  Manage, 28–30
Put Options, 330–332

Rackspace Hosting, Inc. (RAX), 255–256
Ralph Lauren (RL), 250–251
RAX. *See* Rackspace Hosting, Inc. (RAX)
RBC. *See* Regal-Beloit Corporation (RBC)
Real-life trading. *See* Trading Rules
Recognia, 301
Red Hat (RHAT), 12–13
Regal-Beloit Corporation (RBC), 225–227
Resistance, 7–11
Retracement, 87–88, 102, 289, 297. *See also*
  Fibonacci retracements
RHAT. *See* Red Hat (RHAT)
Rich Man's Panic, 5
RL. *See* Ralph Lauren (RL)

Roaring Twenties, 5
Rockwell Automation, Inc. (ROK), 40–41
Rounded bottoms:
  definition, 255–256
  examples, 257–265
  generally, 255, 263
  psychology, 256–257
Rounded tops:
  definition, 267–269
  examples, 270–277
  generally, 267, 278
  psychology, 269–270
Russell 2000 Index ($RUT), 12, 183–184

S&P500 Index ($SPX), 109–110
SBA Communications (SBAC), 38
SBGI. *See* Sinclair Broadcast Group, Inc.
  (SBGI)
Schnitzer Steel Industries, Inc. (SCHN), 73
September 11 terrorist attacks, 168, 335
Setting stops. *See* Stop prices, setting
Ship Finance International (SFL), 209–210
SHO. *See* Sunstone Hotel Investors, Inc. (SHO)
Shock event, 168, 276
Short selling:
  exchange-traded funds (ETFs), 328–330
  overview, 6–7
  philosophy, 325–326, 332–336
  practical guide to, 326–328
  put options, 330–332
  risk management tools, 328
Sina Corporation (SINA), 260
Sinclair Broadcast Group, Inc. (SBGI),
  151–152
Slope of Hope blog, 22
SM Energy Company (SM):
  cup with handle pattern, 72–73
  inverted head and shoulders (IH&S)
    pattern, 212–213
SNCR. *See* Synchronoss Technologies, Inc.
  (SNCR)
SNIC. *See* Sonic Solutions (SNIC)
Sonic Solutions (SNIC), 276–277
STD. *See* Banco Santander (STD)
Sterling Financial Corporation (STSA),
  286–287
Stop prices, setting:
  above resistance, 320–321
  above trendline, 321
  below support, 320

Stop prices, setting (*Continued*)
  below trendline, 321–322
  generally, 319–320
  most recent high, 322–323
  most recent low, 322
  special cases, 323
STSA. *See* Sterling Financial Corporation
  (STSA)
Sunstone Hotel Investors, Inc. (SHO), 144–145
Support, 7–11
Support failure:
  definition, 279–280
  examples, 281–298
  generally, 279, 299
  psychology, 280–281
Synchronoss Technologies, Inc. (SNCR),
  194–195
Syneron Medical, 88–89
Sysco Corporation (SYY), 149–150

Technical analysis basis, 3–6
Tenneco, Inc. (TEN), 52–53
ThinkOrSwim (brokerage), 301

3M Company (MMM), 76–77
Toro Company (TTC), 96–97
Trading rules:
  closing a position, 343
  generally, 337, 345–346
  holding a position, 341–343
  no holy grail, 344–345
  opening a position, 338–341
  time and money, 343–344
Trendline, 281, 294–295
Trendline break, 280, 281
Triple bottoms. *See* Multiple Bottoms
TTC. *See* Toro Company (TTC)

Using this book, 14
UTH. *See* Utility HOLDRS Trust (UTH)
Utilities Fund (XLU), 180–181
Utility HOLDRS Trust (UTH), 13–14

Waddell & Reed Financial, Inc. (WDR),
  145–146
Whole Foods Market, Inc. (WFMI), 264–265
WIRE. *See* Encore Wire Corporation (WIRE)

Printed and bound by CPI Group (UK) Ltd, Croydon, CR0 4YY

23/04/2025

14660929-0003